CULTS

CULTS

FAITH, HEALING, AND COERCION

MARC GALANTER

OXFORD UNIVERSITY PRESS
New York   Oxford

Oxford University Press

Oxford   New York   Toronto
Delhi   Bombay   Calcutta   Madras   Karachi
Petaling Jaya   Singapore   Hong Kong   Tokyo
Nairobi   Dar es Salaam   Cape Town
Melbourne   Auckland

and associated companies in
Berlin   Ibadan

Copyright © 1989 by Oxford University Press, Inc.,

First published in 1989 by Oxford University Press, Inc.,
200 Madison Avenue, New York, New York 10016

First issued as an Oxford University Press paperback, 1990

Oxford is a registered trademark of Oxford University Press

LIBRARY OF CONGRESS
Library of Congress Cataloging-in-Publication Data
Galanter, Marc.
Cults, faith, healing, and coercion / Marc Galanter.
p.   cm.   Bibliography: p.   Includes index.
1. Cults.   2. Sects.   3. Psychology, Religious.
4. Spiritual healing.   I. Title.
BP603.G35   1989   88-25277
291'.01'9—dc19   CIP
ISBN 0-19-505631-0
ISBN 0-19-506658-8 (PBK.)

2 4 6 8 10 9 7 5 3 1
Printed in the United States of America

In memory of my father

Marc Galanter, M.D. is professor of psychiatry and director of the Division of Alcoholism and Drug Abuse at New York University School of Medicine; research scientist, World Health Organization Collaborating Center, Nathan Kline Institute; and director of the task force that prepared the American Psychiatric Association's *Report on Cults and New Religious Movements*.

ACKNOWLEDGMENTS

This book was written after fifteen years of studying the psychology of contemporary charismatic groups. Although this is an unusual subject for today's psychiatric research, I found it compelling because of the remarkable ability of these groups to exert influence on the thought and behavior of their members, often greater than our most potent treatments. An understanding of the "cult" phenomenon might offer valuable insights in areas as diverse as the treatment of mental illness and the understanding of group violence.

Inspiration for this quest lay in the work of observers who had succeeded in defining the nature of group behavior without being distracted by the particulars of ritual or circumstance. Max Weber, a sociologist, drew a perspective on charismatic leadership that could be employed in the most varied cultures. Wilfred Bion, a psychoanalyst, used the psychodynamic approach to understand small groups, and thereby afforded an understanding that went beyond the specific concerns of individual members to the innate forces governing group process. The contemporary sociobiologic paradigm recently articulated by Edward O. Wilson provided the foundation for the approach I developed in empirical biology, a reassuring opportunity for a physician researcher. Ideally, this approach will do justice to its antecedents.

I was fortunate to have skilled and understanding support in securing agreements with the groups I studied. Richard Erlich, Bonnie Blair, Kathy Lowrie, and Nora Spurgin were extremely helpful in this endeavor. Leaders of the groups themselves must certainly be credited for their willingness to undergo independent evaluation, particularly Neil Salonen and Mose Durst, presidents in their respective terms of the Unification Church in America.

Unfortunately, some members of these groups will question having their movements likened to others mentioned here. Conversely, detractors will likely take issue that criticism or even condemnation were not given. To proponents of both views I can only say that this book's purpose is to convey a psychological understanding of the charismatic group. Early on I realized it was necessary to avoid passing judgment on the merit of the groups' pursuits in order to study their operating principles. Very different groups could thus be compared with regard to their psychological and organizational processes but not for the inherent worth of their ideologies or tactics.

I am grateful to my colleagues and collaborators for their support and collaboration, both on conceptual issues and statistical analysis, and especially thank Robert Plutchik, Hope Conte, Mark Mizruchi, Peter Buckley, Alexander Deutsch, and Richard and Judith Rabkin. Assistance with data analysis was also given by my research assistants, Mary Tramontin, Denise Cancellare, Charles Flavio, Virginia Privitar, and Luiza Diamond.

The Department of Psychiatry at Albert Einstein College of Medicine in New York served as a home base for this work, where support was provided by Wagner Bridger, Herman van Praag, and Byram Karasu. I completed this book while at New York University, under the leadership of Robert Cancro. Grants and funding for this and related endeavors were given by the National Institute of Mental Health, the National Institute on Alcohol Abuse and Alcoholism, the National Institute on Drug Abuse, the Commonwealth Fund, and The J. M. Foundation.

My wife, Wynne, was patient and most helpful in offering valuable advice. She, along with Cathryn and Margit, gave inspiration.

New York   M. G.
September 1988

CONTENTS

CULTS

*And the Spirit of the Lord will
come upon thee, and thou shalt prophesy with them,
and shalt be turned into another man.*

I Samuel 10:6

1

THE CHARISMATIC GROUP

Individuals who become involved in a religious cult or radical political group may do things that puzzle and dismay their friends and family. They may don saffron-colored robes, shave their heads, or give away their family legacies. They may accept strangers 10,000 miles away as prospective mates, dedicate their lives to panhandling, or simply disappear. Their families may ask, "How could this happen? Nothing would have led us to expect it."

Strange as these transformations in attitude and action are, they can be understood in terms of psychological principles. These principles in turn can be explained and illustrated by recent research findings from seemingly diverse groups that share a "charismatic" quality. Charismatic groups are highly cohesive. They impute transcendent powers to the group's leader or its mission, and they strictly control members' behavior by means of a shared system of beliefs. Among these groups are cults and zealous religious sects; some highly cohesive self-improvement groups; and certain political action movements, among them some terrorist groups.

Three examples of individual members' experiences illustrate the impact of such cult-like groups. The first involves a young woman whom I interviewed some time ago.

> After breaking up with her boyfriend, Debbie left home on the East Coast to start summer school at a college in California. She was optimistic, if also a bit apprehensive, about her upcoming adventure. Her parents expected her to do well in the school environment, as she had dealt quite successfully with high school and the first year in a local college. Before summer school began, though, she was befriended by a group of youths who suggested that she get to know members of their informal organiza-

tion, dedicated to promoting "social ecology and world peace." Within a month, she was spending all her spare time with the group. Only at this point was she told by them that the group was associated with a small religious cult with an elaborate and arcane theology. She was soon asked by the group's leader to adopt its idiosyncratic beliefs and leave school. Interestingly, she agreed to all this without hesitation, and began to devote herself full time to raising funds to support the cult. For the next three months her parents could not locate her. In the midst of their anxiety, they could offer no explanation as to why she "threw away" the family's values and her own stake in her future. Five years later Debbie described the period as a difficult but meaningful time, and the friends she made there as among the best she ever had.

In recent years, many such young people have had similar experiences. In most cases, neither a psychiatric disorder nor overriding social pressure explains the profound changes in their lives. Was this young woman's mind "captured" by the group? There was no evidence that physical restraint or even psychological coercion was used. Was she only superficial in her previous relationships? Neither her family nor her friends thought so. There was apparently something extrinsic to her in the group experience that exerted an unusual, overriding influence.

Consider another example:

After increasingly heavy drinking that began in his teens, Ted became addicted to alcohol in his mid-thirties. His work performance passed from adequate to irregular, and he eventually lost the sales job he had held since college. Within the next year, his wife left him, taking their child with her (he had recently begun to beat her when he was drinking). Within five years he was hospitalized twice for gastrointestinal bleeding caused by his drinking. Despite frequent exposure to medical advice and the exhortation of his extended family, he expressed no interest in sobriety and had refused to attend meetings of Alcoholics Anonymous. On one occasion, though, he accompanied a recovering alcoholic friend to an AA meeting and found himself agreeing to stay after the meeting to speak with some other members. When I talked with him two years later, he remarked that by this point no one seemed to care whether he lived or died, but he couldn't admit that it might be within his power to change this. He could give no clear reason for agreeing to attend the AA meetings at this point, but he continued to do so. Within two months of regular meetings, he had acquired the resolve to remain abstinent, although he himself still wondered how he had fended off for even sixty days the alcohol that had controlled his life for over two decades. Later contacts would reveal that AA helped him maintain abstinence thereafter.

We have come to view alcoholism as a disease, one reflecting both compulsive behavior and physical incapacity. How can social influence, through a self-help fellowship, so dramatically change this syndrome? How can it achieve such impressive results when family, friends, and professionals have been so limited in their ability to aid alcoholics alter their behavior, even when their illness seems likely to be fatal? As we will see, the mutual support by members of Alcoholics Anonymous serves to engage alcoholics and promote their acceptance of the group's values. The combination of intense social cohesiveness and strongly held, shared belief (in abstinence, in this case) allows for such striking behavioral change.

Consider a different issue. Here is a case of group influence in the political arena.

> In March 1978 a group of youths abducted Aldo Moro, a leading figure in Italian politics, a former Prime Minister and then a potential candidate for the Presidency. While the entire country waited in suspense, they held him hostage and then murdered him. The group who carried out the kidnapping consisted mostly of individuals from stable middle-class backgrounds. They were generally articulate, thoughtful, and strongly committed to the welfare of their fellow man, as they saw it, but nonetheless sought opportunities to injure or kill representatives of the country's establishment—ironically, the very persons their families and friends revered. They belonged to a national network of like-minded individuals who regularly committed murder, while roundly condemned by all segments of Italian society. Their pursuit of terror was fired by the society's dread of their acts.

How does such a network emerge and what keeps it together in the face of widespread condemnation? How does it instill highly deviant norms of behavior in its members, for whom the act of murder was unspeakable before they joined? In psychology, social background, and education, these youths are no different from their school classmates, who moved on to conventional lives in terms of family, work, and politics. How does an all-encompassing philosophy compel political activists to give up their most deeply rooted standards of behavior, sacrifice the lives of others, and risk their own? Are there common mechanisms of group influence at work in these various examples, different as their personal, social, and political aims and outcomes may be?

What Is a Charismatic Group?

A charismatic group consists of a dozen or more members, even hundreds or thousands. It is characterized by the following psychological elements: members (1) have a _shared belief system_, (2) sustain a high level of _social cohesiveness_, (3) are strongly influenced by the group's _behavioral norms_, and (4) impute _charismatic (or sometimes divine) power_ to the group or its leadership.

In a charismatic group, commitments can be elicited by relative strangers in a way rarely seen in other groups. Even Freud, who championed the compelling nature of individual motives, addressed this impressive capacity at length in his book, *Group Psychology and the Analysis of the Ego*.[1] He discussed these forces in terms of the "primitive sympathetic response of the group," and said that, "Something is unmistakably at work in the nature of a compulsion to do the same as others, to remain in harmony with the many."

We will see that the cognitive basis for this conformity is a *shared belief system*. When these groups are religious in nature, their beliefs are often codified, but some groups have no more than an ill-defined ideologic orientation. In some religious cults, as shown in Debbie's experience, converts are introduced to the group's ideology only after they have affiliated. Once they have identified with the group's general orientation, though, they accept the particulars of belief quite readily when these are spelled out.

Members of these groups tend to be intensely concerned about each other's well-being, and are deeply committed to joint activities. Their *social cohesiveness, essential to the group's integrity*, is reflected in the close intertwining of the individual's life circumstances with those of all group members. Meetings are frequent; they serve as a focus for group functions and articulate their cohesiveness. Members often express their need to associate regularly with each other by developing joint activities such as minor group tasks and rituals, which in turn justify such meetings. Both cult and self-help group members are always well aware of when their next group meetings will be held, and look to them as a means of instilling commitment and a sense of purpose. A member's emotional state may be highly vulnerable to disruptions of this routine, and a group gathering missed can become a source of distress. As one long-time AA member noted while describing his despair over everyday problems, "It always feels good to go to a meeting."

The *norms for behavior* in a charismatic group play an inordinate role in determining how its members conduct themselves. Marital practices, for example, may be changed profoundly when the group itself adopts a certain style of betrothal. This emerged strikingly among the American-born members of the Unification Church (the "Moonies"). Although coming mainly from ordinary backgrounds, they agreed to get engaged in mass ceremonies to marriage partners whom they had never met before, selected for them on the spot by Reverend Moon.

Members also look to group norms for ways to behave in new situations. They may respond in a similar fashion to strangers perceived as threatening—in some groups, with a blunted and distant stare. Often they are implicitly aware of their style of behavior in an unexpected situation since it is based on previous instruction to the group. At other times it emerges without conscious appreciation of how they act. I found it intriguing to visit the headquarters of cult members overseas where even the style of socializing, the way food is served, and the response to strangers are the same as in countries several thousand miles away.

Behavioral change may also extend to mimicking the symptoms of mental illness. In these groups, transcendental experiences, often hallucinatory, are quite common. A deceased comrade "literally" stands by a member or a historical figure brings divinely inspired advice. Intense emotional experiences are reported, such as profound euphoria or malaise. Such phenomena, which are often seen among the mentally ill, occur among individuals who give no other evidence of psychiatric disorder.

Charismatic powers are typically imputed to leaders but can also be ascribed to the group or its mission. Some contemporary terrorist groups, for example, are viewed by their members as heralding an inevitable new world order—a remarkable belief, since the general acceptance of their peculiar philosophy is so unlikely.

These traits of charismatic groups are often best illustrated by the way they bring about changes in the thinking and behavior of individual members in single episodes. One example comes from my own research experience with the Divine Light Mission, a Hindu-oriented new religious movement. Janice, an eighteen-year-old American-born high-school senior, had described her problems to a counselor from this group at one of the group's religious festivals. I was studying the group while visiting the festival site, and was able to interview members at the counseling center.

The atmosphere at that center was highly cohesive; strong feelings of camaraderie and a sense of shared belief were evident as members arrived to discuss a variety of psychological problems. Janice came to the unit looking quite distressed. The counselor she encountered was not a health professional, but was contributing her time for Service, as religiously motivated good deeds were called. She allowed me to sit in as she spoke with the girl.

As the counselor approached her, Janice immediately burst into tears, explaining her misery and feelings of helplessness. She concentrated on her difficulty in meditating properly, saying of their Guru, "Maharaj Ji has given me Knowledge but I cannot see his light." This was very important to her, she said, because she could not be a premie, or a member of the sect, without this transcendental experience, achieved through proper meditation. She was further troubled because she felt obliged to do more Service for the Guru to compensate for her inability to meditate properly. This was best done by engaging new converts, but, she reported tearfully, she was too frightened to approach potential members.

The counselor listened to these expressions of distress, implicitly conveying support by her presence and demeanor. Her actions were in keeping with the atmosphere of the counseling center; she was empathic, even affectionate, and alluded to similar problems with meditation other members might experience from time to time. She expressed her perspective from the vantage point of the group's transcendent beliefs, and did not minimize the need for proper meditation or Service. She did, however, give Janice some examples of how problems like hers may be overcome in time with full devotion to the Guru, and reassured her that it was not necessary to perform an undue amount of Service at present. She said that the resolution of this distress might come through a ritual called *darshan,* meeting with the Guru in person, where such difficulties are often remitted. The following exchange ensued.

> COUNSELOR: Now tell me how you feel toward the premies you meditate with.
>
> JANICE: Of course, I am very close to them. They mean so much to me, like brothers and sisters.
>
> COUNSELOR: So you know now that when you are with them you confirm Maharaj Ji's Knowledge. You attend *satsang* [religious sermons] with them, and you will be going to *darshan,* too. You know that Maharaj Ji will see that you are faithful, and this will soon lead to your relief.
>
> JANICE: Yes I do. You *are* right.

By now the girl, like many others healed by faith, was composed and visibly reassured, even serene. I asked her counselor how she understood the girl's distress. She tried to explain, searching for a simple response, as a professional would speak to a layperson. "She had somehow lost the Knowledge. This happens often. She did not know how to rejoin Maharaj Ji's path." This was stated more as literal fact than metaphor, an expression of the charismatic role of their leader.

I was then able to speak with Janice. She had been having an affair with an older married man around the time she became affiliated with the group. When he ended their relationship two months before her arrival for counseling, she became acutely depressed, withdrew from social relations, and was unable to concentrate on her school work. At this point she also began having difficulty meditating, clearly due to the anxiety associated with her depressed state. This only compounded her sense of guilt and probably prolonged the depressive reaction that might otherwise have abated. She began to feel the need to do more Service for the group, in part to atone for the sexual liaison and also because she saw herself as an inadequate sect member. She had not discussed these matters with anyone. She felt her conduct had run contrary to the group's principles and she was ashamed.

The genesis of Janice's difficulties in meditating seemed fairly clear to me, but she had not really put the pieces together herself. Significantly this issue of her disrupted affair did not have to be broached with her Divine Light counselor because the cohesiveness of the group and the explanatory nature of its dogma (Maharaj Ji's Knowledge) were implicitly available without fuller exploration. These group forces were mobilized to relieve her feelings of guilt.

I spoke with Janice the next day after a protracted KNOWLEDGE session, a religious experience conducted for a large group of members by a principle of the Guru, and asked her how she was feeling. She said that the counselor was right to say that Maharaj Ji could offer me other ways to serve him. I could tell that when I was with all the premies today, Maharaj Ji's wisdom was touching me and that what I was doing was right. . . . It's clear that everything will work out; I have the Knowledge in me again.

This young woman had been wrenched into anguish compounded by her *feelings of distance* from the group, and apparently relieved and then healed through a renewed closeness. The norms for behavior set by the group were used to construct her "treatment," and the resolution of her problem was sealed by her commitment to the group's charismatic goal of "Knowledge," or divine enlightenment.

A Research Perspective

The psychology of zealous groups has not been a popular area of research. In recent years, however, scientific interest in such groups, and our ability to investigate their emotional impact, has advanced dramatically. To appreciate this newer perspective, we need to review previous studies.

Although Freud wrote about the infectious nature of cohesive groups, the fate of that work stands in contrast to his contributions to individual psychology. His concepts of the unconscious and the importance of early childhood experiences have been studied in great depth, but his views on group experiences were not extended by psychologists and psychiatrists. William James was aware of the absence of scientific attention to the impact of such experiences even two decades before Freud wrote on group influence. In 1902, this founder of modern psychology wrote an acerbic critique of the profession's ignorance of the psychology of religious affiliation.

> Medical materialism finishes up St. Paul by calling his vision on the road to Damascus a discharging lesion of the occipital cortex, he being an epileptic. It snuffs out St. Teresa as a hysteric, St. Francis of Assisi as an hereditary degenerate.[2]

Why wasn't James' call for attention to the psychological side of such religious phenomena more actively heeded? This can be put another way relative to our thesis. If the charismatic group is a discrete phenomenon governed by psychological principles, why has it attracted so little systematic study? Why have we not developed a coherent body of observation and explanatory principles to make sense of its members' experiences? The reasons for this reflect contemporary attitudes toward psychological research and limitations in our understanding and study of the biologic basis of social behavior. First let us consider "styles" of scientific investigation.

That scientific investigation is shaped by social bias goes without saying. In its extreme such bias was enforced by a trip to the stake. More commonly, it is reflected by inattention to alternative perspectives. The contemporary paradigm of psychological research is based on carefully controlled measurement of observable behavior. It is closely allied to a philosophy of science articulated by the natural philosopher and historian David Hume some two hundred years ago.

> If we take in our hand any volume of divinity or school metaphysics, for instance, let us ask, does it contain any abstract reasoning concerning quantity and number? No. Does it contain any experimental reasoning concerning matter of fact and existence? No. Commit it then to the flames: for it can contain nothing but sophistry and illusion.[3]

From this attitude toward empirical science comes the value we attach to quantifiable observation of measurable natural phenomena. In psychology it fosters an inclination to study psychological phenomena that can be reproduced and measured in a controlled setting, not necessarily those that are most intensely compelling. This general approach has indeed borne fruit in the field of psychology, as in the works of Pavlov, Watson, and Skinner. Needless to say, these investigators did not study charismatic group experiences in their laboratories.

Indeed, the laboratory-based scientific community has long been suspicious of the subjective nature of inference in such areas, where formal, controlled studies are not easily conducted. What scientific approach can consequently apply to charismatic groups? One perspective, derived from evolutionary theory[4] and popularized by Edward Wilson, is sociobiology,[5] which applies the principles of evolution, ethology (the study of animal behavior), and genetics to the study of social interactions.

Population geneticists have pointed out that the survival of biologically grounded behavior traits over generations depends on the traits themselves more than on the person who manifests them. A behavioral trait can persist if it promotes the survival of *relatives* of that person who carry the same genes for that trait.[6] Social affiliation and altruism therefore become important aspects of evolution. In my own studies, I attempted to investigate the nature of affiliative behavior[7] and then relate it to behaviors observed by anthropologists[8] and ethologists[9] to understand how patterns of group affiliation evolved and continued.

My first study of charismatic sects was the Divine Light Mission, a Hindu-oriented group, followers of a child guru. I found among the high membership an intense social cohesiveness, as well as a decline in the level of neurotic distress symptoms on joining the group. There was a relationship between these two observations: a high correlation existed between the degree to which a member felt affiliated with the group and the relief in distress that person experienced on joining.

I later studied induction and membership in the Moonies, and found that potential recruits acquire a high degree of social cohesiveness very quickly during initial phases of the introductory workshops. Furthermore, the psychological well-being of active members was directly proportional to how closely affiliated with the group they felt, in terms of both social ties to other members and acceptance of the group's beliefs.

One might therefore conclude that members of charismatic groups experience a relief in neurotic distress on joining, and that maintaining that relief (i.e, a sense of psychological well-being) depends on the intensity of their relationship with the group: if they disaffiliate somewhat, they experience distress; if they remain close, they keep their psychological well-being. This "relief effect" serves to reinforce members' involvement in the group and also continually reinforces their acceptance of the group's beliefs by rewarding them for their conformity and acceptance. As we will see, both anthropologic and ethologic evidence suggest that such affiliative behaviors and biologically grounded drives improve the ability of a group to adapt and survive.

A different scientific perspective—*a systems approach*—can be used to analyze a group's structure and functioning.[10] In looking at a system, we do not first ask what motivates an individual member to act. Instead we say, "How are the *group's* needs met by the overall behavior observed in its membership?"

From this viewpoint many observations of individual behavior can be synthesized into a model that can help us to better understand motivations. We may consider these individuals' behavior as it is generated by the needs of the social group, even when it seems to run contrary to their interests and personalities. This enables us to see how strongly they can be influenced to conform to the system's need to stabilize and carry out broader objectives.

Many years ago I saw a striking example of how this influence filters the impact of events within one group on another. On a Sunday in November 1978 a banner headline in *The New York Times* read, "GUYANA TOLL IS RAISED TO AT LEAST 900 BY U.S., WITH 260 CHILDREN AMONG THE VICTIMS AT COLONY." It was rapidly becoming clear that a bizarre and frightening situation of historic proportions had arisen in the past week among the followers of the cult leader Jim Jones. A mass suicide of American citizens had occurred in an isolated South American encampment where members of this group had sequestered themselves. Ironically, Jones was a Protestant minister who had been an esteemed member of the San Francisco Bay area religious community only months before.

I was unsure how to relate this tragedy to the Moonies, whose recruitment techniques I was studying. The Moonies themselves had just been the subject of a critical congressional inquiry, and were quite vulnerable to the anxieties that fueled public opinion on the issue of cults. They had been compared to every deviant movement that congressional witnesses might suggest.

Only a few days before, when interviewed about the events in Guyana by a national news magazine,[11] I was reluctant to tar the vulnerable and less ominous new religious movements inadvertently by association with these bizarre events, since it seemed to me that unique circumstances surrounded the People's Temple. (Particularly important was the prolonged isolation of Jones' followers in a jungle setting, with no feedback from outside the group to contradict the paranoid views that Jones himself had come to espouse.)

The vulnerability of the Moonies to public opinion at this juncture was corroborated that morning when I telephoned their workshop center in the San Bernardino mountains of California, where my study of recruitment practices was soon to begin. The workshop coordinator reported with concern that parents of five of the participants had driven up from Los Angeles to wrest their children away from what they feared might be an ominous fate. One family brought the local police to remove them, and the workshop leaders had felt it wise under the circumstances to accede to the parents' demands, even though they recognized no legal ground for removing these members, who were neither minors, nor coerced, nor mentally incompetent.

Later that day, as I entered the Unification Church's U.S. Headquarters in Manhattan, to make final administrative arrangements for the study, I wondered whether some shock wave might have struck the group by now. Were they rushing to prepare for public attacks on their sect? I knew the young man at the reception desk, and remarked how unfortunate it was that events in Jonestown might be used against his church. He said, "It's sad it happened to them. But no one would compare us to that terrible group."

I went upstairs wondering why he would think that, and found an air of calm. It soon became clear that they saw the events in Jonestown as not related to them in any way. It was further clear from discussions with members at large, as well as directors of church departments, that no statement had been promulgated by the leadership about what views the members might adopt toward the Jonestown affair. The Moonie members, functioning as an integrated social system, had somehow developed a psychologically defensive perspective. Their denial of the implications of the Jonestown affair apparently protected the group from being confronted by the similarities that might be drawn between their own cult-like structure and that of the People's Temple. One member gave me his view of the group's detractors while rationalizing what criticisms might be raised.

> We don't really need to deal with them on this. They would pick up on any little matter they can dig up to criticize us. Anyway, if there's one thing we can do here [in the church] it's to do what each of us wants. Reverend Moon would never lead us astray anyway, because of his own Divine Principle.

I soon concluded that the issue was better avoided. Members of this social system had obviously arrived at a consensus that, above all, assured the system's equilibrium by quashing potentially threatening self-examination.

On this basis, we may consider the operation of a religiously oriented charismatic group in relation to one aspect of systems theory—the role of feedback among system components. The group must struggle to preserve its integrity and gain acceptance or tolerance from society at large, since it typically constitutes a small and deviant minority. With the Jonestown events, the Moonies with whom I spoke were clearly moved to suppress any threatening implications. As if by plan, the system "unconsciously" assumed a posture that assured its own stability. It needed to avoid the feedback implied in any acknowledgment that the Unification Church might be similar to the People's Temple. In similar ways charismatic groups may operate to effect their goals. By incorporating members' needs for affiliation into the group's social system, they create a strong social unit capable of exerting much influence over the members' thoughts and actions.

Zealous religious, quasi-religious, and political groups are commonly formed to achieve practical goals. Some address the disparity between members' distress and their desire for contentment by spiritual means. Others may provide relief from an addictive illness poorly managed by the medical community. Still others alleviate the intolerable consequences of perceived social oppression. Whether we can influence the course of these groups, or whether they can be directed toward constructive ends, may ultimately depend on how well we understand their underlying psychology.

I

FORCES IN THE CHARISMATIC GROUP

Few of us are expert in understanding the behavior of people in groups. We arrive at a practical "expertise" in human nature by relying on everyday social exchanges, but such exchanges are mainly with individuals rather than groups. A child begins to learn about human relations as she turns to her mother to elicit a favor, and a youth follows his teacher's behavior, trying to assess how he is expected to behave. As adults, we deal primarily with individuals: a woman studies a co-worker to gain his cooperation, then returns home to puzzle over why her husband seems troubled.

We develop working models of human behavior based on the way individuals are motivated, solve problems, react in anger, expect appreciation. This cognitive set is hard to break when the focus shifts from the individual to the group.

Attempts to influence large groups of people illustrate this point. Only the most practiced actors have developed the facility of standing on stage and reading the shifting moods of an audience so as to tap the forces operating in the group setting. It is an unusual public speaker who can motivate a large group, just as it is an unusual psychiatrist who can develop a strategy for generating a therapeutic response in a group of fifty patients, or for turning a large group's interest away from issues that create conflict. To acquire these skills requires repeated exposure to uncommon situations that give people the opportunity to practice and learn.

Few people have the opportunity to learn firsthand the principles governing the motivations of a charismatic group. And those who do are more likely to operate intuitively than to study these groups in a controlled, scientific setting. Thus, it is not surprising that our understanding of the psychological forces operating in such groups has been slow to develop, certainly slower than a comparable understanding of individuals. We lack means for "reading" these forces, for anticipating the group's motivations.

The psychological forces that mold the intensely affiliated charismatic group cannot be examined adequately through the prism of individual psychology, whether that of the citizen-in-the-street, the clinician, or the researcher. Instead, they must be understood from the perspective of the group as a whole; when properly understood, these forces have a compelling, almost palpable quality. They include group cohesiveness, shared beliefs, and altered consciousness.

2

GROUP
COHESIVENESS

Group cohesiveness may be defined as the result of all the forces acting on members to keep them engaged in the group.[1] When cohesiveness is strong, participants work to retain the commitment of their fellow members, protect them from threat, and ensure the safety of shared resources. With weak cohesiveness, there is less concern over the group's potential dissolution or the loss of its distinctive identity, and joint action is less likely.

Group cohesiveness[2] is seen in informally structured groups, such as a clique of teenagers who make every effort to get together, even when forcibly separated by their elders. It also exists in formally structured groups, such as professional sports teams or military platoons, whose members undergo great sacrifice to assist each other in their common mission, particularly when confronted by adversaries. In most organized groups, however, it is characterized by neither adversity nor great drama; in a fraternal organization, for example, members meet regularly to share experiences and give each other practical assistance.

A Clinical Model

Two group settings in particular attract the attention of clinicians: families and therapy groups. In both settings a body of empirical observation highlights the impact of a group's cohesiveness on the psychological function of members, and although both family and therapy groups are smaller than charismatic groups, they demonstrate the potent role this psychological force can play in shaping feelings, attitudes, and behavior.

17

We will begin looking at the issue of cohesiveness with a review of some studies on the relationships in families that are intensely close-knit, and for this we must rely largely on clinical observations. The concept of the "differentiation of self," developed by family theorists such as Murray Bowen and Lyman Wynne,[3] helps explain the interaction between the individual and his or her family, and can be assessed independently of a person's diagnosis, social class, and cultural background. At one end of this scale lies the highly differentiated individual, characterized by autonomy and even rugged individualism. At the other end family relationships exhibit emotional fusion and an inability to make critical judgments because of a need to assure harmony with others.

Emotional fusion in families is akin to group cohesiveness in its merging of identity and decision-making functions. It occurs in large charismatic groups as well as in families because members of both may be highly dependent on each other and rely excessively on their compatriots for emotional support and decision making.[4] This is also seen among certain disturbed families unable to tolerate disruptions in the balance of their members' relationships. For example, if a psychiatrist attempts to change an apparently harmful pattern of interaction with a family, one way or another that pattern will soon reestablish itself; this takes place without any formal understanding among family members, as if a governing structure existed outside their awareness.

Take, for example, Ann, an unemployed, twenty-two year old living with her divorced mother, who was admitted to the hospital during an acute psychotic episode. Her case illustrates the intense mutuality and lack of differentiation seen in a pathologically cohesive family. Her mother had brought her to the emergency room after a battle between them, during which Ann had become uncontrollable, demanding that she be allowed to seal the windows of their apartment to protect them from poison gas. Ann herself was hallucinating the voices of threatening figures who warned her about her neighbors' plans to kill her and her mother.

Ann and her brother, one year younger, had both been involved since childhood in intense, ambivalent relationships with their mother, but the brother had enlisted in the army three years before, hoping to escape. Mother and daughter now spent almost all their time alone together and were, for each other, their only sources of social support. Soon after the brother left, they began to develop a delusion that was remarkable because it was shared in its entirety by both mother and daughter. This *folie à deux* was the belief that their neighbors were plotting to kill them by injecting poison gas into their apartment. Both women devoted considerable time to averting this eventuality by plugging up spaces in the walls and carefully observing the neighbors' comings and goings.

The current crisis had been precipitated by the brother's return from military service. Ann's closeness to her mother was threatened, and she fell into an unmanageable state. Her involvement with her mother had become so intense that a disruption in the relationship threatened her very sanity, and Ann's perception of the world around her had become grounded in that very relationship. She now began to hallucinate and to assault her mother physically, thereby assuring herself a greater measure of maternal attention since her mother would attempt to restrain her.

The hospitalization precipitated by these events was characterized by a rivalry between the mother and the medical staff, each vying, as it were, to secure Ann's fidelity by providing their respective cures. The staff's medication did indeed stop the hallucinations, although Ann's persecutory delusion abated more slowly. Her mother sustained Ann's attachment to her by bringing in countless packages of preserved fruit, meat, and beverages, which caused difficulty with the nursing staff.

Ann's condition soon stabilized, and the medical staff, with no alternative to offer, planned to return her to her mother's care. It was presumed that Ann's persecutory delusion, like her hallucinations, had resolved in response to the medication since both symptoms had abated. When interviewed with her mother before discharge, however, Ann began once more to speak of the dangers present in the household, subtly abetted by her mother, and one month later mother and daughter again shared the same delusional perspective, although Ann was no longer hallucinating and violent. Their close tie apparently served to reinstate their distorted perspective.

A family like this, albeit pathologic, illustrates how a group's equilibrium can be reestablished in the face of an external threat. In this case, the threat was the brother's return and then intervention by supportive outsiders, the hospital staff.

Preserving intense interrelatedness is also essential to a religious cult. A cult can react similarly to the potential disruption of its social stability when, for example, its leader becomes manifestly deranged. A good example was provided by Alexander Deutsch in his study of thirty followers of Baba, an American-born, self-proclaimed guru.[5] The cult had coalesced in the early 1970s not long after Baba returned from a spiritual voyage to India and began sitting each day on a park bench in Manhattan's Central Park. His followers—"The Family," as they called themselves—ate, sang, meditated, and worshipped their leader at this spot. They also spoke of deep ties to him and to each other. Essential to Baba's philosophy was the concept of "letting go," which required that his followers' detach themselves from worldly desire, ambition, and guilt to achieve unity with God. However, Baba did not speak at all; instead he communicated in sign language, a personal system understandable only through his interpreter.

Within a few years, at Baba's urging, the group relocated to a rural setting. Although their successful transition reflected commitment to the group, Baba soon began to show evidence of psychiatric deterioration. His muteness became increasingly autistic, and the sign language he developed became fragmented, to the point that his devotees could no longer follow it. He began to act strangely. For example, he used a large sum from the group's modest resources to buy himself a Jacuzzi, even though there was no electricity where they lived. He also beat some cult members repeatedly and subjected some of the women to sexual abuse.

All this should have put considerable stress on the group's stability, but throughout this period Baba's "Family" remained relatively intact and sustained its close-knit relationship. The members shared their resources; some contributed considerable personal assets to their guru. Neither the move to the rural commune, their privation, nor Baba's derangement and abusive behavior succeeded in separating them.

They adapted to the situation, compromising their sense of reality but sustaining their dependency on the leader and their cohesiveness in this small cult. They continued to insist that Baba's leadership was benign and his path merely a "hard trip," requiring much faith and fortitude. Paradoxically, they even maintained that he was a model of freedom and his bizarre behavior was a reflection of not being trammeled by socially imposed constraints. They did not deny that Baba might be "crazy" but insisted that this simply brought him closer to the expression of a "divine energy" and that, in his behavior, he was "teaching them a lesson." When a woman was sexually abused by Baba, the group concluded that she had been holding on too tightly to her chastity. The purchase of the Jacuzzi was said to illustrate the importance of letting go of money.

Both Baba's "Family" and Ann's family reflect the dynamics of excessive mutuality in family pathology. Both needed to preserve their cohesiveness and interdependency, to remain stable in the face of internal or external threat. This led to a distorted consensus, a mutually held point of view, that allowed equilibrium to be maintained. The consensus was achieved by denying reality and rationalizing their shared perspective. Reality becomes less important to certain groups than the preservation of their ties.

The aberrant manifestation of social cohesiveness found in pathologic families (and to a lesser degree in normal ones) has its parallels in psychotherapy groups. Contemporary models of group therapy owe much to Wilfred Bion, a British psychoanalyst who pointed out that a group may be moved by latent forces, usually unknown to its members. As a leader of early experimental therapy groups, Bion chose to remain silent, making only occasional interpretive comments. He provided little if any leadership so that he might observe the psychological forces operating within the group. Central among these forces was the desire of the members to be dependent on the leader and remain close to each other. By not acting to fulfill this need and avoiding an active leadership role, Bion allowed the groups' unmet needs to become increasingly apparent as the level of anxiety mounted,[6] reflecting the force of social cohesion.

Bion observed that a group operates on two levels simultaneously: "tasks"—

matter-of-fact functions such as, "When will the next meeting be held?" or "Who will arrange for proper heating in the room?"; and "basic assumptions"—unconscious drives such as the dependency that places pressure on the leader to meet the group's expectation of being held together and led. At any given time the basic assumptions can influence the nature of the group interactions and its task-oriented behavior. Thus, a practical group decision to reorganize its schedule may be compromised by members' fears of having their security in the group threatened.

For the clinical training of group therapists, A. K. Rice at the Tavistock Clinic developed participatory group exercises that shed light on the dynamics of large groups led by trainer-"consultants." By providing little or no structured leadership within these training groups, trainers elicited surprising behavior. For example, members would sometimes become extremely hostile over petty group concerns. Rice commented on the need for a cohesive structure.

> Without an abstract ideal or external enemy its boundaries are difficult to define; without boundaries, and hence without even an elemental structure, action is impulsive and hence potentially dangerous. . . . In this emotional climate the members turn to the consultants for reassurance that they, at least, can control the violence; the fear, and it is shared by the consultants, is that they too will be unable to act quickly or wisely enough to avert disaster.[7]

In charismatic groups, leaders express no such fear. Instead, they channel these inchoate forces into forming, in Coser's words, "a greedy institution." Such "institutions" seek exclusive and undivided loyalty. They reduce the social roles available to members to those provided by the group. They form "social cocoons" that help transform members' identities by forcing the group into social, ideological, or physical isolation.[8]

Freud's observation about group psychology and the pressures that draw individuals into consensual and irrational response is particularly apt here. The evolution of a crowd, he noted, is based on a compulsion in people to do the same as others, "to remain in harmony with the many."[9] This presents both a promise and a threat.

A Charismatic Religious Sect: The Divine Light Mission

A friendship led to my first encounter with contemporary sects or new religious movements[10] and served to highlight the influential role of group cohesiveness in shaping the behavior of charismatic groups. I had known Beth[11] for ten years, and we had kept in touch while living in different cities. Her personal life had been disrupted by a divorce and a move to a new university teaching job. Soon after she gave up a promising academic career to devote herself to the philosophy of a teenage guru who had arrived in the United States the year before; eventually she moved into a commune of the guru's followers. How could she have adopted such a deviant lifestyle after spending her adult years at liberal universities?

The group she joined, the Divine Light Mission, was introduced to the United States in 1971 by a thirteen-year-old boy from India, scion of a family of Hindu holy men; members believed in the lad's messianic role. Divine Light was not unlike a number of Eastern-oriented sects that emerged in the United States around this time. Along with others having a neo-Christian orientation, these groups constituted the bulk of the emerging cult phenomenon, or, depending on one's view, new religious movements. The introduction Beth gave me to the Divine Light Mission led to a series of studies of these movements.

A History of the Sect

Like many groups of Hindu orientation, the Divine Light Mission originated as religious practice in India. It was founded in 1960 by Sri Hans Ji Maharaj, father of the Guru Maharaj Ji and a former member of the Radhasoami Satsang Beas, one of several Sikh religious movements in northern India. Each of those movements operated independently and was headed by a leader regarded by members as a satguru, or perfect master, whose task was to lead his followers along a path to God.[12]

Maharaj Ji was the youngest of four sons of Sri Hans Ji, and even as a young child participated with his family in their public religious programs. Given this status, he was accorded a great deal of attention by his father's devotees and lived in luxury.[13] When his father died, eight-year-old Maharaj Ji was selected to lead the sect instead of his older brothers because of his unusual talent at delivering religious homilies.

Within a few years, the sect began to send mahatmas, or apostles, overseas to preach the young guru's inspired mission, and by the time he was eleven, Maharaj Ji himself had traveled to London. Two years later he came to the United States at the invitation of several American premies (followers) who had received Knowledge (enlightenment) in India. The young guru visited several cities and was accorded a favorable reception by many young people who were experiencing the uprooting of the late counterculture era with its rebellions against established authority. As he traveled, he began to attract a following.

Maharaj Ji returned to India to tend to the members of the Mission there, but came back to the United States a year later and established a national headquarters in Denver. Within months, hundreds of American youths accepted the guru's invitation to receive Knowledge and flew with him to India in several chartered jumbo jets for a festival called Hans Jayanti. On their arrival, his followers were taken to the family's ashram, or religious commune, for several weeks.

By this time, about a thousand members had moved into a dozen Divine Light communes in Denver,[14] and soon there were several thousand members nationwide. Commune residents devoted their full time to the group, and took an active role in developing a national organization for the guru. The study I carried out then provided a profile of sect members,[15] revealing that they were typically single (82%) whites (97%) in their twenties (73%). The distribution of Catholics (32%) and Protestants (44%) was not very different from the general population (38% and 57%, respectively), but there was a greater proportion of Jews (21% vs. 2%).[16] The members' middle-class background was reflected in the large majority that had attended college (76%), as had one or both parents (71%). Typical group members were middle-class young adults, many of whom had interrupted higher education to join the sect.

What were some of the trappings of religious practice in this emerging movement? Potential initiates were usually introduced to the Divine Light Mission at a session of religious discourse called a satsang, where experienced members presented the philosophy of the sect to the assembled group. The satsang could be delivered to active members or to those with only a casual interest. It was something of a polemic interspersed with parables, and because members were bright and sophisticated, these discourses tended to be engaging, making use of both Hindu mythology and Western philosophy.

After a period of acquaintance with the group, a potential member might approach a mahatma from the sect. These were long-time Indian devotees designated by the guru to initiate new members. Although their pronouncements were often obscure, they lent an aura of transcendence to the initiation. In the initiation ceremony the mahatma rubbed the eyes of the newly initiated members, producing a sensation of flashes that were perceived as a divine light. Initiates wee thereafter called premies, or followers of the guru.

The premies undertook four types of meditative experience during daily periods of silent repose, spent with eyes closed. In the first meditation they visualized a light, described as real and intense. In the second they heard music, and this too was reported not to be metaphoric but rather an essential sound of the universe. In the third meditation they tasted "nectar," supposedly a purifying fluid flowing from the brain to the throat,[17] and finally they spoke the "word," said to be a primordial vibration that underlies all existence. These meditations were recounted with great zeal.

Performing Service, or good works, for the sect was a requirement, and giving satsang was one type of Service, as it led others to hear that the knowledge was available. Other Service included helping with the arrangement of speaking tours for the mahatmas and drawing new converts into the group. Premies could live in the ashrams to devote themselves more fully to

Service. These premies often worked part- or full-time outside the ashram and gave a sizable portion—sometimes all—of their income to the movement. They also practiced celibacy, vegetarianism, and frequent meditation. The focus of this ascetic existence was their religious mission rather than personal pleasure or gain.

In 1973, the sect rented the Houston Astrodome for a celebration of world peace and religious rejuvenation, "Millennium '73," billed as "the most significant event in human history." Devotees were flown from overseas, and the event was promoted with considerable advance publicity and a good deal of media coverage. A highlight of the celebration was the participation of Rennie Davis, one of the Chicago Seven anti-Vietnam War protestors who had recently become a premie. The event, however, fell far short of expectations. The stadium was only partially filled; a variety of millennial expectations, such as the arrival of world peace, failed to materialize, and the whole undertaking left members of the movement disillusioned and in debt.

The guru himself, however, was increasingly taken by the enticements of American society. He was, after all, still a teenager, not above spraying his coterie with shaving cream for fun. Such pranks led them to speak of his "heavenly playfulness." He began dressing in western clothes and adopted a luxurious lifestyle that included setting up residence in a mansion and being ferried about in a limousine.

Soon he married his secretary, an attractive American woman several years older. This he did against his mother's wishes, and the event precipitated a schism in the family, ultimately leading to the estrangement of the American branch of the religious sect from its main body in India, where his mother and brothers remained. His mother revoked his title of satguru, an action he refused to accept. Maharaj Ji now began to preach against the betrayal he felt he experienced at the hands of his family, couching his arguments in parables drawn from Hindu mythology. In America too, the marriage caused dismay, particularly among the premies living in ashrams who had followed the strict path of celibacy dictated by the guru himself. Perhaps half of these members left the sect over this issue.[18]

Maharaj Ji now moved his headquarters from Denver to Miami without explanation. This caused a major dislocation among his remaining followers, most of whom did accompany him. In Miami, he moved further away from the sect's traditional Hindu flavor and gave less active direction to sect members. At first, he led religious meetings about once a month in a hired auditorium, where as many as 500 to 600 followers would assemble, but after a while he appeared less often, and rarely visited the ashrams in the community. Maharaj Ji nonetheless was still regarded as a divine figure by his followers.

The movement had apparently reached its peak of expansion and popularity, and in the next few years many members drifted away, although they still retained an attentuated fidelity to their spiritual leader. Some who had interrupted their education or their careers began to look for a more stable identity within the Miami community. As they settled down, they increasingly adopted more traditional roles as young working adults and parents, while maintaining their reverence for the guru and their affection for other premies.

In 1984 Maharaj Ji moved again, with his wife, four children, and considerable assets. This time he went to the affluent beach community of Malibu in West Los Angeles but did not ask his followers to join him. Although he continued to make occasional spiritual tours, he did not appear at most of the religious gatherings held in his name. The diminishing numbers of his faithful, most of them still in Miami, did not appear to be disappointed in the sect's lack of coherence, and often explained it as paradoxically showing the strength of their leader's spiritual message. They continued in their meditations, although these became more of a personal matter and were practiced less frequently and in isolation.

Initial Encounters

My first encounter with the Divine Light Mission came when Beth invited me to visit an ashram at the time the group was expanding. She thought the sect would be interesting for a psychiatrist to observe because some members had experienced a relief from serious emotional problems when they joined. She felt her group had tapped a large area of mental function psychiatry was unaware of.

The atmosphere in the ashram was indeed quite striking. On entering a large apartment on the Upper West Side of Manhattan, I was greeted in a friendly, even intimate fashion by people who were complete strangers. The intense communality of the members was immediately apparent, a quality that was clearly an important aspect of the group's function. One could sense a closeness among those present, and an absence of the minor tensions that would be expected in a setting where two dozen people were living in tight quarters. A college dormitory, a military barracks, or a summer camp soon reveal a certain amount of hostile banter or argument. These appeared to be absent in the ashram. Caring and intimacy, reflective of the group's cohesiveness, seemed to mute any expression of animosity.

There were kind words, offers of food, expressions of interest, and warm smiles, all from people I'd never met before. Any question was soon answered, sometimes even anticipated. Having been invited by one of their members and defined temporarily as one of their own, I was made to feel as if I were entering a supportive envelope, to be protected from the rough edges of relationships in the outside world.

To illustrate the healing offered by her newfound religious experience, Beth told me about Janet, a twenty-six-year-old premie whose case showed the vital role that social bonds within this group play in stabilizing the members' subjective state and behavior. I later corroborated the details in interviews with the woman herself and her relatives and friends. Over the course of several hospitalizations dating back to her mid-teens, Janet had been diagnosed as schizophrenic. She had been placed on a variety of medications, usually major tranquilizers in modest to large doses. Despite this treatment, the intermittent hallucinatory periods, episodes of rage, and inappropriate behavior were not effectively brought under control. When Janet was not in the hospital, she lived with her hapless parents, and was apparently quite demanding and easily upset by their presence. The parents, unable to move her into an independent living situation, were pleased that she at least retained a few friends, some of whom she had met while in the hospital. Occasionally her tenuous equilibrium broke down at home whereupon florid psychotic symptoms appeared, including delusions of persecution, and her unpredictable behavior often led to a return to the hospital. In the most tragic periods of her illness, fearing that her eyes were the source of demonic visitations, Janet actually blinded herself with her own hands.

The sight of her sunken eyelids confirmed this, as did a later physical examination; here was even more convincing evidence of unmanageable behavior than the hospitalizations and trials of psychotropic medication. But Janet was now behaving appropriately, even though she had taken no medication in the three years since joining the group. During my first visit she conversed with companions, apparently in good spirits, and was able to tell her story to me. She said she felt relaxed with other premies and had experienced no psychotic symptoms since joining the group, although she had seen the "divine light" during her meditation, an experience common to other members.

It became apparent from observing her and speaking with other members that the group not only displayed affection and support, but also set clear standards for her social behavior. This was something her parents had tried but failed to do. While engaged within the cohesive structure of the group, she felt compelled to comply with the expectations of her fellow members, a process that aborted the downward spiral of regressive behavior regularly ending in a psychotic state at home. This dynamic was illustrated by the comment of a friend and fellow member: "When she gets irritable or complains, I let her know that it's not the way premies should behave. She knows that we care for her, and that our scolding is done with love." Indeed, other members did not leave her alone for extended periods, even if she did not approach them.

This supportive atmosphere and sense of closeness apparently had a strong impact on the mental state of certain members, especially individuals like Janet. Somehow the sect was reaching some disturbed persons in a way that conventional psychiatry could not. Through intense togetherness and support, it seemed to have turned around their thinking and behavior.

But this was also true for members who had been well adjusted. Beth, for example, was profoundly changed by the sect. She had previously demonstrated herself to be highly intelligent and competent, and excelled academically without great effort. With independent-mindedness, she had assumed a leadership role in the antiwar movement of the late 1960s, yet only a few days before my visit to the ashram she sat with me at the dinner table and seemed transfixed, removed from all worldy cares. Only when she spoke of her newfound commitment did she become animated. She talked of the divine light she could literally see, the sacred nectar she could taste, and the divine music she heard. Under the group's influence Beth had somehow acquired a mental set entirely at variance with her previous attitudes. This development seemed no less surprising than Janet's; both women had apparently been transformed in their behavior, feelings, and perceptions.

Within a few months, I began to study this compelling phenomenom. I enlisted the help of Peter Buckley, a colleague at the Albert Einstein college of Medicine and we conducted interviews and designed a questionnaire to evaluate two issues: first, the relief of psychological distress experienced on joining, and, second, the degree of social cohesiveness felt by these members toward the group. I hypothesized that a relationship existed between the perceived emotional relief and fidelity to the group.

The study was conducted on the outskirts of Orlando, Florida, at a national festival held by the Divine Light Mission, one of the conclaves regularly organized to allow members the opportunity for personal contact, or darshan, with the guru. A field had been rented for the week-long event. Events there showed how the group's cohesiveness could be mobilized as a potent social force and how nonmembers could be excluded.

The atmosphere of belonging was pervasive, as some 5,000 young adults gathered to make preparations. They interacted in a congenial and open manner, even when they had struck up acquaintance only moments before. To say the least, this was not an impersonal work site. It represented a network of people who hastened to assist each other and sought ways to further their common cause of making the festival a shared experience, something valuable to all.

As a group, the members looked as though they had been drawn from the graduate campus of a large university—bright, not too carefully groomed, casually dressed. They were lively, good-tempered, and committed to their mutual effort. Some set up tents; others sold religious tracts and pins with pictures of the guru, his American wife, and their baby. Some handled food; others moved about with an air of eager expectancy. There was no idleness, brashness, marijuana, beer, loud music, or flirtation—all hallmarks of a more typical assembly of people in their twenties.

The administrative structure for the event appeared informal, but no sense of disorganization pervaded. The speakers addressed the group from a large floating stage on a lake. The program moved along smoothly from one event to the next, whether singing for the guru ("He's Got the Whole World in His Hands") or listening to various leaders deliver satsang.

The group's congeniality apparently extended to anyone designated as acceptable, as long as the proper signal was made. Thus, because Beth, who held a position of respect in the group, had labeled my colleague and me "okay," we were acceptable. After being introduced to the appropriate parties, we were greeted warmly and made to feel a part of the group. Help was offered as I began to query various organizers on strategy. Was it possible to pick out people at random from the registration lines to administer the questionnaire? There surely was a way, once I deliberated with them over the options available. Was space necessary for subjects to sit quietly and fill out research forms? Something would be worked out for every need. Soon we were all sitting around and talking about experiences of mutual interest, even of a few remote common acquaintances.

We also saw the other side of the coin—how the group defined and protected its boundary between members and the outside world. The demarcation could be drawn tightly, much as a droplet of quicksilver coalesces and separates from its surroundings, or as family members draw together and limit access of outsiders to their personal affairs. Our own status suddenly changed from inside to outside when a more suspicious member of the administrative group asked me if the project had been "approved" by senior figures from the Mission. In the absence of a definite response, our legitimacy was now open to question. Although it was not entirely clear what this approval entailed, a request was quickly relayed to the upper reaches of the Divine Light hierarchy and was then—to my surprise and distress—peremptorily turned down.

The members I had met quickly withdrew their offers of friendship, providing an object lesson on exclusion from a cohesive group. I soon felt myself to be a nonperson, treated civilly but cooly, having become an outsider as rapidly as I had been made an insider. The very people who had hovered around us to help with our plans now found making conversation uncomfortable. People seemed to be looking *through* my colleague and me rather than at us.

Toward the end of the day approval came as suddenly as it had been withdrawn, with the information that a decision had been made at the "highest" level, presumably in consultation with the guru himself. Acceptance and offers of help came with rekindled warmth. As if automatically triggered, a renewed air of intimacy suffused our exchanges.

This experience illustrates the considerable mobilization of support that such a cohesive group can generate, either informally or with formal sanction, as well as the strength of its controls over actions. The sect's ideology lends the control structure a legitimacy that penetrates the layers of the individual members' own decision making, eliciting group-sanctioned behavior. At no point in the Orlando sequence was there any significant diversity in attitudes expressed toward us. Each group member adhered to the consensus and thereby assured unanimity. As in Ann's family, this intense mutuality reflected the need both for security in the face of an outside world that is perceived as threatening and to prevent internal conflict. Agreement in attitude and views serves to protect the integrity of the group as a social system.

Later in the festival I asked to interview people who had experienced psychiatric or drug problems, hoping that they might help clarify the sect's impact on psychiatric symptoms in individual members, as well as the function of its intense social influence in mediating psychological change. One member brought forward was Ellen, a thirty-four-year-old divorced, part-time clerk whose five children had been remanded to her mother's care by the court because they had been neglected during her protracted bouts of psychiatric and drug problems. These problems had apparently come under control when she joined the Divine Light Mission. Her story illustrates two points. First, like many other initiates, she was attracted to a charismatic group at a time of psychological crisis, as if seeking aid to cope with extreme distress. Second, the support and structure offered by the sect allowed her to pull her psychological resources together. She used the strength of the group as an auxiliary ego to help regain her emotional stability.

Seven years before, Ellen had begun using drugs and was taking ten to fifteen barbituate capsules a day. When psychedelics became popular, she began using LSD and later became addicted to a variety of opiates: morphine, Demerol, heroin, and illicit methadone. Her opiate habit became very expensive, and for four years she survived through prostitution. While on her rollercoaster of drug abuse, she was hospitalized on several occasions for psychiatric problems, typically for a few days or weeks, during which she often smuggled a supply of heroin into the hospital.

The despair that precipitated these hospitalizations led to several suicide attempts. Ellen denied any history of hallucinations and gave no evidence of formal delusional thinking. Significantly, she reported that her mood improved by the time she left the hospital, often without any antidepressant medication. This history, along with her somewhat histrionic presentation of it, left the impression that she did not have a major despressive disorder. I thought she might have a borderline personality disorder, reflecting impulsive and self-destructive behavior and poor coping skills, and that the episodes requiring hospitalization were precipitated by drug use and environmental stress.

At one point, despairing of any escape from heroin addiction and the consequent need for prostitution, Ellen applied for methadone maintenance, which allowed her to stay away from illicit drugs and out of the hospital for over a year. She thought of herself as independent, though, and did not like the regimen of frequent visits to the clinic required by the program. Like a number of patients on methadone maintenance, Ellen mistook her newfound stability for a genuine ability to withstand the pressures of daily life. Wanting to "take control of her life," she withdrew from the methadone program and soon began using marijuana heavily and taking barbituates again. As she said, "I used anything I could to stay off the heroin."

Her drug use rapidly increased, and she began to shoot heroin again. Feeling panicky over a likely full-fledged relapse, she fled to Colorado from her native Philadelphia, in the hope that life in a rural setting would save her from further deterioration. It did not, and she continued to use drugs, settling into life as a street person.

After a month in Colorado, Ellen met some members of the Divine Light Mission. She immediately felt comfortable with them and soon began to appreciate the merit of their religious devotion. She wanted to become part of the group to salvage herself from a profound sense of desolation. Each day she went to their ashram where she was accepted warmly, began to cut down her use of drugs, and attempted to meditate. Though living alone, she felt herself to be part of a "close, loving community." Now, ten months later, she reported only occasionally using half a marijuana cigarette.

Part of my exchange with Ellen was revealing of the role played by the group's cohesiveness.

> M.G.: How did you feel when you were shooting heroin in Colorado?
>
> ELLEN: I was terrified, but I also felt that I had returned to a friend, one who would heal my wounded feelings but then hold me in its claws. I knew I couldn't control it. . . .
>
> M.G.: And the premies, how did they help you?
>
> ELLEN: Once I got to know them, I realized they loved me. They took me up, and it was as if they were holding me in their arms. I was like a baby whose mother guides its moves and cares for it. When I wanted to take heroin, or even to smoke [marijuana], I knew they were with me to help me stay away from it, even if I was alone. And their strength was there for me, even before I could hardly meditate at all. I could rely on their invisible hand, moved by Maharaj Ji's wisdom, to help me gain control.
>
> M.G.: What was it that they did?
>
> ELLEN: After a while it was *everything* they did that made me know I belonged. Just feeling their love was all I needed.

The drug abuse syndrome that Ellen confronted when she arrived in Colorado was serious, and the likelihood of her aborting a decline into full-blown heroin addiction was small. A geographic escape generally is of little value. Few patients in the throes of an addiction such as hers, combining opiates and other drugs, are able to establish control over drug abuse on their own. Her description of the intense support she felt from other Divine Light members suggested an alternative dependency. Her reliance on the group for the strength to face the stress of everyday life paralleled the reliance she had placed on drugs. Both aided her in coping with conflict, but at the cost of independent action.

The sect had exerted a remarkable influence on this woman's addictive problem, affecting her in a way that our usual psychological therapies do not. What produces such influence? We can begin to answer this question by recalling the discussions of the family and the therapy group earlier in the chapter. Further insights came from our studies of Divine Light members in Orlando.

A *Study of Group Cohesiveness*

The objective study of behavior in charismatic groups is not a simple undertaking, and two issues complicating this research are relevant here: investigator bias and limitations in available methodologies. The problem of investigator bias reflects the very nature of charismatic groups. Such groups maintain their views even in the face of contrary evidence, and, as we just saw, do this with a mutuality that stands independent of contrary evidence. They also tend to elicit contrary views and animosity from the surrounding community, which itself may be no less biased regarding an alien sect. As a result, the investigator is almost always pressed to adopt a position that either favors or opposes the stands taken by the charismatic group. For example, at times my studies on charismatic sects were attacked as a reflection of my being "duped" by the Moonies; at other times the same studies were seen just the opposite, as evidence of the use of my "professional credentials to discredit" these groups.[19] A dispassionate middle ground is not easily defined.

A second problem in carrying out this research lies in designing a valid methodology. We had to adapt approaches and techniques from a variety of disciplines, including psychiatry, social psychology, anthropology, and sociology. In addition, questions often had to be framed so as to make use of the methodology available, rather than what might be the most interesting to study. For example, my principal interest in initiating the Orlando study was to examine the major psychopathology found among some Divine Light members. Practically speaking, this could not be studied in a controlled fashion because reliable self-report measurements for the relevant diagnostic categories were not available. Instead we had to use a more general psychological adjustment scale.

Even more broadly, the choice of a proper context in which to study the interrelatedness of group members in a charismatic group also presents a major paradox. The group phenomena observed among its members—their intense closeness, feelings, and beliefs—can hardly be recreated in a laboratory. Yet so many real world variables impinge on the phenomena to be studied that to observe them outside the laboratory setting, without ample controls, would leave researchers vulnerable to a circus of external issues, let alone their own subjectivity.

This paradox is illustrated by my previous research on the influence of social context on drug use and abuse. Volunteers in a laboratory setting smoked either active marijuana, placebo marijuana, or no drug at the outset of each of a series of professionally led encounter-group meetings.[20] The controlled setting was too artificial, however, to create the degree of cohesiveness usually associated with drug use. The question remained as to how such a controlled evaluation of group interrelatedness could be undertaken effectively.[21]

Outside the laboratory, studies on the peyote rituals of the Native American Indian Church in the Southwest United States[22] show that the tribe's cohesive social structure was closely integrated into this religious experience when the hallucinogen is taken in the context of a close-knit community. This religious context clearly cannot be reproduced in an ad hoc fashion, but one can surmise that these close ties are an effective vehicle for transforming a potentially disruptive hallucinogenic experience into a constructive and therapeutic one.[23]

In what setting can the role of the naturally emerging social ties of a religious sect be best studied? My access to the Divine Light Mission appeared to offer an opportunity for analyzing group cohesiveness in a systematic, controlled way within its natural setting. Specifically, a statistical assessment could be made of the relationship between such variables as group cohesiveness and other measures of the members' emotional status. In this respect, the sect presented an "experiment of nature."

To conduct such an analysis, a fairly large sample of subjects was needed, and consequently it was not feasible to rely primarily on interviews, since personnel were not available. We developed a seven-page multiple-choice questionaire and gave copies to 119 subjects who were active members of the Divine Light Mission, selected at random from the festival registration lines.*

In framing the questionnaire, we had to address certain technical problems. One was the need to choose symptoms of mental illness or health that could be queried within this format. Some scales for evaluating major mental illness, such as the SCL-90,[24] have limited specificity and are fairly lengthy. It was best to use a scale that drew on symptoms experienced by a large portion of the population, such as anxiety, depression, and suicidal thoughts. Since we needed to ascertain the subjects' perception of their psychological state both before and after joining the group, the scale had to be short and easy to fill out relative to the subjects' experience during more than one period in their life.

---

*Members of charismatic groups are remarkably compliant in filling out long questionnaires, so long as it is sanctioned by their leadership. I have found, however, that more independent sorts in less zealous groups can give an investigator no end of trouble.

Table 2-1. *Psychological Distress Items (and Implied Symptoms)*

Subjects indicated how much they felt this way, on a scale of 1 ("not at all") to 5 ("very much").

1. I felt nervous and tense. [anxiety]   ( )
2. I felt depressed and glum. [depression]   ( )
3. I had thoughts of ending my life. [suicidal ideation]   ( )
4. I had the feeling that I was being watched or talked about by
   others. [referential thinking]   ( )
5. I was unclear about how to lead my life. [anomie]   ( )
6. I got into trouble with my job, at school, or with the law.
   [behavioral]   ( )
7. I heard voices that other people did not hear. [hearing voices]   ( )
8. Emotional problems interfere with my adjustment in life.
   [general emotional maladaptation]   ( )

For a brief ad hoc scale, it also seemed best to develop items that would have face validity, that is, they would clearly reflect the symptoms of psychological distress. This approach contrasts with self-report psychological scales such as the Minnesota Multi-Phasic Personality Inventory (the MMPI), a widely used but quite long schedule whose validity has been tested by standardizing items on large groups of people with different psychiatric diagnoses. Each of the MMPI questions in itself (comparable to "I like to collect stamps"), however, does not have an obvious relationship to the symptoms measured by the test.

Table 2-1 gives the items developed for this Psychological Distress Scale, each rated from 1 ("not at all") to 5 ("very much") by the respondent.[25] The total points for the eight symptoms indicated the psychological distress score. Subjects evaluated each symptom during four two-month periods: the worst they had felt; right before their first contact with the Divine Light Mission; immediately after joining; and at present. This made it possible to compare their estimation of the psychological distress they had experienced before and after joining.

In addition to psychological distress, a second "outcome" variable, drug use, was studied. Each of six common drugs of abuse was listed, and subjects were asked to rate how often they used each drug during the same four two-month periods on a scale from 1 ("none at all") to 5 ("more than once on most days").

Responses were then related to specific aspects of the group membership to find out how group membership might have led to any psychological and drug use changes. Group cohesiveness as a predictor of change, as well as other group issues such as meditation practice, to be discussed later, were also considered.

Group cohesiveness was measured on the scale given in Table 2-2, adapted

Table 2-2. *Social Cohesiveness Scale*

Subjects rated their feelings toward the group on each item, on a scale of 1 ("not at all") to 5 ("very much").

1. How much do these descriptions apply to the group?
   a. They care for me   ( )
   b. They are happy   ( )
   c. They are suspicious of me [scored in reverse]   ( )

2. How would you describe your feelings for them?
   a. I care for them   ( )
   b. They make me happy   ( )
   c. I am suspicious of them [scored in reverse]   ( )

3. Do they have the qualities a *premie* [member] should have?   ( )

4. Do you like being part of their activities?   ( )

---

from the earlier study on marijuana use and social interaction. A member's cohesive feelings about three different groups were recorded: the ten members of the sect whom the subject knew best, all the sect members, and the ten nonmembers the subject knew best. This offered a contrast between the subjects' feelings of affiliation toward people inside and outside the group.

Results of the Study

The survey produced revealing findings regarding the psychology of the charismatic group. First, the members' reports reflected a relief of distress on joining. Second, the members' cohesiveness toward the group was closely associated with this relief. From these findings emerged a beginning sense of what motivated members to comply with the group.

Members who had joined the sect roughly two years before reported a considerable decline in psychological distress and drug use after joining. Many had a history of psychological problems and several had sought professional help (38%) or had been hospitalized for emotional disorders (9%). These findings formed the first objective evidence of the role psychological distress plays in recruitment to such groups. Furthermore, members' level of distress symptoms decline over the course of conversion. The average incidence for the items on the Distress Scale is given in Table 2-3, as are the figures for marijuana and heroin use, which reflect the all-around decline in both psychological distress and drug use.[26] This observation revealed an apparent overall improvement in psychiatric state derived from conversion and its retention through continued membership. These findings were confirmed in later research on the Unification Church where it was possible to study recruits as well as disaffiliated members.

The cohesiveness scores showed that respondents felt considerably closer

Table 2-3. *Outcome of Initiation into the Divine Light Mission*

These figures indicate the percentage of subjects who reported the presence of symptoms during each of four two-month periods.

	The Four Periods			
Three Sample Items	*The Worst Ever*	*Right Before Joining*	*Right After Joining*	*Now*
Psychological Distress Scale, average for the 8 items	80	71	45	37
Daily marijuana use	65	45	0	7
Any heroin use	14	7	1	0

toward members of their sect than toward nonmembers whom they knew best.[27] Almost all of the respondents (99%) said they cared a lot for the ten members they knew best, and most (56%) felt similarly toward the membership overall. Only the minority of members (39%) responded this way in relation to the nonmembers they knew best. If valid, this would mean that most members felt closer toward the sect overall (few of whose members they had actually met) than toward the ten people outside the sect they knew best. Their connection to the group far outweighed their attachments to outsiders.

To examine the relationship, if any, between the feeling of cohesiveness and the symptom changes reported, we statistically analyzed the average decline in symptom scores.[28] Social cohesion accounted for 37% of the overall decline in psychological distress that occurred after subjects joined the group. That is, a large part of the enhanced well-being derived from joining this sect could be attributed to the members' feelings of relatedness with fellow members.

Such findings were notable since the degree of neurotic distress experienced by individuals is determined by many factors, including differences in temperament, quality of life, and how people see themselves in relation to the rest of the world. But for the young adults in our study, the decline in feelings of psychological distress was directly proportional to the degree of cohesiveness they felt toward the group.

One might have thought that members like Ellen, who were most emotionally troubled before entering the sect, would have benefited the most from joining. Yet the survey indicated that serious emotional problems before joining were not specifically correlated with either a greater or lesser decline in psychological distress. Nor were serious emotional problems correlated with a higher social cohesiveness score.[29] All members, whether seriously distressed or not, reported an improved emotional state after joining.

These findings naturally raise the question of whether subjects overestimated the degree of distress before joining and the amount of improvement after. While this may well have occurred, a later study on the Unification Church (see Chapter 8) supported the view that the effect on psychological well-being of joining the group was real.

Such emotional gains reinforce members' involvement in the group by effectively "rewarding" them for their fealty to it. The reward, specifically, is enhanced well-being when the members feel closer to each other. And this reward may help explain the members' remarkable conformity to the group's expectations, since acceptance and conformity bring relief from distress.

3

SHARED
BELIEFS

The beliefs held in common by members of cults are a vital force in the group's operation. They bind members together, shape their attitudes, and motivate them to act in self-sacrifice. I began to appreciate the importance of such beliefs in following the career of my friend who had joined the Divine Light Mission. At first it seemed certain that Beth's involvement would be ephemeral; surely this sensible and successful young woman would soon turn back to her roots in the Western mainstream. But this assumption proved wrong. Beth moved her home across country more than once to follow her youthful guru, and took a number of trips to India along with his followers. Several years later she married a fellow premie. After having a child, she obtained a university position and returned to teaching, but remained deeply committed to her belief in the guru.

A few years after Beth joined the Divine Light Mission, it was obvious that she believed very strongly in something the group offered and that her involvement reflected an abiding faith, not easy to fathom but quite telling in its implications for the psychology of charismatic groups. Consider a letter in which she spoke of her belief in the guru, whose actual contact with thousands of followers must have been limited.

> His revelation of the Kingdom of Heaven within us all is a completely practical experience for each and every individual. . . . The gift of Knowledge that Maharaj Ji has given me is so deeply satisfying and joyfully constant that I can't imagine another being conveying the truth as he has revealed it.

Beth accepted the guru's transcendent message in a way that others before her might have embraced the prophets and messiahs of old. This literal

37

faith was hard to understand since it came from a woman whom I had known some years before as agnostic and even cynical, and was clearly at variance with the underlying attitudes one would expect in a person with her background and pluralistic views. To understand the role such strong beliefs play in charismatic groups, we will examine a related historical example.

Communities of Shared Belief

A Utopian Commune

In the mid-nineteenth century several Utopian communities, each rooted in its particular interpretations of Christian dogma, were established in northeastern United States. Most were limited in both size and duration. They included the Oneida Community, the Shakers, the Harmony Society, and— transplanted from Central Europe—the Hutterites. Though short-lived, these communities had a high degree of social cohesiveness and shared belief, were typically led by a charismatic leader, and exacted conformity to their unusual norms of behavior. Particularly striking is the important role that religious creeds played in sustaining these groups. Rosabeth Kanter[1] studied thirty sects and found that those with the greatest social stability and longevity were all founded on the basis of shared religious beliefs: their respective systems of belief and ritual were essential to the groups' stability, allowing members to sacrifice their own needs in rejecting the material world. In addition, the groups' transcendent moral codes serves to support the primacy of their leaders.

Among the more successful of these groups was the Oneida Community, which was established in 1847 in upstate New York and dissolved thirty-two years later after the departure of its leader.[2] It was part of a widespread religious renewal that began in the early 1830s. Around this time, John Humphrey Noyes graduated from Dartmouth College and served unsuccessfully as an apprentice in a New Hampshire law firm. During his subsequent disillusionment, he attended a four-day camp meeting in his native Vermont and underwent a religious conversion. Noyes declared himself to be without sin, drawing this position from his own interpretation of Christ's redemption, and began to seek followers for his emerging system of idiosyncratic beliefs. Within a decade, he developed a following of a few dozen people who adopted the practices of economic communism and spouse sharing that were remarkably deviant for the time. Under threat of indictment for adultery, Noyes had to remove his group to an isolated location in upstate New York. The commune Noyes established there grew to over a hundred members within a few years and nearly three hundred before its decline. The intensely held beliefs of these Perfectionists, as they were called, were striking. They espoused a utopian goal of "creating heaven on earth," a pursuit centered for the sect's duration in a large communal residence called the Mansion House. Here their society was organized around group-oriented facilities, such as a community dining room, a library, and common recreation areas. Even three generations after the commune dissolved, descendants still lived near this house, reflecting their lingering fidelity.[3]

The members' strong belief in the principles of communal ownership is seen even in the activities of its children. At one point the principle of shared property was reinterpreted so that each little girl might possess a doll of her own, rather than share in the community's dolls, as done with all other possessions. When the adults observed that the youngsters spent too much time with these dolls and not enough on household chores, all were summoned together and told to destroy them, each girl throwing her own doll into a fire. Noyes' son later wrote that, "Throughout my childhood the private ownership of anything seemed to me a crude artificiality to which an unenlightened Outside still clung. . . . it never occurred to me that I could possess a sled to the exclusion of other boys."[4]

In a charismatic group, shared beliefs are best established by a close-knit communications system in which acceptable views are directly or implicitly encouraged and dissenting ones suppressed. Control is most effectively exerted through social pressure rather than forcible prohibition of dissent, which would only generate disillusionment and passive conformity. In the Oneida Community this was evident in the group's daily communal meetings. Every night the Oneidians met in the Big Hall of the Mansion House to combine religious rituals with secular functions and discussion. Hymn singing and Bible reading were part of the evening fare. Noyes himself would speak, relating the group's religious practice to the behavior and attitudes of the members. Members could also bring up personal concerns, so that issues not usually voiced in public settings were discussed by the group and then resolved by recourse to Noyes' religious ideals. This enabled the community to establish norms in all areas of social interaction and promote social conformity. Meetings were referred to by one member as "the most cherished part of our daily lives,"[5] reflecting the way in which the group's influence on a shared set of values was accepted by members, and not seen as intrusive.

In rural isolation, the group developed an ideology and related rituals deviant from those of the general population. It became known for the nature of its sexual relationships in particular, and these eventually led to widespread public criticism that contributed to its dissolution.

Noyes believed that monogamous marriage among commune members was harmful to the communist principles of his sect because it excluded others from sharing in a vital affectional tie. Although this view may have arisen from his own personal disappointments, he cited the Bible for his rationale: "In the Kingdom of Heaven, the institution of marriage—which assigns the exclusive possession of one woman to one man—does not exist" (Mt. 22:23). The system he implemented in Oneida allowed a man who wanted to have sexual intercourse with a particular woman simply to ask her. If she agreed, he would spend the night in her room. Contraception was achieved by terminating intercourse before ejaculation, a procedure practiced with apparent success. Some years later, the use of a "go-between" became conventional. This person judged the acceptability of any given liaison and discouraged "amatory" relationships, which were seen to run contrary to the group's communal ideology.

Management of marital and affectional ties by means of the belief system of a charismatic group can be a powerful component of social controls, and the go-between system clearly served this purpose. Indeed, later in its history the system was organized so that decisions on couplings were made by Noyes himself, thereby centralizing his control over the group.

The Oneida Community is an interesting historical illustration of how a group's beliefs can be integrated into its system of social controls. It also demonstrates the central role a charismatic religious leader can play in their implementation. These techniques stand in sharp contrast to the crude, coercive ones described by Lifton and others in their studies of brainwashing by the Communist Chinese.[6]

Faith and Healing

Assumptive beliefs, communication patterns, and, ultimately, norms for behavior were all determined within the confines of the Oneida Community. A step removed from this is the less clearly defined entity of a subculture, which does not exist in physical isolation from the broader social environment but nonetheless shapes communication among its members by means of consensually held beliefs.

Most often, we apply the term faith healing to treatments used in cultures whose fundamental beliefs are alien to the contemporary values of scientific medicine. In their classic studies of Navajo healing, Alexander and Dorothy Leighton[7] emphasized the role of belief, group support, shared emotional experience, and the paraphernalia of communal rituals, such as eagle and owl feathers. A disruption of the members' usual psychological and physical state (discussed later under altered consciousness) further intensified the way the group called on its shared belief system. For example, emetics were frequently consumed by participants in these rituals, and hot pokers were often applied by shamans both to the patient and others present at the healing ceremony. Syndromes treated by the Navajo have been classified in accordance with that culture's own subtypes of mental illness, and some may also be described in terms of contemporary diagnostic criteria as major psychiatric illnesses, including schizophrenia, agitated depression, hysteria, and pathologic intoxication.[8]

An upsurge in religious commitment in the United States in recent decades, particularly in fundamentalist religion, has brought faith healing closer to the cultural mainstream. Church attendance has increased dramatically in the past half-century. Currently, for example, about half of all married couples attend church regularly, compared to only one-quarter fifty years ago, and the ratio of church buildings to the population has gone up by almost two-thirds.[9]

Mansell Pattison and his associates[10] have studied contemporary American faith healing by evaluating psychological traits of individuals who underwent Pentecostal healing. Those who had been "healed" avowed that they could place their full faith in God and so there was consequently little reason to be concerned or upset about their problems. A systematic assessment of their mental status by psychiatric interviews showed scant evidence of major mental illness, but their responses to the MMPI indicated that these people relied heavily on the psychological defense mechanism of denial. Using this defense, an individual who is unable to tolerate an objective reality or its implications literally thinks and acts as if that reality did not exist; this occurs even though the person may be regularly confronted by unpalatable facts. Pattison's subjects perceived their faith-healing experience as a definitive treatment *regardless* of the presence or absence of physical symptoms afterwards. He and his colleagues concluded that the primary function of faith healing was not necessarily to resolve symptoms, but to reinforce the group's religious perspective and thereby provide sick people with a means of avoiding harsh realities. Although healing was the declared purpose of the ritual, in actuality it functioned to integrate members into the group.

The ability to blind oneself to reality through religious ritual may serve as a solution to certain psychological problems. This is evident in research on the plasticity of people's responses to the physiologic changes underlying their emotions. In a study conducted by Stanley Schacter and Jerome Singer,[11] subjects were given a dose of adrenalin, a naturally occurring stimulant, and were then led to experience either euphoria or anger, depending on the sham setting into which they were introduced. Those who were exposed to an actor who feigned anger tended to feel anger. Those exposed to a giddy, silly actor tended to become euphoric themselves. The study was important because it suggested that people's emotional responses to drugs can be determined to a large degree by the social context. Hence, it is not surprising that a zealous religious service could prime individuals to accept a group's own interpretation of how they *should* be feeling and how they should perceive their physical state.

Another interesting study by Pattison[12] concerned a group with long-standing histories of overt homosexuality. After joining a Pentecostal Church group and adopting its belief systems, these men eventually became exclusively practicing heterosexuals. Did religious commitment lead to a genuine change (healing, as it were) in sexual orientation, or was the tendency toward homosexuality only suppressed? This is difficult to answer definitively, but the men reported the emergence of satisfactory heterosexual relationships with women, both as newfound friends and spouses, and in time homosexual fantasies among these converts became quite limited or nonexistent, essentially at the level of the heterosexual population.

How could these men have changed their sexual orientation through religion? Within the belief system of the Pentecostal Church, homosexuality was defined as an immoral attitude that the individual himself can expunge, and members were expected to refrain from all homosexual practices. By virtue of their personal experience in the group, and the behavior expected of them, they apparently relinquished what is thought by many to be an almost irreversible trait.

The Pentecostals did not regard homosexuality as a deviation from an innate characteristic or a physically grounded condition. Thus, the afflicted person could take an active role in changing his own attitudes and behavior, in collaboration with the church. Interestingly, investigators found that these "converted" homosexuals, committed to their Pentecostal beliefs and actively complying with them, experienced much less emotional distress than a comparable sample of practicing homosexual men in the general population.

A Psychiatric Hospital

Systems of belief sometimes clash in psychiatric wards. Physicians committed to the values of science and rationality often do not make allowances for alternative perspectives with patients whose cultic views have brought them to the hospital or seem intertwined with psychopathology.

A few years ago, I was asked to help evaluate Carol, a twenty-nine-year-old black woman from a disadvantaged background, shortly after she was transferred to our psychiatry service. She had just undergone exploratory abdominal surgery because of a life-threatening and self-inflicted gunshot wound. During the course of her hospitalization, I was able to trace Carol's encounters with three systems of shared belief, each exerting its influence over her behavior. The first was a delusional belief system that brought her to the hospital; the second was the world view espoused by her physicians; and the third consisted of the Pentecostal religious beliefs she later adopted.

Though Carol was at first reluctant to provide details, her mother reported that she and another woman had shared the same lover who had driven them to a variety of bizarre behaviors. Bobby, the lover, once paraded the two women naked into the street. He occasionally boasted of having special powers, of being a "genius" who would "change the course of history and bring on the Black kingdom." Carol often parroted his words and ideas, saying that, "White devils are going to leech the color out of the world." Other informants also reported that both women sometimes seemed to go into a "trance" while with Bobby, and would tell of seeing images on the television screen placed there by him. Once Carol told her mother that Bobby literally controlled her feelings from day to day.

The episode that precipitated Carol's hospitalization occurred a day after Bobby had shown her a picture of a gun, along with a book entitled *The Power of Decision,* leading her to conclude that he wanted her to shoot herself. After doing just that the next day, she telephoned him, and he suggested she call an ambulance and get to a hospital.

The staff was puzzled when Carol was transferred to the psychiatry service. They felt they were confronted by a phenomenon at the interface of a shared delusion (therefore "crazy") and a cult (presumably cultural). Psychiatry does have trouble dealing with pathology shared by groups, for it is primarily a discipline that addresses individual disorders rather than social phenomena. The staff's inclination was to treat Carol as a "routine" psychotic.

I interviewed Carol at the request of the staff and found that she had no thought disorder and no overt symptoms of delusional thinking, although it was possible she was keeping bizarre thoughts to herself. She did not appear to be suffering from a schizophrenic psychosis. Nor was she particularly depressed, although she was fairly anxious and confused about her motivations when confronted with the tale told by her mother. I suggested her psychiatric symptoms would abate now that she was removed from Bobby.

In several days, a shift in Carol's thinking was indeed apparent. She made the following statement, reflecting the distance she had begun to place between herself and the beliefs she shared with Bobby.

> I used to think that Bobby could explain everything, but what he said didn't always make sense. I think I should forget the Kingdom he promised; it was just his own crazy idea. I hate to blame him for the shooting, but maybe he had a bad influence on me.

Carol had been affected by the rational world view of the hospital staff, who explained to her how she had developed delusional ideas under Bobby's influence. In casting out her devil, however, her doctors had not offered Carol an alternative set of beliefs that was compelling to her, unlike persons engaged in religious ritual. Explanations about delusions and mental function meant little to this young woman who had ended her formal education at age fifteen.

During her hospital stay, Carol herself stumbled on a solution. She was given a Bible tract by a fellow patient involved in a Pentecostal sect, and quickly developed a strong interest in reading Scriptures. A commitment to Pentecostalism, which she had encountered as a child in her grandmother's house, soon followed, and she began to explain both the events of the shooting and a clear-cut relief in her malaise in terms of her growing belief in Jesus.

Three weeks after admission, Carol stated that she planned to move to her grandmother's house when she left the hospital. She explained:

> When I used to go to bed at night in the old days, I felt the devils coming onto me before I could fall asleep. . . . There was no way to escape them, so I stayed awake till dawn to protect myself. Bobby told me that the devils would always follow me, and that I was going to act out their sins. Sometimes he said I had to run out into the street without my clothes on so they would be shamed into leaving me, but now the devils are gone forever, and it was Jesus who made them go. They left when I returned to Him, and that's why I'll be safe with my grandmother and with the Church.

Carol had now adopted the perspective of Pentecostalism, which seemed more comfortable for her than any offered by the medical staff. She made this clear on the fourth week after her admission to our service.

> Look, I'll tell you this. Jesus says it's evil to shoot yourself, but He'll forgive me, and I'm ready to plead for His mercy, and start again. You folks should take a lesson from Him. He's the one with the answers. . . . Bobby? The Devil must have sent him; that's for sure.

She looked forward to going home, and the edge of anxiety in her earlier manner was gone, replaced by an appearance of certitude. She was experiencing no delusions or hallucinations and was soon discharged to her grandmother's custody.

Carol had begun to move from one system of shared beliefs, Bobby's delusions, to a second one, the psychological perspective of the hospital staff, but she finally accepted a third that was more viable for her: Pentecostal Christianity. That her first set of bizarre beliefs had been validated by two other persons may reflect a bit less poorly on the integrity of Carol's mental function. Nonetheless, she was clearly disturbed. The Pentecostal beliefs provided Carol with an explanation of her illness she could accept, ascribing it to satanic influences external to herself and allowing her to feel intact once she renounced those influences.

In Carol's case, we have seen how a very small charismatic group can generate a delusional belief system. These vigorously defended views can then lead a member to pathologic thought and behavior, even to self-destructiveness. In the end, acceptance of such bizarre beliefs may be difficult to distinguish from true mental illness.

A second case of conflict between belief systems in a psychiatric ward involved a member of a well-organized charismatic sect. When I was asked to evaluate Tom, a single twenty-six year old at a nearby hospital, conflict was apparent from the outset: the hospital staff had become agents of Tom's family, who suggested his admission.

On arrival, I saw from the hospital's Tudor-style buildings and commodious rooms that it catered to a class of patients with access to whatever services the mental health professional might offer. The resident psychiatrist who had treated the patient in the hospital presented the case and explained that Tom had been admitted to this hospital by his private psychiatrist. He came from an affluent background, and his family was prepared to provide whatever was necessary to assure his return to a "normal" existence. He was judged to have two problems. One was the depression precipitating his hospitalization; the other was his commitment to Shri Rajneesh, an Eastern guru. The second problem concerned Tom's family most. After three months with the sect, Tom had all but severed his ties to his family, much to their anger and distress, and after four years moved to a remote spot in Oregon where the guru's followers had recently relocated.

The resident psychiatrist emphasized a conflict that, in her estimation, had developed in Tom's family. The depression began, she explained, when Tom was confronted by his father, whom he had visited in the hospital shortly after the man had been in a serious auto accident. The father insisted that Tom was pursuing a senseless course and that it was time for him to abandon his foolish ideas and return home, where he could enter into their business and have a proper future. As on previous occasions, Tom refused to accept this offer. The resident surmised that Tom felt guilty about his father's condition but was unable to express his resentment over the man's demands, given his precarious medical condition.

After the confrontation Tom spent a few weeks with followers of Rajneesh in another city but then returned home. He was apparently feeling depressed now, and over the next few weeks became more withdrawn. Eventually he agreed to be hospitalized, since he was not motivated for any activities other than meeting with local followers of the guru.

To protect Tom from further tension in the hospital, the resident psychiatrist had prohibited members of his sect from visiting him, although he was allowed to see his family. Tom resented this at first, but later accepted his isolation from his co-religionists, and soon developed a comfortable relationship with his doctor. While being treated with psychotherapy and antidepressant medications, he began to improve. When he was ready to be discharged, Tom was referred back to his skilled private psychiatrist who continued his therapy on an outpatient basis.

The whole process served to isolate him from his fellow cult members. Since his adherence to the group's unusual beliefs depended on sustaining a mental barrier against the common culture, his psychiatrist's therapeutic regimen effectively undermined the stability of his religious world view.

Tom's private psychiatrist had also come to the resident's presentation to discuss the case. He remarked on his own distaste for the "cult," and was pleased to say that in time Tom was able to put aside preoccupations with the group and attend to the matters at hand, which revolved around the need to consider an appropriate role for himself in the family's business and reestablish a secure identity in the general community.

I was a bit suspicious of the history presented, having encountered many young sect members who had shed commitments to their families when their parents opposed their involvement in a zealous sect. Indeed, in many such groups, parents were regularly eschewed when they intruded on sect activities. Why did Tom turn away from the sect at this time and return to his family? In addition, it was routine practice for any member in trouble to turn to fellow sect members, however far away they might be.

When I spoke with Tom, it became clear why he hadn't contacted other Rajneeshees. Apparently he experienced conflicts with senior figures in the Rajneesh movement while living in their religious community in Oregon and was beginning to question his ability to achieve the religious goals they had outlined for him, although he did not doubt the merits of the goals themselves. Tom insisted that he had otherwise been content during the previous years in the group, and had established close relations with other members. He had been involved for a while with a young woman in the group and was considering returning to her, but was not prepared to face his fellow members because of the difficulty in resolving his spiritual impasse.

Three months before his hospitalization, Tom had volunteered to organize a regional center for the Rajneeshees on the West Coast, hoping to work out his conflicts in this setting, but he apparently ran into difficulties with some members in that task too, difficulties that mirrored his prior trouble in relating to the group's hierarchy. Because of all these events, he was becoming increasingly disenchanted with himself when the call came from his family about his father's accident.

As Tom described the situation, his problems with the sect were mainly responsible for his feelings of failure. His decision to remain with his family was primarily an attempt to create a setting where he might resolve these conflicts and then return to the sect since his commitment had not wavered. His sense of failure depressed him and he was uncertain whether he would be acceptable to sect members should he turn to them for help. When the option of hospitalization was offered by his parents, he saw little alternative but to accept, even though he feared they were using this to wean him from the movement.

By preventing Tom's continued contact with the sect, his resident physician was implicitly pressing him to give up an identity and the related beliefs that had been most important to him. Both psychiatrists in effect worked to move him further from the group, identifying a "healthy" outcome as a return to the beliefs and values of the broader culture. Whether he would be better off adopting his doctors' and family's perspective was a question that troubled him, for Tom still spoke of the option of returning to the sect. He was no longer suffering from depression but was clearly unhappy, as he now felt unable to accept either option. He was torn between two belief systems.

In its attempt to provide assistance, the medical community was clearly promoting a set of beliefs in conflict with those Tom had espoused on entering the hospital. Perhaps he would be happier with the advantages and values of his family or maybe he would be better off returning to the sect where he had lived for the previous five years. But this value judgment was being made for him, at least implicitly, by his physicians.

Also troubling was that the doctors, because they shared the family's values, were unaware of making a subjective judgment and hence misconstrued some of Tom's conflicts. Specifically, they presumed that Tom's depression stemmed from guilt over his response to his father, rather than his feelings of having failed as a member of the sect. They saw his affinity for the sect as pathologic in contrast to entering the family's business and social world, whereas in Tom's mind it was a reasonable choice that he had not yet made.

In the end, Tom chose to stay with his family, and was closely monitored by them for several months after his release. During that time he held an office job in the family business and gradually reestablished contact with the friends he had made before becoming a follower of Rajneesh.

This case may convey the way in which subjective judgments can enter our assessment of the shared beliefs of members of charismatic groups, and how difficult it is to stand apart from one's own beliefs in making such judgments. It becomes even more difficult to decide on a proper course of treatment for sect members when psychiatric disorders occur. After all, Tom's parents brought him in. Unlike Tom, many individuals have resisted reacculturation at the hands of mental health professionals.

The Treatment of Schizophrenia

The issue of zealous beliefs in the treatment of mental illness is relevant not just to a small minority. Hope for the future, based on commitment and belief, is one of the vital components of all psychological treatments. Patients must accept an assumptive system (such as psychoanalysis or self-help) that implicitly explains how they will get well.

Jerome Frank[13] pointed out that a central aspect of the psychotherapeutic process is the instillation of hope. Sadly, this is lacking in the treatment of many seriously ill psychiatric patients because it usually focuses on acute symptoms, after relying on the use of psychotropic medications. All too commonly, acute schizophrenic patients are successfully medicated for relief of hallucinations and delusional thinking and are then seen ready for discharge, without serious attention to their attitude toward future readjustment.

It is also true that schizophrenics admitted to psychiatric hospitals are often unable to face their own disillusionment with themselves and their lives—only chemicals can suppress their disturbing thoughts—and they have no beliefs relevant to their illness around which they can build a positive view of the future. To maintain a measure of hope, they sometimes deny the very reality of their past problem, and may even be unable to acknowledge the immediate circumstances that brought them to seek help.

In an attempt to address the problem of disillusionment in recovering schizophrenics, a compelling experiment was conducted by Loren Mosher and Alma Menn under the auspices of the National Institute of Mental Health. They established a psychiatric treatment center called Soteria House in a modest residential building, and tried to instill a different perspective in their patients. Mosher and Menn applied many of the psychological principles we have observed at work in charismatic groups in an explicitly therapeutic context. Specifically, they created a cohesive group setting that provided an explanation for the patients' illness and also gave them a reason to feel optimistic about their return to a healthy mental state.

The experimental Soteria Program was not hospital based to avoid the feeling of a large, impersonal institution. Also missing were psychotropic medications, which were used only as a last resort for uncontrollable residents; the overwhelming majority (92%) of Soteria residents received no drugs. They were cared for by a nonprofessional staff that worked closely with them in 48- to 60-hour shifts, allowing for continuous and intense interactions.

What did this experimental treatment actually offer its patients? Caregivers did not have a professional or scientific rationale for viewing schizophrenia as an innate disease; rather they regarded Soteria residents as having reacted in an unusual but *meaningful* way to their problems of living, and were able now, with the aid of those around them, to rebuild their lives by using their unique experiences.[14] This attitude is far removed from the biological view of schizophrenia most psychiatrists hold today. Mosher and Menn used the term *belief* to characterize the way in which the Soteria staff framed its conception of the psychotic experience.[15] Indeed, a shared belief in the value of the schizophrenic's personal experiences is conveyed to the Soteria residents, thereby affording them a basically optimistic viewpoint to which they may be "converted."

This gives the endeavor a transcendent quality. It falls within a tradition in which madness is associated with sacred quasidivine attributes; residents and staff alike take a philosophic position broadly applicable to the altered consciousness everyone may potentially experience.[16] From this derives a behavioral norm: patients, to move on to the next level of personality integration, must now adopt a constructive and positive set of behaviors. They do this with hope of moving toward this next stage rather than from a sense of needing to suppress some innate failing. That is the ideal at Soteria, and there is evidence that schizophrenic patients can develop active control over symptoms of their illness when properly motivated by their social milieu.[17] Sadly, this perspective is still alien to most established caregivers.[18]

Shared Beliefs in the Unification Church

The Unification Church, or the Moonies, was one of the best known of the charismatic sects to appear on the American scene in the 1970s. The mistrust that arose between members and the surrounding culture received extensive media coverage; it pitted proponents of different belief systems against each other in a society that had worked hard to achieve religious tolerance.

The sect gained considerable notoriety for the way it acquired youthful converts, since conversion represented a major disruption in family ties and religious beliefs. New members moved into communal residences, and for weeks, even months, refused to associate with their families. Distraught parents felt they had lost their children forever; some resorted to deprogrammers who would forcibly abduct and sequester their children, pressing them to recant their newfound beliefs. Most of those treated this way (who were, in fact, not minors) escaped their captors and returned to their co-religionists, where they were usually sent to remote church centers and protected from further abduction.

Initial Encounters

My first contact with the Moonies came through Dr. Richard Rabkin, a psychiatrist at New York University, who had heard about the Divine Light Mission project. After giving a talk on the psychology of contemporary religious sects at a nearby university, he had been approached by representatives of the Moonies, who asked whether he would be interested in learning more about this group. He felt that I might be able to organize a systematic study of it.

The opportunity was appealing because I had already begun to experiment with a treatment approach for alcoholism modeled on the psychology of charismatic groups and I now wanted a better understanding of how such groups operated. I was particularly interested in learning how dissemination of the group's beliefs and concomitant control over communication in the sect affected members' psychological states. A project on the Moonies might shed light on the remarkable beliefs these zealous groups could engender and how they motivated their members to such high levels of commitment.

Rabkin and I were soon joined in the study by Drs. Judith Rabkin of Columbia University and Alexander Deutsch of New York University. Our principal liaison with the sect's hierarchy was a likeable and frank woman in her late twenties, who served as the Director of Public Affairs for the U.S. church. The necessary arrangements were made in a lengthy meeting with Neil Salonen, the president of the Unification Church of America. No doubt he too felt it necessary to have a firsthand sense of the researchers' attitude and chose to be directly involved in any final understanding. Salonen was an affable and outgoing Caucasian in his late thirties, who seemed more like the regional manager of a middle-American corporation than a religious zealot or scion of subversive aliens. He had worked in hospital administration before joining the church, and had only reluctantly left that position after an extended period of membership, when he decided to contribute more actively to the work of his newfound religion. He and his wife, both members for ten years, had borne and raised two children since joining.

The rationale I presented Salonen for supporting his members' participation in this study was the same offered for subsequent projects. I pointed out that the sect often received poor press, as he well knew. Participation would offer the opportunity to have the nature of their sect brought forth objectively and would further show they had nothing to hide on the issues of brainwashing and coercion, since they were willing to have outside observers evaluate the membership experience. I felt their openness to these studies did indeed reflect well on the group's credibility.

Conversion and Belief

Interviews with members of the Unification Church revealed several different routes of induction into this charismatic group. Some converts did not actively seek out any new order, and were only introduced to the sect's beliefs by means of *subterfuge*. Others became engaged only after their own protracted journey as *seekers* of an acceptable creed. Some were initially attracted to a group whose idealistic commitments allowed for their *identification* with an admired figure or ideal, while others felt compelled to accept church dogma they had initially *opposed*. We will now examine more closely these four ways of engagement.

My first chance to speak in depth with a church member, whose mental competency I was asked to evaluate, was with Jerry, a twenty year old, who had become involved in litigation over his parents' attempt to remove him from the sect. His case shed light on how new members were sometimes converted by subterfuge, often in surprising ways.

SUBTERFUGE

Three weeks before I met Jerry, his parents had been designated by a local court to serve as his legal guardians. He was alleged to be mentally incompetent, based on two pieces of evidence. The first was the statement of a family physician who had last seen Jerry when he was fifteen, when he became anxious during a family crisis; the second was Jerry's current involvement in a putative cult. The doctor now wrote that Jerry had "schizophrenic tendencies and was unstable, depending on the environment."

I spoke with an attorney assigned to the case by the American Civil Liberties Union. This organization had long defended the rights of people espousing unpopular causes, and recently provided attorneys for members of new religious movements such as the Unification Church. The attorney emphasized the overriding importance of the First and Fourteenth Amendments to the Constitution—freedom of religion and due process. New York State, for example, required that for someone in Jerry's situation to be placed under conservatorship, he must appear to be mentally ill and likely to cause serious harm to himself or others. I was well acquainted with this rule since it was also used as a criterion for the involuntary commitment of psychotic patients.

On interviewing Jerry, I found that a conservatorship on these grounds was unjustified because he was lucid, content with his circumstances, and without signs of mental illness, by any standard diagnostic criteria. His discussion concerning the nature of his beliefs was similar to those of members of other organized zealous religious groups. From Jerry I learned one way converts can come to accept a highly deviant belief system. The sect's members had introduced him to a set of nonspecific beliefs, which later served as a bridge to his involvement in the church's specific dogma. Jerry effectively joined before he even realized the group's identity, but throughout the conversion process had been fully mentally competent and able to query his hosts at will. Like many others he did not do so, and instead became entrained first in a more popular cause that later led to acceptance of the church and its dogma. Induction into the sect's beliefs, in effect, was carried out by subterfuge.

Although he had adapted well in high school, Jerry ran into difficulty when he left home for college. From what he said, he had become very distressed over his father's alcoholism, which had just recently reached a crisis. Also on his mind were uncertainties about choosing a career, accentuated by his father's own failing prospects.

After his first year, Jerry decided to take a leave of absence for one semester to work in an anti-poverty program, hoping to resolve these feelings of inner turmoil. He returned to college the next spring, but did poorly and felt isolated, even among the friends he had made the year before. He told his parents that he missed the previous semester's sense of commitment, which he had found fulfilling, and was considering leaving school again. This troubled his father, who was now expressing undue expectations for Jerry, perhaps hoping to compensate for his own recent reverses.

While visiting a friend at a nearby college, Jerry was approached by a young Japanese-born woman who engaged him in a discussion on "the future of the world's poor," and then, after an animated exchange, invited him to a day-long workshop for the One-World Crusade, which he agreed to attend. The workshop dealt with a variety of general issues related to the welfare of the poor in America and abroad. The young woman telephoned the following week to ask Jerry if he would be interested in going to a second, weekend-long workshop on the issues they had discussed, but at first he declined. When she offered to pick him up, he agreed, and was then taken to a nearby workshop center. During a weekend of group discussions, sports, and singing at the workshop, Jerry became increasingly attracted to the group's ideals of universal brotherhood and its commitment to a Divine Principle. Among the workshop guests, though, few if any appreciated that the Divine Principle was actually the basis of the religious belief system of the Unification Church. Jerry acknowledged that if had he known this at the outset, he would not have chosen to participate.

Before the weekend workshop was over, the sponsors asked the eight people in attendance if they would like to spend the rest of the week in a retreat. For Jerry, this did not entail a major disruption since he had no classes during the upcoming spring break. In addition, he said, "I found in the group some principles I could believe in, and a true concern for people." Along with two other workshop members, Jerry decided to continue with the week-long program, and these three, along with four members participating in the One World Crusade, embarked by van for the retreat. He did not yet realize that they were heading toward the Unification Church Seminary in Barrytown, New York, a facility recently purchased from a monastic order.

In the van, Jerry heard another recruit mention the Moonies while speaking with the driver. He recalled turning to the young Japanese woman who had originally invited him to the workshop, and reconstructed the following dialog.

JERRY: Say, does the Divine Principle have something to do with the Moonies?

SHE: You mean the Unification Church?

JERRY: I don't know. Are they related?

SHE: Reverend Moon wrote the Divine Principle.

JERRY: Oh? Is he that Korean guy who spoke at Yankee Stadium?

SHE: Yes, he's a very wise man who gave us the ideas we've been talking about the last few days.

JERRY: Oh, I see. How come you didn't mention it?

SHE: People criticize Reverend Moon unfairly; they would turn you away from joining the workshop, and you would lose the chance to hear his words. We just want you to have the chance to find out what he has to say.

Jerry did not remember being very surprised or distressed at this point. In fact, he gave surprisingly little thought to his growing involvement with a system of beliefs likely to have a profound influence on his life. The transition from views tenable to the population at large to ones that were clearly deviant took place through such casual subterfuge that it provided little cognitive dissonance in the convert. Jerry made the transition from a general support for the poor of the world to engagement in the church's unusual beliefs without even noticing—a telling reflection on the plasticity of belief when those vested with authority promote such a change.

The day after he arrived at the seminary, Jerry telephoned his father, describing in general terms where he was. He recalled subtly trying to avoid identifying the Moonie movement itself, as he knew his father would not

approve. Within a few days his family heard from him again and they insisted that he leave, but he felt strongly that it was his option to finish the
week.

By this time, however, Jerry's parents had seen a lawyer and a family
physician, and appeared at the seminary with a document that gave them
the right of conservatorship over their son. Jerry quickly consulted the church
leaders. After some deliberation over strategy, he opted to slip away from
the compound and seek refuge in a remote Unification Church center, while
members of the group began to obtain legal advice for preparing his defense.
The adversity Jerry was facing contributed to the consolidation of his beliefs. He not only espoused the creed of the church, but also had to defend
it.

Jerry may have begun his involvement with the Moonies under a misap-
prehension, but his affirmation of their beliefs was now clear, and his mental competency to stay on (or undertake any course of action he chose) appeared intact. He was introduced to a new set of beliefs by subterfuge at a
time when his own distressed mental state made him vulnerable. The malaise he felt over his father's alcoholism and his own uncertain career plans
had left him open to the offer of a universalist solution. He was gradually
drawn into a belief system that provided a sense of certainty and a needed
dose of hope and commitment. Proponents of unpopular belief systems have
long revealed only what they felt wise during initial recruitment.

SEEKERS

Unlike Jerry, however, some converts have had long careers as seekers[19] of
spiritual experience before joining one of the new religious movements. Becoming involved in an active quest for a comprehensive approach may represent an effort to resolve conflicts about life's meaning. Such preoccupations are of course common in adolescents, but for some they can become
compelling and protracted, and may serve as a primary focus for intellectual
commitments. The culture in which a youth grows up can also do a great
deal to prime the person for such a mental set, and the counterculture perspective of the 1960s and early 1970s led many young people to seek a guid-
ing philosophy. Yet, for many seekers, the specifics of ideology in the sects
they joined were apparently less relevant in their particular choice than
coincidences surrounding their initial encounters with the group. That is,
if the time, people, and place were right, any movement might have caught
their attention.

One person who ended a protracted quest by joining the Moonies is named
Bill; his experience illustrates the career of a seeker. Like his parents, Bill
thought of himself as agnostic from an early age, and maintained no formal
religious identification. In his mid-teens, he became interested in his Jewish
cultural background and traveled to Israel after his high school graduation.
While spending a week in Europe, he ran into members of the Unification

Church, but was not, as he later recalled, attracted to their lifestyle or religion.

The next year, as a college freshman, he took two courses in philosophy hoping to gain a better understanding of "essential issues," and spent much of his spare time with a neo-Hindu group, but eventually lost interest in it.

He went to a lecture at the campus headquarters of the Unification Church, looking for "some ideas about the way the world turns." Although the group offered interesting views, he chose other opportunities to find a meaningful identity. For some months he "became a hippie, to see if drugs were a route toward understanding," and then, as he put it, an "intellectual; I read a lot. I was big on the value of 'ideas' as the essence of life."

Bill began participating actively in the antiwar movement during his second year at college; he again went to Israel to spend the summer in a Hassidic Moshav. Here, too, he became disenchanted, feeling that he could not accept the Hassidic position that Jews have a special place as God's chosen people.

Bill returned to college that fall, but only as a part-time student, feeling uncertain of his future goals. He dropped by the campus headquarters of the Unification Church again, but remembers feeling no great camaraderie and no sense of connection with his own experience. Still, the Divine Principle interested him and he offered to help with tasks around the building, regarding this as a convenient way to make an acquaintance with "off-beat" aspects of the local scene. As we spoke, he surmised that he was feeling the need for some group he could relate to more permanently, having exhausted his role as a movement "buff."

Bill was soon invited to a four-hour lecture on the Divine Principle, which he attended with misgivings, thinking that its origins were not compatible with his own Jewish background. After the lecture, though, his response to the group's philosophy was one of "glee. I had found my purpose in life. I now had conviction and belief, something which had been lacking before." He had reached a resting place in his career as a seeker, and six years later, in recounting his experiences, he pointed out that subsequent exposure to the group's beliefs had strengthened his commitment.

IDENTIFYING

Other converts joined as a way of identifying with values they perceived in their own parents; for them the group often represented a meaningful cause from the outset. One young woman, Barbara, remarked that the most important reason for her joining was that its members had the same kind of dedication to social values as her own mother, whom she had admired greatly since childhood. Her mother had been deeply involved in the struggle for racial equality and had worked actively for peace from the early years of the Vietnam war.

As a college freshman Barbara became interested in the women's movement, and wrote a comprehensive paper on contemporary woman musicians. On her professor's suggestion, she adapted the paper for an article in her college newspaper. She said, "I pursued this idea because I was committed to change, but I decided that we were only scratching the surface. Like my mother, I wanted to believe in a philosophy of action to build an ideal world, and as soon as I became acquainted with the Church, I sensed that their beliefs could bring it about."

OPPOSITION

In contrast to Barbara, a potential convert may assume an oppositional position. Many youths like to engage in conflict with an established authority, in this case represented by a new religious movement. What is at first most visible is the blustery autonomy and rebelliousness of adolescence. But in the end their underlying need for dependency, against which they do battle at this stage of life, emerges in their attraction to the group's totalistic demands. An independent stance may serve as the basis for conversion to the very position they oppose, as they become involved in battling over the sect's ideas. Similar observations have been made in studies on the social psychology of attitude change.[20]

One young man, Carl, was introduced to the church at a time when he felt relatively content with the circumstances of his life. His friend joined the Unification Church, and Carl tried to convince the friend to leave, relishing the opportunity to argue against the sect's position. The friend prevailed on Carl to attend a church workshop, claiming that he could not really communicate effectively unless exposed directly to the Divine Principle. Carl recalled the workshop as an "interesting" experience, but said it left him tense and irritated since he felt compelled to refute the views of its leader as they spoke together after the formal sessions.

The crucial point in Carl's conversion came three days later when he was challenged by two acquaintances to justify the interest he seemed to be showing in the church. An argument followed and, in insisting on his own neutrality, Carl's ambivalence shifted to more positive feelings. Later that evening, he decided on impulse to telephone his friend at the church center. He found himself saying that he would be coming over the next day to a session at the center to "get more familiar" with the church. That night, Carl felt an intense longing for the church, and the truth it now seemed to offer. "Now I wanted to believe in the Principle so that I could find comfort in it. The next day I decided to join."

This experience is similar to that of many alcoholics who join Alcoholics Anonymous, also a charismatic movement. Their association with the group is born out of a need to establish a safe base in opposition to their compulsive attraction to alcohol, but they are often skeptical about the quasireligious commitment inherent in AA. Nonetheless, the alcoholics' own oppositional position against dependency on the group and its creed can ultimately yield to a strong commitment. This is reflected in the comments of one alcoholic concerning the First Step of AA, the acknowledgment of helplessness before a Higher Power.

> I thought it was preposterous at first, submitting to a Higher Power. I knew better than that, and I even argued the point with some members. Then, after a while, I realized that they *were* right and that all along I had *wanted* to acknowledge my belief, but had fought it off for too long. The strength of these principles became clear when I realized how hard I had to fight to avoid them.

Often the need to aggressively oppose the creed of a charismatic group is fired by a convert's psychological defense against dependency needs, which are heightened by the seductiveness of submitting to a set of absolute beliefs. As the convert becomes more intimate with the group, even in rebellious anger, the need for dependency may produce submission.

A Study of the Members

As I began planning for a study that would address the issue of shared beliefs in a charismatic sect, it became clear that church officials would not impose *a priori* restraints, so it then seemed feasible to touch on some sensitive topics such as drug use, physical coercion, and attitudes toward sex. I prepared a questionnaire on these as well as other psychological and demographic issues from the Divine Light study. The questionnaire was to be completed anonymously to avoid concern by members that their responses might somehow be monitored.

The group's leadership was also quite cooperative in helping with arrangements for administrating the questionnaire at a large meeting at the New York Church headquarters, where members would attend a routine program of evening entertainment. The meeting was typical and because of the considerable mobility of church members throughout the United States, this sample included individuals from all regions of the country.[21]

Our research team was present to distribute the questionnaires and coordinate a cadre of members whom I had previously prepared to answer questions that might be raised. As we began, the National President introduced the exercise, asking that members be frank in responding so that an accurate picture of the church would be given. There were 307 members present that evening, and, of these, questionnaires from the 237 who were native-born Americans were analyzed; they had been members for an average of almost three years.

Responses showed that the backgrounds of Unification Church members were similar to those observed among the Divine Light Mission. Also reflected, however, was a dislocation that preceded their joining the sect, both in terms of disruption of their education and emotional problems, as well as antecedent interest in other sects. For example, members began to withdraw from the usual sequence of education before they encountered the group, since less than a third of those who were students right before conversion were actually enrolled full-time. In addition, although most (58%) had begun college, only a minority (25%) actually graduated. Although most (67%) regarded themselves as moderately or strongly committed to their family's religious orientation before they reached the age of fifteen, the overwhelming majority (90%) reported a subsequent history of some commitment to one of the other new religious movements—reflecting at least some experience as religious seekers.

Psychological difficulties before joining also were not uncommon (as also shown in the Divine Light Mission study). Thus, a sizable portion (39%) felt that they had experienced serious emotional problems in the past, problems that led many to seek professional help (30%) and even hospitalization (6%). The nature of the members' current emotional status was ascertained by means of a standardized instrument developed by the National Center for Health Statistics, the psychological General Well-Being Schedule. This instrument allowed us to compare Unification Church members to a representative sample from the general population based on national survey data.[22] From their responses, it was apparent that even at the time of the study, members' sense of well-being was notably below that of a matched group from the general population.[23] This is all the more significant because members' Psychological Distress scores for the period *before* joining were considerably (48%) higher than those obtained for the time of the survey. This suggested that members had as a group been experiencing a notable level of psychological distress prior to joining, which no doubt left them vulnerable to a set of beliefs that promised to provide them a renewed sense of purpose. Furthermore, the data on members not completing their college education and reports on their contact with other sects suggested a behavioral concomitant of this emotional disruption.

To examine the relationship between members' acceptance of the Unification Church beliefs and their current emotional well-being, I had developed a scale for religious commitment (Table 3-1), in which subjects rated a series of items according to how they had felt at three different times: for the period immediately before joining, the one immediately after, and at the present time.

Not surprisingly, members' current commitment to their religious beliefs was very high. For example, the bulk of the members (74%) felt a "close connection with God . . . very much." Their proselytizing zeal was also reflected in their strong feeling that nonmembers should "adopt the same religious beliefs" as their own (80%). In addition, in relation to transcendental religious experiences, most (90%) reported that they had "intensely

Table 3-1. *Religious Belief Scale*

Each item is rated from 1 ("not at all") to 5 ("very much") relative to the period in question.

1. I feel a close connection with God.   ( )
2. My religious beliefs give me comfort.   ( )
3. I should avoid thinking about sex.   ( )
4. I should avoid getting "high" from alcohol.   ( )

   People who are not members of my religious group should:
5. adopt the same religious beliefs that I do.   ( )
6. avoid thinking about sex.   ( )
7. avoid getting "high" from alcohol.   ( )

8. Prayer or meditation give meaning to my life.   ( )
9. Prayer or meditation raise my spirits when I felt troubled.   ( )

. . . seen a special new meaning in life . . . during daily prayer."[24] These feelings were reported much more strongly than for the period before joining.

How did this degree of commitment affect members' emotional status? In the first place, a large majority (91%) indicated that their level of psychological distress was lower for the period right after conversion than the one right before. The average decline was equivalent to a change from "moderately" to "slightly" anxious on the Distress Scale (from a score of 3 to 2). Equally important, the actual decline in symptoms was directly correlated with the strength of members' religious feelings, so that those who improved the most in their distress had shown a markedly greater increase in religiosity scores over the course of conversion.

Three variables in question could now be considered together, so that we could evaluate the impact of the members' religious belief and cohesiveness on their emotional well-being. This analysis showed that items from these two scales of group affiliation—belief and cohesiveness—were strong predictors of members' sense of emotional well-being (that is, together they predicted 36% of variance in General Well-Being scores). Two items of religious belief, "My religious beliefs give me comfort" and "I feel a close connection with God," were the highest ranking predictors in this analysis.[25] A member's ongoing emotional state was strongly related to the degree of affiliation felt to the church. If the member were closer to the group in terms of beliefs and social ties, he or she would experience considerably more psychological general well-being than if more distant.

It was also interesting to ascertain the extent to which members' beliefs affected their actual behavior, since behavioral change is certainly a test of true commitment. Two areas of attitude and related behavior were considered: sexual relations and use of drugs and alcohol. Members indicated a striking increase in constraints over sexuality after joining. Only a few (11%)

reported that they had felt very much that they "should avoid thinking about sex" immediately before they joined the church, but by the time of the questionnaire, the large majority (76%) felt this way, and a similar portion of the respondents believed that such avoidance was appropriate for non-members too. Members also put these views into action, since sexual contact of any sort was unheard of among the many members I interviewed, and proselytizing to bring in others to accept these norms was a principal activity. As I later observed in studying members engaged to be married, a prohibition on all sexual contact was adhered to over the course of more than three years of engagement and even afterwards, for months of a prescribed "separation period" following the marriage.

The impact of people's beliefs on their behavior was further seen in the changes in their use of drugs and alcohol. As creatures of their contemporary culture, members had used intoxicants fairly extensively before joining, so that a fair portion of them (23%) actually reported having serious drug problems in the past. The large majority had smoked marijuana (79%) or drunk alcoholic beverages in the past (90%), and almost half (45%) had used hallucinogens. At present, the bulk of the members (88%) strongly accepted the preferred norm, to "avoid getting high from alcohol," and only a small minority (13%) had drunk any alcoholic beverage during the previous two months. Only one respondent (0.4%) had used alcohol daily during this period, in contrast to a fair number (17%) who had done so at some point before joining. In my subsequent study on the induction experience (discussed in a later chapter), I found that such religiously grounded attitudes were acquired quite rapidly: Workshop participants expressed levels of commitment similar to those of long-term members after no more than two days of exposure to the group.

What emerged from the interviews and survey was a picture of the individual convert's pliability in acquiring strong beliefs over a relatively short period. Once receptive to the charismatic group and then part of it, the convert's psychological status becomes engaged with these beliefs. A state of well-being is maintained insofar as one adheres to these beliefs, but distress emerges when one feels less committed to them and to fellow members. This close relationship between affiliation and emotional well-being reinforces compliance and continued ties to the group, without need for external coercion. This mechanism is not consciously perceived by the member, any more than most people routinely ponder why they go home to their families each night or why they repeatedly seek out their friends for social engagements. Norms for belief and associated behavior become internalized very rapidly and considerable distress would emerge if some undue circumstance led a member of a charismatic group to violate these commitments.

We are often surprised at the deviant behavior of cult members when it is dictated by beliefs at variance with our own. When a Moonie spends his or her day soliciting in the street, we find this incomprehensible, just as we think it bizarre when a Hare Krishna member appears in flowing robes with shaven head. Nonetheless, so long as a particular behavior pattern has been adopted in association with a system of cultic beliefs, and in association with a charismatic sect's close-knit social network, it is not experienced as unusual or strained by the members themselves, even though it may shock or repel the general public.

The Attribution of Meaning

To consider further how the convert acquires a set of beliefs different from prior attitudes, we may draw on attribution theory. Originally outlined by the social psychologist Fritz Heider,[26] this theory deals with how people ascribe meaning to events by drawing on their existing attitudes and environmental cues. It has been applied to the way people interpret their experience in spheres as diverse as psychotherapy, politics, and religion.[27]

One way people acquire their attitudes is literally by observing themselves. Daryl Bem[28] pointed to this aspect of self-perception when he wrote that individuals come to "know" their attitudes, emotions, and other internal states, partially by "inferring them from observations from their own overt behavior, and/or the circumstances in which this behavior occurs. . . . The individual is functionally in the same position as an outside observer, an observer who must necessarily rely upon those same cues to infer the individual's inner states."

People may, for example, attribute meaning to important experiences in life by recourse to their family's religious background, but usually they had adopted these attitudes without formal intention, in part because they *observed themselves* engaged in that faith as they grew up. One does not necessarily arrive at a conscious decision about one's religious orientation, but rather acknowledges "I am a Catholic" or "I am a Jew" because one has repeatedly carried out practices associated with that faith.

This type of attribution also applies to more transient experiences. A person can be thrust into uncertainty by a confusing series of events, and then draw on any readily available explanation suggested by the *social context* in which those events took place. The individual may then use that explanation in other situations where it seems relevant. Given an uncertain state of mood and perception, the individual responds with the most readily available credible explanation. We tend to deal with uncertainty by looking to past experience or cues in the situation, and may then come to an understanding without carefully evaluating all available data. Certain situations actually tend to increase the likelihood that an individual will be influenced by circumstantial cues rather than making careful observations and verifying them. Harold Kelly[29] proposed that this is most likely if someone has

1. Little social support.
2. Prior information that is poor and ambiguous.

3. Problems difficult beyond one's capabilities.
4. Views that have been disconfirmed because they were inappropriate or incorrect.
5. Other experiences engendering low self-confidence.

These ideas shed light on the way potential recruits begin to acquire new beliefs while attending the workshops of the Unification Church. For example, when the recruiter telephoned Jerry at college and asked him to attend the weekend workshop, Jerry met these criteria for dislocation. He had recently quit the job he had taken while on leave from college, was uncertain of his future career, and felt adrift. His father's difficulties with drinking were also weighing heavily on him, contributing to his malaise and low self-esteem. In the Unification Church workshop, he was subjected to an unexpectedly intense group experience, one that forced him to develop some perspective, if for no other reason than to make sense of the unanticipated affection showered on him. In addition, the contrast between the uncertainty he felt before and the certitude shown him by members of the One-World Crusade (as these Moonies called their group) primed him to attribute some broader meaning to the experience. At this point, the workshop leaders offered him the transcendent role of their Crusade as an explanation for this remarkable display of commitment.

Jerry was also influenced by observing his own behavior, as he found himself mobilized into taking part in the workshop: a full schedule of group discussions, singing, sports, and the sharing of intimate feelings. Participating in these group activities shaped his perception of himself as a member of the Crusade who shared the group's values. Thus, his own behavior in complying with the group's exercises and the messages imparted by the workshop's leadership both attributed meaning to his experience.

Once established, this attribution helped guide his subsequent behavior, and implicitly served as an explanatory model around which he defined his later experience. This becomes clear in what he told me about his feelings after the weekend workshop.

> It was strange, but the intensity of the two days left me much clearer about why I had been so uncertain, and where I might head for the future; it was as if a haze had been lifted. I began to understand things that had made no sense before, why most people rushed around for no reason, without any lasting sense of purpose. I had a sense that I could look for direction to my friends in the One-World Crusade.

In later joining the Unification Church, Jerry acquired a small community of comrades whom he knew personally, but in addition a much larger *pseudo-community* now existed for him—the full membership of the church. This group, most of whom he had never met, was becoming as much a reality as the members he actually knew. This use of a large interpersonal network, existing only in the individual's mind, allows the charismatic group member to feel close to many people who support the attributions he or she had just established. A deviant belief, an idiosyncratic mission, and fidelity to a cultic figure are all more tenable if there are thousands who hold the same position. A newly acquired philosophy is more likely to be maintained when its tenets are accepted by many others.[30]

The concept of the pseudo-community is also relevant to the understanding of certain types of psychopathology, particularly paranoia. For the paranoid, a pseudo-community is autistic—it is conjured up without any consensual validation from others. As originally described by John Cameron,[31] the pseudo-community consisted of persons whom the paranoid imagined to populate the world, usually potential assailants, who might be members of the FBI, the Mafia, or similar menacing and powerful groups.

For Carol, a pseudo-community had included the devils she and Bobby were battling. In the hospital, she was able to free herself of this deluded state by adopting a different attribution set—a Pentecostal religious perspective—and her alienation was relieved by joining a new pseudo-community, that of the Pentecostal believers awaiting salvation. Jerry, the seeker, on the other hand, provides an interesting contrast. His exposure to the Unification Church before his weekend workshop had been brief, and the group's beliefs bore little relationship to his prior attitudes. One might wonder what led him to acquire a commitment to the broader community of the Unification Church and its transcendent mission. This should be most revealing, reflecting on the remarkable capacity of church workshops to engage participants into the sect's system of beliefs.

Two studies highlight the role of group conformity in altering individuals' judgment. Solomon Asch[32] had an experimental subject join a group of six people seated around a circular table. The six were actually collaborating with the experimenters, and had been rehearsed on how to behave. All seven were shown a board with a vertical line drawn on it and then shown three other lines and asked to select the one identical in length to the first. The task was structured so that the correct choice was easily made. A series of trials was carried out in which the six collaborators, each responding *before* the subject, gave correct answers. In a final trial, however, all the collaborators made the same *incorrect* response. When his turn came, the subject could either conform with the unanimous majority and make an incorrect choice or choose correctly and be at variance with the group. In a series of these experiments, only a third of the subjects gave the right answer every time. Less than one in ten conformed and answered incorrectly on almost all occasions, while most responded incorrectly intermittently. Here we see a prototype for a nonmember's acquiescence to the group view.

The importance of unanimity among the collaborators was revealed in a subsequent study in which one gave the *correct* response during the last trial while the other five did not. Conformity to incorrect responses among the subjects declined considerably (from 32% of trials in the original study to 6%).

These experiments indicate why cults must maintain a high degree of conformity to the group's views in their recruitment efforts. The Unification Church typically includes a majority of active members in its induction workshops, rather than a lone member as leader in a group of nonmembers. The tenor of communications is thereby more easily managed by the committed majority. Similarly, in Alcoholics Anonymous, recruitment generally takes place at meetings in which the majority of persons present are active members who tell of their salvation through AA and their commitment to maintaining complete abstinence.

During the Unification Church workshops, Jerry conformed to the group's activities and observed himself acting like other adherents to the One-World Crusade, individuals he had come to like and respect. As he said, "I went along in all the activities because they were sincere people doing things for a good cause, even though sometimes it seemed silly." As time went on though, his perception of his own attitudes was no doubt influenced by observing his own behavior. As Bem suggested, after a point the person who willingly acts out a set of attitudes will come to feel that those attitudes are his or her own.

As the workshop progressed, the group's values gained credence through his observations of his own behavior and the emotional well-being he was beginning to feel. Jerry recalled that, "I realized the Principle had to be important. I could see what it was doing for me." Increasingly, he saw the group as a reference point for his perceptions of the world around him and as the basis of his decision making.

Consider the nineteenth-century Oneida Community in this regard. Members' acceptance of its utopian beliefs and their compliance with the ideals of their leader were reinforced at daily meetings of the entire community in the Mansion House, in which personal problems were raised and arbitrated by recourse to group values. Decisions regarding daily activities, from kitchen work to sexual practices, were explained and implemented by recourse to the views of John Noyes, the group's charismatic leader, thereby promoting attribution of all experiences to the Community's world view.

Attribution to the group's perspectives may also be carried out in small group meetings, as in Synanon, a therapeutic community for drug abuse treatment that originated in Southern California in the late 1950s. The Synanon "games" are protracted group sessions in which participants meet several times a week. In these games, members aggressively address minor problems in their relationships and deviations from prescribed norms among members' attitudes until they achieve a consensus for compliance with the community's values.[33] This small group format is potent; it has allowed members to achieve abstinence from heroin addiction early in the group's history and later served as a basis for establishing a rigidly controlled, closed community with its own self-contained residential and occupational arrangements. Throughout its history, this community was tightly controlled by its charismatic leader, Charles Dederich, whose views were transmitted to members through a network of these games. Controlled communication in the small group also characterizes coercive persuasion, or brainwashing, where the individual is forced to adopt a group's views *against* his or her will. Robert Lifton has observed that brainwashing like that in Chinese Communist prison camps required full control over the context of communication[34] but in voluntary conversions contact must be maintained in a subtle (or deceptive) way, without forcing the individual to comply with the group's views.

Individuals in highly structured group situations can be led to make judgments in ways very different from their decisions while on their own. When properly primed by the social setting, they may accept unusual beliefs that the group they have affiliated with continually reinforces. As we will see, these beliefs can be further intensified when an individual's feelings and state of consciousness have been altered within that group setting.

4

ALTERED
CONSCIOUSNESS

People are more vulnerable to social influence when they are made to think, sense, and feel differently than usual, when someone or something disrupts their emotional balance. Such changes in subjective experience (or alterations in consciousness) can undermine the psychological matrix in which our views are rooted, so that we lose track of customary internal signposts. They may also introduce a feeling of mystery, or a sense that forces beyond our control are operating. Thus, they can prime us to accept unaccustomed explanations for our experiences and adopt new attitudes implied in these explanations. In this respect altered consciousness can help shape members' attitudes in a charismatic group.

I was struck by the significant role of alterations in consciousness when studying the Divine Light Mission. From my first contact with this group, members mentioned the importance of the four "meditations" to their personal commitment. Each drew on a different sense, causing unexpected visions, tastes, and music. The sect itself was named for one of these sensory experiences, the "Divine Light," that members reported seeing during their personal meditation. At first these meditation practices did not seem compelling, perhaps because of my own inclination to dismiss as self-deceptive or pathologic those experiences that could not be verified by independent observation. Their importance became clear, however, as I spoke with one person, Raymond, whose views I tended to take more seriously, since he too was a psychiatrist. Sharing a profession made it easier to empathize with him. In addition, Raymond was a bright young man, well-versed in contemporary psychological thought, and willing to consider all sides of an issue.

Nonetheless, in his recounting he seemed almost obsessed with the alterations in consciousness he ascribed to his religious experience.

While in medical school, Raymond wanted to be a general practitioner and decided to do his internship in family medicine. Then he took a position in a small-town clinic to have the personal contact with patients he had long anticipated. After two years in this crowded clinic, he became disenchanted with the limited opportunities for working closely with patients and began to wonder about other possibilities. An acquaintance invited Raymond to attend satsang, the religious sermon of the Divine Light Mission. He did and found in the group members a sense of conviction lacking in his own life. He had begun to feel bored and the group offered a focus of interest. He attended satsang again, and described the following experience from his third visit.

He was sitting comfortably in a group of a dozen people, mostly members, listening to a young woman speaking about the importance of the guru's mission. He was not attending too closely to her words, but was instead lulled into relaxation by the rhythm of her speech. Suddenly, he saw a bright light emanating from her body, forming a halo around her. He later recalled

> The light was intense. She glowed as if she were a religious figure in a movie, and it gave her the appearance of holiness. It was a real light, as real as the light bulb in a lamp. So I sat there listening carefully to her words, and they were no different from the ones she had spoken minutes before. Now I'm a fairly cynical guy, and I don't take the unexpected at face value, so I did a double take and looked away, expecting the light to disappear—but it was still there. No one had even told me to expect a light like this, and no one else seemed to see it.
>
> When she finished I got up to leave and, as I walked toward the door— she was still glowing—I realized that something had happened to me that I couldn't dismiss. The experience would somehow have to become a part of my understanding of the world around me. Over the next few weeks I found myself getting involved further with the group, and soon decided to ask to receive Knowledge [to join].

Raymond continued to work at his clinic for a few months, but then decided that he had to carry the group's message to others, so he took a position in an alcoholism treatment program where he hoped to help his patients by conveying to them the sect's message. After six months in that program, his patients were unresponsive to his message, and Raymond decided that a career in psychiatry would offer him a better opportunity to deal with the spiritual issues his conversion had raised. He took his training in psychiatry and continued to meditate, occasionally experiencing intense visual and bodily sensations and changes in his sense of time.

This episode of altered consciousness was not very different from many in the literature on religious conversion, but was nonetheless difficult to explain from a psychiatric perspective. Raymond's vision of the halo might be construed as a hallucinatory experience in conventional psychiatric terms, and thereby ascribed to causes of perceptual change such as a dissociative reaction, transient psychosis, or even mass hysteria. But his history, his behavior, and his demeanor as we spoke gave no hint of such a diagnosis. This "vision" also fit in nicely with his later experiences in meditation, and could not be dismissed as an isolated phenomenon.

I was left with a tale told by a perceptive and lucid observer who described a phenomenon that did not fit into my handbook of diagnoses. Nonetheless, the experience had clearly served as a basis for the attribution of a new meaning to his life. It set him off balance and he turned to the philosophy of the sect to explain the puzzling event. From that point, Raymond's relationship with the Divine Light Mission followed with seeming inevitability, and served as a basis for his understanding of his own role in life. This experience had many counterparts in my interviews with other members of the Divine Light Mission, as it became clear that altered consciousness in the form of inexplicable perceptions and transcendent emotional states was common in their conversion and subsequent religious experience.

These reports made a compelling argument for the role of altered consciousness as a force in the charismatic group, even though the phenomena reported were difficult to integrate into contemporary models of psychiatric function. Research on mental function is generally conducted at the level of observable behavior or neurophysiology, and does not usually address subjective aspects of experience. Nomenclature is based on what can be seen and measured by independent observers, whereas altered consciousness is usually only subjectively perceived.

Altered consciousness, however, can be a prime motive force among both well-adapted and disturbed individuals. Like group cohesiveness and shared beliefs, it acts as a vehicle for the identity transformation and engagement that draw people into a charismatic group.

As a starting point for understanding the role of altered consciousness in charismatic groups, we must turn back nearly a century to the work of William James. James reasoned that "the distribution of consciousness shows itself to be exactly such as we might expect in an organ added for the sake of steering a nervous system grown too complex to regulate itself."[1] This concept of consciousness as a meta-organ is useful, and serves as a credible basis for Arnold Ludwig's definition of an altered state of consciousness:

> any mental state(s), induced by various physiological, psychological, or pharmacological maneuvers or agents, which can be recognized subjectively by the individual himself (or by the objective observer of the individual) as representing a sufficient deviation [from] . . . alert, waking, consciousness.[2]

But given these definitions, what specific aspects of perception are actually altered in the altered state of consciousness? We can consider consciousness as if it were a multidimensional space, with each dimension representing some aspect of perception or sensation.[3] Different altered states may then be defined in relation to the dimensions altered. We will discuss a variety of dimensions relating to charismatic groups, such as time sense, personal identity, appetite drives, and visual perception. Each dimension contributes to the totality of a person's state of consciousness and allows for mapping out similarities and differences between altered states. When altered by a charismatic group experience, each can serve as a nidus for the attribution of new meaning to one's experience.

Consciousness and its alterations are grounded in physiology, so that states subjectively perceived as similar may also have similar physiologic characteristics. This is illustrated by the changes in neural function found in some states of mental relaxation and reflection. For example, electroencephalographic (EEG) studies of experienced practitioners of Transcendental Meditation reveal an increase in alpha wave activity[4] during meditation. This calming state can be compared to that experienced during marijuana intoxication when people are allowed to relax in the absence of social input. Here the EEG is characterized by alpha waves of greater amplitude.[5] An increase in alpha-wave activity coupled with similar mental relaxation can also be achieved through biofeedback training.[6]

The fact that altered states may be substituted for each other also suggests similarities. For example, many members of the new religious movements switched from drugs to meditation to achieve similar mental effects. The Divine Light members who previously had "serious drug problems" and frequently experienced altered consciousness from drug use were more likely to practice meditation routinely after joining the sect than those who had not used drugs extensively.[7] Crossing over between one vehicle for achieving altered consciousness to a second one suggests an inherent relationship between these subjective states; it also complements the observation that states may be induced by different means.

Meditation

The important role of altered states in the Divine Light Mission was set in relief by the responses from members describing their own transcendental experiences during meditation, which almost all of them (95%) practiced daily.[8] In answering the questionnaire summarized in Table 4-1, they used a scale designed to register increasing levels of hallucinatory-like phenomena, and thus more profound alterations in consciousness. In the auditory sphere, for example, members were asked whether they had "heard something special that no one else could hear," the first item on this scale. The large majority (92%) reported having such experiences during meditation. Of these, about half (49%) reported hearing it "only inside" them; a small number (14%) answered, "I could almost hear it in my ear"; but almost a

Table 4-1. *Altered Consciousness During Meditation*

Each respondent indicated the extent to which he or she had the following experiences during meditation, using a scale of 0–3. The first figure after each item is the portion of members who reported any such experience at all (scale responses 1–3); the second figure is the portion who reported the experience most intensely (response 3).

1. I heard something special that no one else could hear. [92%, at all; 29%, I heard it with my ears]
2. I saw something special that no one else could see. [92%, at all; 30%, I could see it clearly with my eyes]
3. I had strong sexual feelings without physical sexual contact. [39%, at all; 14%, clearly more intense than orgasm]
4. I had a special and unfamiliar feeling in my body. [91%, at all; 49%, very intense]
5. Time passed faster or slower than usual in a very special way. [90%, at all; 34%, very intense]
6. I felt myself to be different from my usual self in a very special way. [94%, at all; 56%, very intense]
7. I saw special new meaning in my life. [96%, at all; 61%, very intense]
8. I felt better than ever before in a very special way. [96%, at all; 66%, very intense]

third (29%) gave the most literal response for such hallucinatory experiences: "I heard it with my ears." This response is most striking since it would be compatible with a diagnosis of psychosis outside the context of religious experience.

Table 4-1 reflects a widespread alteration in subjective and sensory states during meditation, but the way in which meditation was practiced is also important. Members not only set aside a specific time to meditate, they also practiced it while involved in daily activities, as suggested by the guru. Almost all (99%) did this sometimes and a majority (54%) did it "usually."

The relevance of such experience to participation in a charismatic group may be clarified by considering how these members attribute meaning to their daily experiences. A compelling alteration in a person's subjective state, whether from drugs or to a novel social context, leaves the person open to ascribing new meaning to experiences. This certainly applies to the altered consciousness associated with meditation, which serves as a vehicle for destabilizing old attitudes and preparing the meditator to accept the group's beliefs. It acts to support the group's cohesiveness and stabilize and even enhance a member's acceptance of the group.

As in Raymond's case, meditation also serves as a basis for *joining* the charismatic group. This is illustrated by the responses of the Divine Light members, who were asked whether the experiences of altered consciousness listed in Table 4-1 had taken place at the time of their conversion. It turned out to be almost as high then as it was during their subsequent meditation, even though their exposure to the group had been modest up to then. A large majority reported that during the conversion period to some degree they "saw something special that no one else could see" (90%) and "heard something special that no one else could hear" (83%). Such experiences must have made them more responsive to the group's influence.

Over the long term of membership, meditation also played an important role in supporting a convert's continuing involvement. An analysis of the relationship between the time members spent in meditation and the decline in their level of neurotic distress revealed that greater meditation time was associated with diminished neurotic distress. This association suggests that the emotional response to meditation acts as a reinforcement for its continued practice.[9] That is, the more a member meditated, in general, the better the person was likely to feel. Members apparently used meditation to relieve distress, both at scheduled times and on an ad hoc basis. This tranquilizer, as it were, had its own reinforcing qualities and no doubt helped cement commitment to the sect. In this way, it had an addicting effect.

The role of meditation in altering individuals' perspectives on life is shown in an interesting manner by American practitioners of Transcendental Meditation (TM), followers of Maharishi Mahesh Yogi. This sect initially had a straightforward approach to achieving a meditative state, based on a formula in which the meditator concentrated on a personal code word, or mantra. The ability to facilitate relaxation with this technique made TM popular in the early 1970s and aroused interest in both lay and medical communities. Certified trainers would impart the technique to clients who paid for a course of instruction, taught with a minimum of cultic trappings although there were some, such as the secrecy surrounding trainees' mantras. By the mid-1970s, 350 TM training centers were scattered across the nation, with 10,000 persons taking up the practice each month, most of them well educated and successful. Professionals involved in the economic and cultural mainstream reported having transcendent experiences while meditating. One senior editor at a New York publishing house had mild hallucinations if she exceeded the prescribed forty minutes per day, "not frightening ones; just flowers and birds and fountains."[10] Acceptance among health professionals was widespread too, and TM was used to allay everyday tension, provide pain relief in dentistry, and for other clinical purposes.[11]

In time, TM evolved into something of a charismatic movement, with a belief system that transcended the domain of its practice. The scope of the movement broadened considerably with the establishment of Maharishi International University, named after the guru of TM, in Fairfield, Iowa. A variety of unreasonable beliefs came to be accepted as literally true by the more committed members, such as the ability of experienced meditators to levitate. Group meditation was thought to effect direct changes in international political and economic affairs, and even to reduce traffic accidents in remote cities. Indeed, at one point movement leaders mobilized a conclave of thousands of Maharishi's followers who expected by their conjoint efforts to shape the course of ongoing military conflicts in the Middle East and Southeast Asia.[12] In this movement, the altered state associated with meditation clearly contributed to members' acceptance of an unlikely set of beliefs.

Drug-Induced Altered Consciousness

Because of their potent effect on perception, thought, and feeling, psychoactive drugs such as marijuana, cocaine, heroin, and alcohol can shape social behavior and social structure. Quite aptly, the term social pharmacology[13] has been used to describe the interplay between the physiologic effects of drugs that alter the mental state and the impact these drugs can have on social interactions. Psychoactive drug use is almost always part of the fabric of rituals and accepted behavior within a society, and thereby usually contributes to the stability of the social structure. Alcohol, for instance, is so closely associated with norms of accepted social behavior in contemporary culture that it is difficult to change such customs, as we learned during Prohibition. Cross-cultural studies indicate that psychoactive drugs generally help integrate members of a society into patterns of social conformity. This observation has been made in diverse social settings and in different historical periods, from primitive to complex cultures. In preindustrial cultures where ritual use of psychoactive plants is found, little if any abuse occurs, and drug use almost always is a means to a socially approved end, such as contacting the supernatural.[14] Even in nineteenth-century United States, where opiates were used widely in tincture form, their role was accepted as part of the standard pharmacopoeia.[15]

Drugs and the Counterculture

Consciousness-altering drugs played a prominent role in spearheading the acceptance of counterculture values in the 1960s, abetted by their ability to alter the individuals' subjective state and thereby prime the person for acceptance of a new world view. The psychedelic movement, fueled by marijuana and ignited by psychotomimetics such as LSD, psilocybin, and mescaline, came close to meeting the definition of a charismatic group. Participants acquired a good measure of social cohesiveness, a mix of shared ideologies and beliefs, and considerable changes in personal values.

Some of those experimenting with LSD attempted to generate new perspectives rooted in the presumed value of self-realization inherent in altered consciousness; we will examine these attempts since they illustrate the incomplete development of a potential charismatic movement rooted in the use of mind-altering drugs. Best known was Timothy Leary, who emerged from the relatively value-free perspective of a psychological research laboratory. Leary was exposed to LSD in the context of his early investigations into its psychotomimetic effects. The motto he later popularized—"Tune in, turn on, drop out"—became a catch phrase for the counterculture, but was primarily a negation of values. His subsequent flirtation with establishing a more transcendent quasireligious movement, the "League for Spiritual Democracy," whose acronym is LSD, did not carry sufficient meaning to engage young people. As an effective orator, Leary drew sizable crowds at first, but interest in the nascent movement evaporated, and drug use did not become the basis of a new religious movement.

Because little historical relationship exists between psychedelics and Christian mysticism, drug-induced altered consciousness was also not seen as the high road into Christian tradition. One attempt at studying how drugs can help attain transcendent experience within the framework of an established religion is fascinating. Walter Pahnke [16] was a researcher who undertook a variety of investigations into the consciousness-raising effects of psychotomimetic drugs. In one notable study, he gave the psychotomimetic psilocybin to ten Christian theology students, and an active placebo (one whose marginal effects might lead it to be mistaken for the drug itself) to an equal number of control subjects, also theology students. Both groups had been prepared for the possibility of a heightened spiritual response and were brought to a Good Friday service in a chapel right after.

Pahnke found that those who received the active drug rated themselves appreciably higher on descriptors of mystical experience, such as feelings of unity and transcendence of time and space, than did the controls. On the basis of a six-month follow-up, he reported that the experience also provided "life-enhancing and -enriching effects similar to some of those claimed by mystics" and had a profound impact on the lives of eight of the ten subjects given the active drug. He emphasized that the experience took place in the context of a religious service whose use of symbols was familiar and meaningful, and that the design of the study provided an appropriate framework for the students to derive meaning and integration from their experience.

Such an approach to promoting a Christian mystical experience was quite interesting, but, in the end, Christian mysticism is associated with asceticism and denial of bodily pleasures, whereas the use of psychedelics, at least within the counterculture generation, came to be allied with a hedonistic orientation and a rebellion against traditional values. Ultimately, the contradiction between these two perspectives made their combination unlikely.

Others sought to revive established religious values through drugs, but drew on Eastern religions rather than Western views. This was more apt because of the acknowledged place of altered consciousness in Eastern meditation. Although Eastern spirituality is not traditionally associated with psychedelic drugs, a lack of familiarity with these traditions allowed youths to relate the drug experiences to their newfound meditation practice. American-born drug experimenters exposed to Indian culture, such as Richard Alpert, who later took the name of Baba Raam Dass, articulated this position.

For many a natural transition occurred from drug-related altered consciousness to the altered states associated with meditations within an Eastern charismatic sect. Engagement within the cohesive setting of the Divine Light Mission helped many fend off their abuse of drugs, but the experience of these young people also reflects the interchangeability of drug use with the meditation practice of this Hindu-oriented group. Ellen's case was presented as an illustration of how a woman about to return to full-blown heroin addiction had been able to respond to such an experience. She was on the verge of relapse when she encountered the Divine Light Mission in Colorado, and was drawn into its supportive network. She initially accepted the social support offered at the ashram, but later found that the group's meditation practice was essential to stabilizing her abstinence. As she said,

> At first all I had to hold on to was the other premies, but I still kept thinking about heroin. After a week or two I was able to meditate, and after a while the meditations began to stand in for the drugs I was craving. At times the sensations I had while meditating felt like the high I used to get from drugs, and soon I could put myself into a drug-free space just by meditating—for a few minutes at first, and later for most of the day. Eventually I could summon it up when I had to.

Some Eastern sects were quite explicit about the direct transition to mystical meditation they offered drug users. For example, Alexander Deutsch [17] studied a small Eastern-oriented cult, and found that most members had made at least moderate use of LSD prior to their encounter with the group. Indeed, Baba, their leader, referred to the psychedelic experience as a "preview of coming attractions." Devotees saw their use of psychotomimetics as influential, even essential, to their embrace of this cult, and reported that those drug experiences with a mystical content were most important to their entry into the group.

The adoption of irrational beliefs in this group was also clearly supported by members' experiences with psychedelic drugs. As one follower of this guru reported, "Baba says that he knows that someone is coming if that person thinks of him on the way here. At one time that would have seemed ridiculous to me, but after all the unusual things I've experienced under LSD, I can believe it." This statement reflects the potency of altered consciousness in preparing the individual to accept unaccustomed beliefs.

The psychedelics spearheaded the introduction of a movement espoused with great zeal by many counterculture members, but it lacked the leadership or mission to crystallize into a true charismatic group. Since it was incompatible with traditional Christian mysticism, it could not coalesce with established Western belief systems. Experiences of altered consciousness, however, did leave a vacuum of commitment among the young that primed many of them to accept the new religious movements of the 1970s, particularly insofar as they offered meditative states as a substitute for drug experience. For many parents it served to generate a contrary movement in their explicit battle against drugs.[18]

Social Induction

Inducing an altered state of consciousness in group religious experience by suggestion from the social milieu is not a contemporary phenomenon. The mystical experience of trances, visions, and speaking in tongues has for the most part been undermined by the influence of rational empirical thinking. The success of the physical and biological sciences in yielding material progress has appeared to validate objective observation and experimentation as the only legitimate basis for inquiry, and with this a world view based on spiritual values has been dislodged.

Although religiously grounded transcendent experience has waned in recent centuries, certain charismatic denominations within contemporary Christian practice espouse a tradition of altered consciousness and mystical experience, particularly during group prayer. These groups assert the validity of nonrational subjective experience guided by belief as a definitive basis for seeking out a "higher" reality. They introduce their adherents to altered consciousness in a social context where the culture of the group leads them to anticipate transcendent experience. This anticipation primes members for intense and moving experiences, like those from previous centuries.

On the contemporary American scene, this is found among Pentecostal Protestants and charismatic Catholics, as well as members of the Unification Church. We will consider each of these movements, and then examine socially induced altered consciousness of a different sort, in a contemporary *non*religious setting, the self-help-oriented est workshops.

The Unification Church

Altered consciousness may be experienced among devotees of religious sects who publicly tout its importance. Typical of these are the Eastern, meditative new religious movements. In other sects, they may occur often but are only infrequently discussed with outsiders. Although the Unification Church is not known for such experiences, these are both common among its membership and important to their continuing sense of religious commitment. Their role in conversion is illustrated by the story of Ed, a Moonie who had unusual perceptions at the time he decided to join. Ed was invited to a recruitment workshop by an older member who participated in the group experiences along with him, serving as a spiritual mentor. After a few days, the mentor became concerned that Ed's attitude did not reflect a proper understanding of the group's mission and advised that he devote his time to prayer for two full days; he also gave him suggestions on how to heighten his spiritual awareness. For example, he told Ed to eat no solids, but drink whatever juices or other fluids he chose.

Ed spent most of the next two days at home, visiting the workshop center each day for a short time. He soon began to experience an unfamiliar state of consciousness, which he described as follows.

> I felt a bit weak, but less cluttered inside, and in my body could sense that I was closer to liberation from my old concerns. The prayers soon developed a rhythm of their own, and now that I had removed myself from my friends, there was a loneliness I could almost feel. It was strangely pleasant.

At the church center he had been told about dreams in which spirits could appear, and indeed did have vivid and intense dreams on the first of the two nights. He also heard about how one may enter into a "condition of indemnity" in which a rapport is established with supernatural spirits.

On the second night, he finished his prayers and read from the Divine Principle while alone in his apartment. Suddenly he felt he was in the presence of Reverend Moon, and heard the minister speaking to him directly

> as real as we're talking now. I didn't turn around but I knew that Reverend Moon was there. His presence was as real as any person I've sat with. He told me that I was doing the right thing and should continue on my course, that I would find spiritual enlightenment.

Ed could not fall asleep, and paced back and forth until after sunrise, when he broke his fast. He had never had an experience like this, nor was he suffering from any psychiatric disorder so far as I could tell.

The demand characteristics of the group (expectations implicit in the social context) had primed this young man to experience perceptual distortions. He had been exposed to a seductive social setting in the church center and its workshop, and the church members whom he had come to trust had convincingly stated that they could experience alterations in perception and consciousness. Furthermore, his isolation, prayer, and fasting had altered his mental state so that his usual sense of his place in the world was destabilized, leaving him open to accept the group's perspective.

A social setting's demand characteristics can determine a person's behavior in unexpected ways. This can happen even if those setting up the group *don't* want to prejudice events, a problem sometimes arising in psychological research laboratories, where the demand characteristics of a scientific project implicitly lead participants to be "good subjects" and perceive their state in a subjective way that will give the experimenter results that will fit his or her hypothesis.[19] Ed wanted to be a good disciple, and tried somehow to feel in a manner that he implicitly knew would please the group and his mentor. Both the demand characteristics of the workshop setting and the altered subjective state Ed established through prayer and fasting led him to attribute his unaccustomed feelings to the church's "spirit world." The consequences of this attribution may have been startling, but they were nonetheless in keeping with the group's expectations.

Members of the Unification Church do indeed experience alterations in sensation and perception like those reported by Divine Light members. In our study of the Moonies, we applied the same questionnaire items as in the Divine Light study to reveal similarities between the two groups.

The Moonies' experience *outside* formal prayer was particularly relevant, as their lives were often touched by transcendent states during the routine of their daily activities. This is illustrated by changes in time sensation. A majority (72%) had experienced a distorted sense of the passage of time outside the prayer experience, and most of this group (50% of the total) felt it "clearly" or "very intensely." [20] Such experience is not without consequences for an individual's judgment and perception of everyday events.

A parallel can be drawn from an experimental study by Fred Melges and his associates on subjects who smoked delta-9-THC, the active component of marijuana. [21] They studied the change in time sense produced by the drug and examined its effect on attention and goal-directed thinking. Subjects became susceptible to alterations in their perception of themselves (feelings of depersonalization) and delusion-like ideas (such as feelings that they were being influenced by outside forces). The researchers likened the situation to one observed in some psychiatric patients and also in normal individuals who may report feelings of clairvoyance. Under these circumstances, subjects drew intuitive "connections" while often disregarding common-sense considerations.

Similar changes may occur in the subjective distortions of time sense promoted by the social context of Unification Church membership. For the majority of Moonies, transcendent experiences may help effect changes in their usual style of thinking. They may draw conclusions they would not otherwise arrive at if they applied the norms for inference accepted within the general society. In this altered state of mind, however, they are more likely to accept unusual attitudes and beliefs promoted within the group, and perhaps to be open to further hallucinatory experiences.

Repeated experiences in which the parameters defining consciousness are altered also serve as opportunities for renewal of commitment to the group's views—mini-conversions, as it were. For example, most members reported experiencing outside the context of prayer "a special and unfamiliar feeling in my body" (52%) and seeing "a special new meaning in my life" (90%). And some members had more intense alterations in the sensations that define consciousness: more than a third (39%) reported feeling themselves "to be in the physical presence of someone important to [them] even though most people couldn't have seen him" or seeing "something special that no one else could see" during their usual state; half of this group (18%) reported that they "could see it clearly with [their] eyes."

Consider how these experiences are integrated into the group's belief system. A sizable majority of members (74%) reported that they *strongly* felt a "close connection with God," and that they had "no doubt at all about the relevance of the Divine Principle in [their] personal life." These feelings were associated with a strong commitment to the sect, so that transcendent episodes were likely to be perceived as divine messages, interpreted within the framework of the group's expectations, associated with the "spirit world" and a member's "condition of indemnity."

Accounts of visions were, of course, much more common in medieval times. Could it be that the world view brought about by the age of empirical science has stamped out the consensual acceptance of mystical experience? Might not such experiences be more accessible today if they were more widely perceived to be a valid part of our subjective existence?

Closer to the Mainstream: Pentecostals and Charismatics

The Protestant Pentecostal movement claims several million American members and its influence has spread to millions more overseas.[22] What makes the movement distinctive is its zealous religious experience characterized by rituals involving a significant degree of altered consciousness in many participants. Among these are speaking in tongues, or *glossolalia,* strange utterances thought to represent the voice of God; *possession behavior,* during which a person may dance and gyrate or roll on the floor; and the *testimonial,* a fervent and spontaneous statement of the person's faith, typically made after rising to speak in the course of a Pentecostal service. Interestingly, careful empirical study of the Pentecostals reveals that all three behaviors associated with altered states are also associated with the relief of emotional distress; the more frequently members of a Pentecostal congregation engage in these rituals, the less likely they are to report symptoms of distress on a standard psychological measure.[23] This offers a parallel to the relief of distress associated with meditation among Divine Light members.

Glossolalia is a form of pseudolanguage said to be available to all persons that can be acquired by inspiration or determined practice.[24] It derives from citations in the New Testament and Pentecostals consider it to be evidence of baptism in the Holy Spirit. The contemporary Pentecostal movement dates to 1901, when the Reverend Charles Parham left an established pulpit in Topeka, Kansas, and began to practice faith healing. Despite local opposition, he soon established a Bible college. Parham assigned some students the task of investigating the experience of "baptism of the Spirit," sometimes called the Pentecostal Blessing, and asked them to report back after the school's Christmas holidays. He later wrote that to his "astonishment, they all had the same story. . . . The indisputable proof on each occasion was that they spoke with other tongues." [25]

The identicalness of all the stories came to assume great importance for the growing Pentecostal movement, and similar experiences were soon reported elsewhere in the Western states. Within a few decades Pentecostalism had spread across the country, and the phenomenon of speaking in tongues came to be seen as the culmination of the rediscovery of Christ as a personal savior. As Pentecostal religious services took shape, they acquired a free and loud participatory style, with sermons and songs frequently interrupted by cries of "Amen," calls in "tongues," and testimonies of faith and supplication. Some of these raucous outbursts and physical paroxysms helped label the Pentecostals as Holy Rollers.

The practice of glossolalia frequently (but not always) serves as a vehicle for achieving a trance-like state. In a process called "driving," [26] the leader of a congregation, typically a gifted orator, impels the audience into a high state of excitement. Driving often takes place in stages; the first is singing of hymns with clear repetitive beats and clapping in time, often enhanced by musical accompaniment. A particular supplicant is next prayed for by members of the congregation and by the leader, usually very loudly and in beat. Soon this evocation passes into a final stage of glossolalia where singing and prayer merge into unknown tongues, usually shouted by the supplicant, who may now enter into a trance.

States of altered consciousness may act as the basis for stabilizing highly idiosyncratic group rituals. Within the Pentecostal movement, snake-handling cults of the Southeastern United States exemplify this. In rural Tennessee, for example, members of the Holiness Church of God in Jesus' Name draw their religious practice from the literal interpretation of the following Bible verses.

> In my name shall they cast out devils; they shall speak with new tongues; they shall take up serpents; and if they drink any deadly thing it shall not hurt them; they shall lay hands on the sick and they shall recover (Mark 16:17–18).

While speaking in tongues, often to the accompaniment of screams and lashing, jerking movements, members of this congregation not only practice faith healing but also expose themselves to the risk of death by drinking poisons and handling poisonous snakes. One member described how he would wait for the right state of mind, or "anointing," during a church service so that he would be ready to handle the congregation's poisonous cottonmouth snake.

> When I get anointed, a numbness starts in my face and in my hands, and it feels like oil dripping out of my fingers. It's symbolic, too, as if your arm went plumb to sleep. But it's full of joy . . . a real good feeling. I feel like I'm walking in another world. It's hard to explain.

Another congregant described the experience in these terms:

It's just like a small still voice. Calmness comes over me from the top of my head to the bottom of my feet. When I hear that voice I go ahead and move. But I want to be doubly sure that it is God . . . [Then, discussing a time he was bitten by the snake,] it stings just like a bee. Like two needles. I hurt for about 12 hours on this one. I suffered, but it didn't make me sick. Both arms swole up. . . . I don't believe in going to a doctor when I get serpent bit. See if God lets the serpent bite you, I don't see that you have the right to do anything about it. God can heal you.[27]

In actuality, between 1910 and 1960 at least nineteen persons were reported to have died in the United States from snake bites incurred during such religious services, and the first of the two congregants just quoted estimated that ten persons in his church alone were fatally bitten over a period of ten years. Indeed, the Holiness Church to which these speakers belonged gained international attention because of court disputes over their right to such practice when two members died from drinking strychnine during a religious service.

More than half a century after their emergence in Kansas City, Pentecostal practices began to spread to the American Catholic Church. In 1966, two young faculty members at Duquesne University in Pittsburgh made a pact to pray for their spiritual renewal. They attended a Protestant prayer meeting and soon became inspired to speak in tongues. With other faculty members and students at the university they formed a prayer group involved in charismatic activities, and their mission spread to the campuses of Notre Dame and the University of Michigan.

In a typical Catholic charismatic meeting at that time,[28] neophytes would report their experience of religious revival, often revealing that this had followed their involvement in the drug subculture. States of altered consciousness were called "gifts of the Holy Spirit" and were expected to lead members to a spiritual rebirth. These experiences included glossolalia, involuntary motor activity, and trances, all generated by the dynamics of the prayer meeting.

This movement spread rapidly and, within the decade, as many as 350,000 Catholics across the United States worshipped in derivative prayer meetings.[29] As the similarities in the ritual practice of the Pentecostals and Catholic charismatics began to surpass the differences, they soon served as a basis for bringing together many members of the Catholic and Protestant traditions in interfaith services and joint religious publications, an ecumenism long considered difficult to achieve.

Experiences of altered consciousness, however, are not restricted to religious settings since they are also reported among the public at large. Andrew Greeley studied a representative sample of Americans, asking them if they had ever felt as though they "were very close to a powerful, spiritual force that seemed to lift you out of yourself," and found that more than a third (35%) answered positively. When this group was then asked what situations triggered these experiences, the most common responses were religious in nature, such as prayer, attendance at a church service, and being alone in a church.[30] Cross-cultural evidence also provides support for the widespread potential for such altered states. Erika Bourguinon[31] reviewed data on 488 societies drawn from the *Ethnographic Atlas,* a standard cross-cultural reference; most were preindustrial and tribal in structure. A full 90% were found to have institutionalized practices that included some form of altered consciousness, trance-like in nature, and, in the majority, trances were ascribed in one way or another to possession by some religious force. Indeed, the linkage between beliefs and trance states is thought to date to Upper Paleolithic times.[32]

In the Secular Mainstream: est

For another view of the role of altered consciousness in promoting membership in a charismatic group, we might ask how a contemporary population can be made susceptible to such influence when the right social setting is established. Consider an "experimental" problem in the psychology of the charismatic group: How might one engage a population of sophisticated, well-educated adults from metropolitan centers in a new, zealously espoused ideology, where the techniques employed can include the development of a cohesive group setting and the promotion of attitude change via altering consciousness? One answer comes from the example of est, an acronym for Erhard Seminars Training.

This secular movement was started in 1971 by Werner Erhard, a man with no formal experience in mental health, self-help, or religious revivalism, but a background in retail sales. Within only five years of its founding, est had reportedly put over 83,000 generally affluent and well-educated people through its training, aimed at "transforming your ability to experience living." Erhard and his trainers combined aspects of a number of popular philosophies, from Eastern religion to psychoanalysis, in a program that would supposedly make participants appreciate the need to confront their own conflicts and social circumstances and dismiss longstanding illusions.

The training program consists of two weekend-long workshops with evening sessions on the intervening weekdays. Workshops with about two hundred enrollees are led by a trainer designated by Erhard and several experienced assistants. Over the course of nine days, enrollees are cajoled and emotionally battered, and encouraged to regress up to the point where they have finally "got it," a state akin to a conversion.

Certain alterations in consciousness and subjective state within this large group context are apparently used to promote this conversion-like experience. Workshop members are subjected to a variety of unsettling circumstances for long hours at a stretch that act to peel away those layers of psychological stability that normally bolster their usual state of consciousness. Several injunctions are issued: no watches, no talking unless recognized by the trainer (which means rarely), no leaving one's seat, no smoking, no eating, no going to the bathroom except during breaks separated by many hours. Participants undergo long periods during which they must keep their eyes closed and listen to diatribes, abuse, and obscenity dispensed by the trainer. They are also generally kept in rooms where there is no daylight, at temperatures that may become uncomfortable (such as 40°). In addition, they are usually exposed to a number of individuals within the group who respond with intense emotion, crying copiously or screaming. A variety of physiologic and emotional parameters are therefore disturbed, disrupting the enrollees' homeostasis. Participating in the program is not without psychiatric risk, and a number of cases of psychotic reaction have been reported among those enrolled.[33]

What it means to "get it" in est is hard to define. After an initial correspondence with Werner Erhard, I met at some length with the movement's director of research so that we might consider studying this transformation. Our discussions of getting it, however, yielded no operational definition (or any viable basis for a study, for that matter).[34] One account of the attitude of an est trainer may be helpful in defining this observation further. Just before graduation, the trainer always asks if people "got it." Some say yes and are applauded. Another group isn't sure. The trainer talks to them and they all say they got it. Finally, one or two people are sure that they haven't got it, and the trainer says, "Well, you got it, because there's nothing to get." The whole thing is treated as a joke, discomforting the new converts.[35] Nonetheless, one study of a large sample of est alumni who had completed the training at least three months before revealed that the large majority felt the experience had been positive (88%), and considered themselves better off for having taken the training (80%).[36]

Psychological sophistication does not seem to breed skepticism among those exposed to the program. In the study of est alumni, for example, there was no significant difference in the proportion of professional therapists or laypeople who gave positive reports. In another study, an experienced clinician evaluated a series of his psychiatric patients who took the est training and concluded that the majority derived some benefit from the program.[37]

One psychologist who had been through the training told me of his distress at the psychological assaults against some of the more labile workshop members, but his words also revealed the role of altered consciousness in overcoming these apprehensions.

> The physical discomfort and badgering left me horrified, and feeling very weird. Time had stopped running in any usual sense, and I was having unexpected feelings of all kinds. At one point, when the trainer called my friend an asshole for trying to console a woman who was crying, I got

enraged; I wanted to see the trainer dead. I realized that I was beginning
to lose any sense of where I was in the real world, and even who I usually
was.

And then suddenly it came clear! I was the prisoner of *my own* compulsion to help everyone and be kind to them. The trainer was right; I didn't
have to be tied down by this attitude. I was free to choose what I might
think and feel, independent of forty years of programming. Then the whole
room seemed to slip away, and I no longer cared about eating, peeing, or
how long the whole damn thing would run on. I felt liberated, released
from a long prison term.

In one sense, this represented a transition to a full-blown "culture of
narcissism" in which the individual owes allegiance only to the self. Participants in the est program often feel released from the commitments born out
of fidelity to their fellow humans, allowing them to indulge themselves without guilt. In another sense, however, est underlines how much we each act
on our own set of comfortable misconceptions. Whether or not the realiza-
tion of this psychologist ultimately proves useful to him, it did indeed come
after his feeling and thought had been altered from their usual state.

II

A MODEL OF
THE CHARISMATIC
GROUP

We have discussed the psychological forces that allow a cult to exert its potent influence on members, and now turn to developing a model that will explain how these groups actually function. To do this, we must link three levels of human organizations—biology, psychology, and social structure. Behavior is rooted in biology, even though it is moved by psychological forces affecting the individual as a whole; the individual group member is engaged in social organizations that themselves assume a life of their own.

5

BIOLOGY AND
BEHAVIOR

We have examined the remarkable power of psychological forces within the charismatic group to shape its members' attitudes and behavior. We will now consider the origin of these forces. Are they innate in human nature, or merely the product of culture and circumstance?

The inclination to participate in local social groups is observed in the most diverse cultures, emerging no doubt from the advantages a community confers in meeting daily needs and contending with adversity. This inclination is intensified, even caricatured, in the paramilitary groups that arise in nations racked by internecine conflicts, such as contemporary Northern Ireland and Lebanon. The intense commitment that participants in military groups can develop toward each other may entail extreme self-sacrifice, as in the human wave tactics involving young Iranian boys in the war with Iraq.

In the Unification Church, as in other contemporary sects, members put themselves at risk in a variety of ways out of fealty to the group. They may go through long periods of arduous work, subject themselves to public ridicule, and postpone childbearing for many years.

The inclination toward such self-sacrificing group behavior is observed in almost all cultures; it can obviously help meet the needs of a group to wage war, endure dislocation, or survive in times of economic privation. This pattern of behavior may even serve as the mechanism for survival of the group and its conjoint goals.

The human affinity for close-knit groups is a ubiquitous and apparently innate trait. If so, how would this trait have evolved? Is an instinct for group affiliation based on the evolutionary advantage that the group—including the charismatic group—confers on its overall membership, particularly at times of crisis and outside threat?

In *The Descent of Man*,[1] Charles Darwin revealed his interest in developing a method of psychology that would explain the appearance of similar social traits in very different species. He even incurred allegations of "extreme anthropomorphism"[2] in writing

> with what care male birds display their various charms, and this they do with utmost skill. . . . it appears that actions, first perhaps intentional, have become instinctive. If so we ought not to accuse birds of conscious vanities; yet when we see a peacock strutting about, with expanded and quivering tailfeathers, he seems the very emblem of pride and vanity.[3]

Konrad Lorenz[4] would have considered the vain strutting observed in both peacocks and Homo sapiens as behavioral *analogues*. Lorenz observed that such analogues arise as two different species independently develop similar biologically grounded means for adapting to their environment. To be analogous, the traits must be found in species that are separated in the chain of evolution by others that do *not* carry such a trait. For an example of a social analogue, Lorenz looked to the behavior of geese, a species he studied at great length. He acknowledged that terms like "falling in love, marrying, or being jealous" might seem awkward when speaking of birds, but pointed out that behaviors comparable to these human ones may be found with little difficulty among monogamous pairs of geese. In addition, they have very much the same role and survival value in both species.[5]

The possibility that ethologic insights may help explain some puzzling aspects of human behavior is therefore most attractive. For our purposes, we may invoke evolutionary paradigms to address the following central paradox of charismatic group behavior: Affiliation with such groups is observed in many settings, both in full-blown or muted form, and appears to represent a universal potential in human beings; nonetheless, such affiliation frequently runs contrary to the interests of the individual, sometimes contrary to the person's very survival. Why should people have retained such a potentially self-destructive trait over the course of evolution?

We do find that most social traits confer a clear-cut adaptive advantage for the individual carrying the trait, such as the strutting behavior of the peacock or the assertion of status in a regional band of primates. Some traits, though, are not clearly adaptive. For example, the inclination to assist others in need offers an adaptive advantage to *other* members of a social group, but does not necessarily enhance the fitness of the individual with that trait. Such an altruistic trait may often operate to the individual's detriment, when he or she sacrifices self interest for other members of the social group. This trait is similar to the human inclination to join a charismatic group, which often demands great personal sacrifice. Explanations for the evolution of altruism may therefore shed light on behavior in the charismatic group.

The altruist who saves a drowning swimmer or the worker honeybee who stings an assailant and thereby loses its life have one thing in common with the person who becomes engaged in the charismatic group. From an evolutionary standpoint, each sacrifices individual interests and survival potential for the group's benefit; they will diminish their fitness for subsequent reproduction by virtue of carrying the trait. How do such traits persist over the course of evolution, if their carriers are *less* likely to survive? Let us consider the following. A trait observed in a given individual may serve to improve the reproductive advantage of *other* individuals who themselves may carry genes for that same trait. The enhanced genetic fitness of those other carriers then promotes transmission of the trait to the next generation, since they are now more likely to survive and transmit it themselves. When such principles of population genetics were elaborated and applied to a variety of puzzling ethologic observations such as the self-sacrificing behavior, a new outlook on behavior emerged, one Edward O. Wilson termed sociobiology,[6] which has become both provocative and controversial in recent years.[7]

The concept of inclusive fitness goes to the heart of sociobiology. As proposed by William D. Hamilton,[8] this form of genetic fitness reflects not only the fitness of a given individual carrying a genetic trait, but also the fitness of all others who might carry that trait, since their survival also ensures its transmission. Inclusive fitness can therefore allow a trait to persist in a species, even if it does not aid the individual carrier to survive.

Consider, for example, the concept of *reciprocal altruism*. Robert Trivers[9] pointed out that an altruist trait need not be based only on the advantage it gives actual relatives who are assisted. It can reflect the reciprocal benefits in a family or a larger population of remotely related individuals who act toward each other in an altruistic fashion, thereby assuring some measure of reciprocity when later in need. Furthermore, interesting models have been developed by Lumsden and Wilson[10] for conceptualizing how certain engrams of cultural behavior may be transmitted. All this, we will see, offers an explanation for the survival of traits that do not necessarily endow a given individual with greater genetic fitness.

The inclination to join cohesive groups per se may well have emerged over the course of human evolution as one particular manifestation of inclusive fitness. In the first place, individuals may not have experienced greater personal fitness because of this inclination. The groups they affiliated with, composed of many individuals with this same trait, *could* work together better in the face of adversity and therefore survive better.

The Relief Effect

When one joins a charismatic group, one gives up the opportunity for independent decision making and complies with the group's norms, which may conflict with one's own adaptive needs. The human inclination to join such a group can therefore lead to diminished personal fitness.

Persistence of this inclination may be explained by inclusive fitness—the enhanced potential for survival of all carriers of the trait in the group, as distinguished from personal fitness alone, the potential for survival of the individual. Thus, if a trait found in a given population promotes the survival of the population overall, we say that the inclusive fitness of the population is enhanced—even though any given individual may be less likely to survive when manifesting this trait. We will now see this demonstrated with regard to the enhanced inclusive fitness conferred by affiliation in a cohesive group. Individuals carrying this trait may suffer from the self-sacrifice it engenders, but the cohesive group as a whole, consisting of carriers of this trait, is more likely to survive and thereby assure its transmission.

The enhanced fitness conferred by the group derives from how this social entity as a whole can act as a highly adaptable instrument of social organization, particularly in times of crisis. A zealous cohesive group can mount collaborative efforts that a more loosely cooperating group cannot. The persistence in the gene pool of a trait that leads individuals toward such zealous group behavior is thereby promoted at the same time that the group's needs as an entity are met.

In some circumstances this behavior may be the only way of guaranteeing that individual members undertake the considerable sacrifices necessary to ensure the group's genetic survival. But what psychological mechanism implements the inclination for maintaining affiliation with the charismatic group? What motivates people to join and stay, often disregarding their own personal interests? To understand this, we must posit a mechanism that ties the individual to the group, one rooted in human physiology. Furthermore, if this mechanism is grounded in the human evolutionary past, it should have homologs in the behavior of other primates.

At the heart of this process lies the relationship between a pattern of social behavior and a biologically grounded motivation, or instinctive drive, that I have termed the *relief effect*. It operates as follows. *When people become involved in a charismatic group, an inverse relationship exists between their feelings of emotional distress and the degree to which they are affiliated with that group.* Individuals' capacity for commitment to the group is mediated by the relief of neurotic distress, relief that they experience on affiliation and continued membership; the closer they feel toward the group, the less distress they feel. Conversely, if they disaffiliate from the group a bit, they are prodded to return by the increased distress they are likely to feel. Thus, zealous group members feel unhappy or dysphoric when removed from their group. A committed member of Alcoholics Anonymous, for example, typically reports feelings of unease or being out of sorts when he or she misses a number of meetings.

A member is therefore poised between reward for closeness and punishment for alienation. Each minor episode of reward and punishment, on moving closer to the group or further away, functions as an operant learning experience that conditions subsequent involvement. The process is indeed similar to a conditioning experiment in which an animal is rewarded each time it spontaneously carries out a particular behavior or punished for acting in a contrary way. After several such spontaneous acts and their associated consequences, the experimental animal will carry out that behavior consistently, even when further rewards are given only infrequently. For example, a mouse can be rewarded with cheese every time it taps a lever. Eventually, it will tap the lever frequently although bits of cheese are few and far between.

A charismatic group member resembles an experimental animal or human subject in an operant conditioning study. He or she can be made to adopt a behavior pattern if at first rewarded whenever the person acts in a particular way. If, whenever the member feels close to the group, his or her distress is relieved, the member will tend to stay close, and the feeling of closeness to the group becomes the source of operant reinforcement. Such habituation can occur without the individual's awareness. Similarly, the repeated dysphoria associated with feelings of alienation tends to make members avoid distance from the group; it is a negative reinforcer for staying close.

After a member undergoing induction has come close to the group a number of times and been rewarded each time, the member "learns" to comply with the group so as to feel close to it and experience the consequent well-being. The new group member, a product of a reinforcement process, will continue in a pattern of maintaining closeness even if rewards are provided only intermittently. The relief effect thereby serves as a reinforcer for continued group involvement.

Thus, by relieving neurotic distress individuals are engaged into the charismatic group and learn to comply with the behaviors it promotes. The relief effect is mediated by the affiliative attitudes of social cohesiveness and shared beliefs—that is, by both social and cognitive means. A series of propositions, supported by data on members of the Unification Church and Divine Light sects, may explain how this effect underlies affiliation within such groups.

Evidence in Contemporary Sects

I will now review a series of propositions based on findings on members of the Unification Church and the Divine Light Mission. These will be used to support the model first described on the origins of affiliative behavior.

When joining a charismatic group, an individual experiences relief in neurotic distress in direct relation to how closely affiliated he feels with the group. Initiation into a group involves remarkable personal commitment. For a member to become fully involved, there should be a dramatic psychological impetus to commitment, and engagement should yield considerable relief. Using the Unification Church and Divine Light findings, we may consider whether this is so.

The needs of potential recruits before joining contribute to understanding the nature of this relief, since those who were attracted most to the group had experienced the greatest distress, as evidenced in the reports of 104 participants in Unification Church initiation workshops. Scores on the general psychological well-being scale revealed that those experiencing the greatest stress were more likely to join.[11] Those who remained after the initial weekend but did *not* join were less troubled; those who left earliest were least distressed. Importantly, though, each group was well below the average in psychological well-being in relation to a comparable sample of young people drawn from the general population. Yet when a cohort of longstanding members was studied, their well-being scores were much closer to the level found in the general population, reflecting a considerable improvement in their psychological well-being over the course of induction and membership.[12]

This is also corroborated by reports given by members of the Divine Light Mission for the periods both before and after joining. Two years after joining they described their psychological distress as having been a good deal less (37%) right after joining than immediately preceding. For example, a considerable decline occurred in the degree to which members viewed emotional problems as interfering with their adjustment in life (35%), with a similar drop in feeling nervous and tense (41%). This decline was highly correlated with the members' feelings of cohesiveness toward the group. Those who felt closest to the group were more likely to experience a relief in neurotic distress. Altogether, the items reflecting group cohesiveness accounted for a large portion of this decline in neurotic distress and these observations are at the heart of the relief effect.[13]

Furthermore, it can be said that mobilization into a charismatic group is most likely in times of distress. From the standpoint of group adaptation, a bold course of action involving mutual commitment and self-sacrifice is in fact usually needed at such a time, so as to address pressing problems that face the group.

In the proper group setting, it is possible to elicit commitment to the charismatic group quite easily. Members or potential members are not necessarily open to involvement in a group for extended periods of time, and it must be possible for engagement to take place when the need arises. The experience of participants in the Unification Church induction workshops was striking in this regard. Of those participants who remained beyond the initial two days, all rapidly developed an intense feeling of affiliation to the sect, whether they eventually joined or not. Their answers reflected very high levels of cohesiveness toward members in their immediate induction group, and rapid acceptance of basic church tenets. Indeed, the attitudes of those who later left differed from those who joined only in that those who dropped out had stronger ties toward persons outside the group. That is, those who refrained from joining did not do so because of a lack of strong feelings for the group—they left because of commitments to family and friends.

This rapid development of affiliation during the induction experience demonstrates how easily a person can become psychologically engaged in the group setting, as long as he or she demonstrates some initial interest. Recall the rapid transition to commitment that Jerry, the depressed college student, experienced when he entered the Moonie induction program. Within several days he had thrown off his previous social bonds and chose to become a fugitive from a court order rather than cut his ties to the church.

Over the course of induction, individuals' attitudes and behaviors came to conform with those expected of group members. In addition to acquiring a cohesiveness toward the group and belief in its creed, recruits also adopt the group's standards of behavior. In the Unification Church, inductees' attitudes and behavior regarding the use of alcoholic beverages illustrate this point; the Church discourages intoxication with alcohol, but does not prohibit its use. The large majority of longstanding members (86%) reported using alcoholic beverages right before contact with the sect, but only a third still used them at all two years later. More important, daily use disappeared entirely.

This pattern was a reflection of newly acquired attitudes. Members' agreement with the statement "I should avoid getting high from alcohol" increased appreciably with members' length of membership. Whereas a minority (42%) said that they strongly agreed with this statement before joining, more than twice that number (89%) felt this way right after joining, and the same proportion concurred after a period of membership. Among Divine Light members, hallucinogen and heroin use almost vanished over the course of membership (hallucinogen use went from 35 to 3%, and heroin use from 14 to 0%).

The relationship between the relief of neurotic distress and affiliation with the charismatic group continues over the course of membership. This relationship is essential to the group's perpetuation since it assures that members will maintain their commitment. The proposition is supported by our data on the psychological status of longstanding members of the Unification Church. Two aspects of their affiliative feelings toward the group were examined: social cohesiveness and shared beliefs. Scores on a scale reflecting group cohesiveness accounted for an appreciable portion of members' psychological well-being at the time they were studied, indicating a very strong relationship between the strength of these social ties and level of well-being. Furthermore, a scale of shared religious beliefs added even more to the statistical correlation between members' well-being and group affiliation. The two items on religious belief that best predicted a member's psychological well-being were "My religious beliefs give me comfort" and "I feel a close connection with God." The relief effect apparently continues to operate over the course of long-term membership in the charismatic group, thereby serving as a motivation for continued commitment.

Conformity to a group's behavioral norms is implicitly perceived by members as necessary for maintaining their well-being. This motivation for conforming was seen in the longstanding Unification Church members who had been matched for marital engagement by the Reverend Moon.[14] These members had been born into typical American families but were nonetheless going along with the betrothal—something that few, if any, youths of their background could be expected to accept. They were, in fact, pleased to have their spouses selected for them with no input of their own. Here was a remarkable example of conformity to the behavioral norms of a charismatic group. The vast majority (95%) of these engaged members were still active in the group four years later, almost all now married to their designated mates. Clues as to why these members so readily complied were found in the way they implicitly perceived their emotional vulnerability to disruptive life events.

It has been established[15] that people are more likely to suffer psychological problems when they have recently experienced life events requiring appreciable social readjustment such as a change in residence, the illness of close relatives, or being fired from a job. With this in mind, these Moonies' recent histories of disruptive life events were assessed with a standard scale. As with other populations, a higher incidence of such events was associated with lower levels of psychological well-being. More important, members were buffered from this emotional vulnerability by the degree of their commitment to the church. Those who felt closest to the church were least likely to undergo emotional distress after experiencing disruptions in their lives, and those who were less close were more vulnerable.[16] Specifically, life events predicted 15% of the variance in well-being; this percentage would rise to 31% when affiliation items were incorporated.

A member's responsiveness to the group's expectation is therefore likely to be supported by the person's implicit perception that he or she is protected from life's emotionally disruptive experiences by commitment to the sect; the member comes to see the group as a shield from threatening experiences. This relationship is succinctly expressed in the high percentage of members (88%) who strongly agreed that "My religious beliefs give me comfort."

This mechanism of conformity was again observed in the same group of engaged members followed up three years after their engagement. By now, the large majority (91%) had been married for one year and many (24%) of the wives were already pregnant. For most of these members, the previous year was full of numerous disruptive life events, such as moving out of church residences, setting up new households, assuming responsibility for their own finances, and for many, being uprooted to serve on mobile fundraising teams. Nonetheless, their scores on the belief and cohesiveness scales had not changed significantly, and these were still strong predictors of their level of psychological well-being. Members' vulnerability to disruptive life events was still muted by the degree of their commitment to the group. This leads to the following corollary proposition.

The group acts like a psychological pincer, promoting distress while at the same time providing relief. This is evidenced in an ironic sequence of events. The group promotes behavioral norms that may expose a member to potential distress. Then, as we just saw, the member comes to feel that the relief of this distress depends on fidelity to the group. This in turn makes the member more responsive to the demands of the group and its leadership.

A cycle of this kind is evident in Alcoholics Anonymous, which uses group dependency as a means of escape from alcohol addiction. Recruits are made to feel that they must give up their use of alcohol when, over the course of induction, they accept the group's creed of abstinence. Giving up alcohol, however, raises fear in recruits over their inability to do so without considerable craving and anguish. The group heightens this fear by making recruits face what they have attempted to hide, that they cannot effectively control their drinking. It then offers an answer to this conflict: as AA becomes more important to the new members, they are told that regular attendance and acceptance of AA's rules are necessary for maintaining abstinence. Since they have come to see their psychological well-being as dependent on abstinence, they are trapped into depending on this large group and agree to go along with its demands. In this way many AA members attend meetings on a regular, even daily basis for months or years and succeed in staying sober. But they become highly dependent on the group.

The magnitude of the relief effect is not enhanced by a history of psychological disability. If emotional distress is relieved by affiliation, wouldn't a background of psychological illness make for a more committed member? In a psychological sense, this might make sense, but from an evolutionary standpoint it does not, for if the relief effect were a correlate of disability, sounder members would tend to disaffiliate, and such groups would retain only their most troubled members, while losing their most able. That obviously would not improve the group's chances of survival.

Our own findings showed that a serious emotional disability is not related to the strength of members' ties to the group. Among members of both the Unification Church and the Divine Light Mission, those who reported that they had experienced "serious emotional problems" at some time prior to joining (39% in both samples) were compared to those who had not. No significant correlation existed between this background trait and the degree of relief experienced on induction or the degree of cohesiveness felt toward the group.[17] Thus, among those who joined, responsivity to the group did not depend on a background of serious emotional problems and therefore did not come at the expense of diminished personal fitness.

The relief effect is correlated with a sense of exclusivity. In the Divine Light Mission, the single item on the cohesion scale most highly correlated with the relief of neurotic distress was "I am suspicious of nonmembers,"[18] reflecting a gulf between attitudes toward insiders and outsiders, a mistrust of outsiders that serves as a basis for excluding them. The factor is among the differences between the Unification Church, a self-contained charismatic group, and the Federation of Parents for Drug-Free Youth, composed of zealous community-based parent groups who share a commitment to combat teenage drug abuse. The Federation of Parents is a more conventional self-help program, well integrated into the community. Although Federation members exhibit considerable cohesiveness and shared beliefs, the movement does not function as a socially circumscribed, self-supporting large group, meeting its own economic, social, and cultural needs. Moonies and Federation members did not differ significantly in cohesiveness scores toward their own respective compatriots. With regard to outsiders, however, the Moonies had much lower scores.[19] This difference in feelings toward outsiders indicates that the benefits of Unification Church members' considerable sacrifice will not be casually available to outsiders and reflects the self-protective nature of the true charismatic group.

These propositions help to explain how members of a charismatic group experience a decline in neurotic distress relative to the intensity of their involvement in the group. Since all these propositions are based on measurable psychological characteristics of large-group members, they provide empirical support for the operation of this relief effect.

We will now look for further support for the relief effect hypothesis to very different sources: our knowledge of our evolutionary past and contemporary studies on the behavior of primates. These anthropologic and ethologic data complement studies on contemporary groups to support the ideas about social bonding just presented.

Ethologic Observations

If the relief effect, presumed to underlie charismatic group behavior, is a valid sociobiologic model, supporting ethologic evidence should exist, for example, in homologous behaviors among other primates.

Australopithecus, a direct ancestor of Homo sapiens, inhabited forested areas of East Africa from about five million to one million years ago. Over many generations they developed stable patterns of large-group social organization to sustain adequate nutrition by hunting large game.[20] Indeed, Australopithecus is thought to have formed groups of thirty to one hundred members, as do hunter-gatherer tribes today. In addition, it was necessary to develop behavior patterns allowing them to share in the allocation of spoils of the hunt, and ensuring that outsiders would not gain access to the spoils without having contributed to that communal activity.[21]

Like contemporary hunting tribes, prehistoric bands are thought to have dispersed at intervals, depending on their immediate needs and ecologic circumstance. They consistently reaggregated, however, thereby establishing stable regional groupings.[22] These behaviors also bespeak the value of a psychological mechanism that would ensure cohesiveness among the individual members of large groups.

Complex social traits such as speech, empathy, and interactional skills make for more effective group behavior. In lower species, complex traits may evolve relatively quickly.[23] Nonetheless, the extent to which social traits have evolved since the emergence of Australopithecus is striking. Hominid cranial capacities, for example, doubled between Australopithecine times and the appearance about a million years ago of Homo erectus, a more recent precursor of Homo sapiens.[24] Such massive increases, in cortical matter primarily, have underlain significant changes in the behavioral repertoires of our hominid ancestors.

The social cohesiveness in early hominids is also represented in homologs among nonhuman primates. As with hunter-gatherers, social band size of forty to eighty individuals is common in the community organization of several monkey and ape species. It is seen in the discrete groups formed by chimpanzees in the wild, who migrate, collaborate, and maintain proximity to each other in groups of this size.[25]

There is also experimental evidence for homologs of the relief effect in lower primates. A body of empirical research involving rhesus monkeys supports the relationship between group affiliation and good mood. In classic observations, Harry Harlow[26] demonstrated the emotional vulnerability of lower primates to loss and separation, using the model of mother-infant separation.

Of more direct relevance to behavior in large groups, Stephen Suomi[27] followed Harlow's work with a series of studies inducing depression-like behavior among young monkeys by separating them from their peers. Removal of a young monkey from the cage where he lived with other young monkeys with whom he had been raised eventually resulted in diminished activity, a doleful expression, and a crouched posture. Thus, severing the bonds that these monkeys had to peers in their social network seemed to produce behavior similar to that associated with depression and anxiety in humans. Interestingly, Suomi then studied two ways in which he could overcome the experimentally induced depression in these monkeys—either by reestablishing social ties to peers or by administering antidepressant medications. In one study, the isolated monkeys were introduced into groups of nondepressed peers and thereby achieved relief from their depression. In a second study, imiprimine, a common antidepressant drug, relieved the depression without return to a peer group. Both social and physiologic intervention were thereby able to mimic a relief effect.

Changes in affect may serve in additional ways to ensure cohesiveness and thereby stabilize large social groups—not only by means of the relief effect. Russell Gardener,[28] for example, has drawn attention to the alpha and omega roles (dominant and submissive positions) observed in bands of lower primates. The alpha member of a monkey troupe, the highest in its hierarchy, aggressively initiates action and continually asserts control over other members, much like a manic or hypomanic human. The omega, on the bottom of the heap, moves slowly, acts with hesitation, and is not able to prevail when confronted by assertive members, much as depressed human beings behave. Among monkeys, these contrasting roles are determined in large part by heritable factors and are also shaped by individual experience. The potential for expressing these behaviors serves to stabilize the social structure of primate troupes by determining the ongoing rank of its members and hence helping define its working organization.

This is of interest to us as an additional example of the role of affect in regulating social structure. Its function of maintaining a dominance structure in a large social group is different but complementary to that of the relief effect. Affective status, in terms of depression or contentment, probably helps regulate social functions secondary to group affiliation, such as dominance roles, mating behavior, and work satisfaction.

Shared beliefs also have a place in the paradigm of the relief effect, and the biologic underpinnings of this conception can be introduced by considering how the religious symbolism implicit in these beliefs may be mediated in neurobehavioral terms. One useful model for relating symbolic function to brain physiology deals with the imagery reported in dreams.[29] Just as the symbolism of dreams is generated in the biology of brain function, so is the symbolic nature of religious belief.

Recent research has demonstrated that the occurrence of dreams depends on periodic activation of the forebrain by lower brain centers during sleep. Because of this, the existence of a dream "generator," rooted in reticular, oculomotor, and vestibular neurons is posited, one that provides a programmed neural basis for the drive to dream. The random, but nonetheless characteristic nature of these generated signals serves to provide "frames" for dream imagery, and clusters of runs of generator signals constitute time marks for dream subplots and scene changes. In a sense, these neural signals serve as the bursts of current that will produce the dream images. Ultimately, the forebrain, automatically activated by such generated signals, synthesizes the dream by combining the stimuli initiated in the brain stem circuits with "remembered" information stored in the cortex.

On the basis of current understanding of the physiological roots of emotionality, it is reasonable to posit a psychobiologic mechanism from which man's *beliefs* may gain expression, as follows. Man's vulnerability to dysphoria is mediated in large part by lower centers of the brain that developed earlier in the course of evolution, by the limbic system of the midbrain in particular. Among limbic centers, the hippocampus, cingulate gyrus, and septal region are thought to be most concerned with emotional states related to interpersonal relations. These limbic centers may serve as a generator for driving higher cortical centers to ensure the presence of affiliative ties. This takes place by virtue of two presumed functions: the ability of limbic centers to produce an affective state vulnerable to changes in these ties, and the capacity of the neocortex to create the imagery associated with previous social relationships and learned symbols related to such social interaction. Thus, the affective components of one's need for social affiliation may be generated in lower centers but experienced on a conscious level in relation to symbols and content introduced from memories stored in the neocortex. The generated need may be requited by expression in action, such as by establishing ties with one's peers.

Rules for generating the ideas, symbols, and communication patterns that compel behavior are in good part grounded in our evolutionary past, just as the ties of social cohesiveness are. Consider the *innate releasing mechanism*, a device found in lower species, which has its counterparts in observed human behavior. This neurosensory pattern triggers behavioral sequences in lower species when certain stimulus configurations are automatically recognized by virtue of an engram that is genetically predetermined. When the animal is exposed to that stimulus configuration, it will instinctively undertake a complex sequence of behavior. The recognizable behavioral trigger is called a *sign stimulus;* it clearly bespeaks a rather specific inborn neurosensory mechanism, one that can yield the release of a specific inborn behavioral repertoire.

Anthropologic findings also shed light on the role of shared beliefs in cohesive groups. In one classical formulation, Radcliffe-Brown[30] emphasized the importance of religious ritual in assuring linkage among members of primitive societies and suggested a mechanism similar to the hypothesized relief effect. He draws on ethnographic observations, pointing out that anxiety emerges among individual members of tribal societies who fail to uphold the religious rituals of the tribe and suggests, with some irony, that "magic and religion give men fears and anxieties from which they would otherwise be free." But he also makes it clear that these rituals assure the upholding of communal standards of behavior. In this way, an inverse relationship between dysphoria and affiliation is suggested, quite similar to the one described in the relief effect. The social norms associated with the group's symbols and rituals help to guide its members' behavior and ultimately enhance the entire group's adaptive capacities. In this chapter, we initially saw how the concept of inclusive fitness might be applied to affiliation in the charismatic group, particularly evident in certain cult-like settings, and then considered its role in relation to two aspects of group affiliation, group cohesiveness and shared belief. In both cases, physiologic, anthropologic, and ethologic observations were found to support an evolutionary basis of this affiliative behavior.

6

THE CULT AS A
SOCIAL SYSTEM

At the interface between the charismatic religious sect and society at large, strange things happen. Many people have noted the glazed look of members of such sects as the Unification Church when they venture outside the fold and mix with nonmembers. It has been suggested that such behavior is symptomatic of psychopathology, specifically a dissociative state. Others who studied the sects, however, have not made such observations. In this chapter, we will see how the discrepancy represents different aspects of behavior at the boundary of a social system.

Another common observation is the animosity cults elicit from outsiders. In a pluralistic society such as the United States, one may wonder why such hostility exists. Again, we will see how this reaction represents a characteristic process that occurs at a sect's boundaries and will explain some troublesome interactions between members and nonmembers.

All social systems have certain functions that act to protect their integrity and implement their goals. The two previous examples are products of the group's boundary control function, its means of securing its perimeter in a potentially disruptive environment. To view sects more clearly in the broad social context, and to understand their interactions with society better, we will draw on systems theory.[1] We will try to see the cult group as a functionally integrated whole. Four functions characteristic of systems are transformation, monitoring, feedback, and boundary control, and we will consider each.

Transformation

Systems have been likened to factories: they take input from the outside, which can be raw material, energy, or information, and process it into output, a product. This function, called transformation, allows the system to carry out operations essential to its own continuity or to the needs of a larger suprasystem to which it belongs. In a given system, the most important transformation—the one that typically defines its identity—is its *primary task;* most components of the system are geared toward either carrying out this primary task or preventing its disruption. The primary task of most cults is to prepare for the messianic end they envision.

An unstable system, such as a cult in its earlier stages, is particularly susceptible to dissolution. Members may disaffiliate at any time since the ties that bind them together have yet to be woven into the stable network of a social structure. In this regard, the concept of transformation can be used as a model for the persistent attempts of certain charismatic groups to stabilize themselves by acquiring new members. This may be why members can become so deeply involved in conversion activities; they themselves are motivated only by an inchoate need to become engaged in the charismatic group, but they begin conforming to the group's needs as a system. Members would not on their own be inclined to go out and recruit for the group, but as parts of its system they come to act in accordance with its goals.

At some point in their evolution, most charismatic groups focus on making converts as a primary task. The process may ensure a larger and stronger group and, when successful, can also help confer legitimacy to the group's own ideology, thereby consolidating the commitment of its longstanding members.

Another important aspect of that transformation function is how it disrupts the psychological stability of potential recruits, the "input" to this process. Since an intensive mobilization of a charismatic group's psychological and material resources may be directed at the conversion of new members, they can create deep turmoil in the individual convert. On the one hand, the group is intensely seductive in its attempt to attract new members; on the other, it demands a disruption of antecedent social ties and a metamorphosis in the convert's world view. Thus, when the full resources of the group are focused on a recruit, the potential for tearing the fabric of that individual's psychological stability is considerable. The result may be psychiatric symptoms in people with no history of mental disorder or psychological instability. The genesis of these symptoms may lie more in the conflict between the convert's needs and the group's demands than in an underlying psychological impairment of the convert.

The overriding importance to the group of these transformation activities helps explain a number of puzzling phenomena associated with religious conversion experiences, in particular, the manner in which the eruption of behaviors among potential converts may appear to meet standard criteria for psychopathology. Several pathologic categories outlined in the Diagnostic and Statistical Manual of the American Psychiatric Association[2] set in relief the congruence between syndromes associated with conversion and those designated as psychiatric illness. Among the illnesses to be considered from this diagnostic manual are dissociative disorders, pathologic adjustment reactions, major depressive disorders, brief reactive psychoses, and paranoid disorders of a psychotic nature. Each can be generated by the charismatic group as its forces are mobilized to implement the transformation function. An experience recounted by an ex-member of the Unification Church illustrates the potential within a charismatic group for creating a searing force as its transformation function operates against an inductee's resistance. In this case, the group's ability to engage and transform was great enough to disrupt an otherwise stable psychological condition, cause much guilt, and result in a severe psychiatric reaction.

Annette was working in a restaurant in a university town when she and her husband of two years separated. At first, the separation had been very difficult, but she invited her younger sister to move in with her and was beginning to readjust. She was dating occasionally, and had become involved in camping and mountaineering, interests that predated her marriage.

After Annette had been separated for three months, her sister became interested in the Unification Church at a sidewalk recruitment display. A few weeks later, the sister decided to leave Annette's house and move into one of the Church's communal residences. This caused Annette anguish, and she rushed to her sister to dissuade her from joining. The sister first refused to speak with her, but then agreed to discuss the matter if Annette would attend some of the church's classes and discussions to gain a better understanding of the movement's philosophy. Annette did attend, and then vehemently pressed her sister to recognize the importance of reestablishing her independent life. In the classes, Annette was at first argumentative, then sullen.

Soon she realized she was under considerable stress, and found herself becoming emotionally unstable. She often cried, but at other times felt euphoric. The world around her began to seem unreal and she herself felt unreal, sometimes imagining that her body was "separated from her mind," operating independently and automatically. This feeling would persist for hours and even a full day, leading her to fear for her own sanity. She took two weeks off from work and told a male friend whom she had dated for several weeks to stop seeing her because she could no longer "handle a relationship."

Annette now became compulsive about discussing with her sister the problems she had precipitated in joining the sect, but at the same time she also began to feel attracted to the group's ideology and well-ordered view of life. At this point her need to save her sister was coming into direct conflict with the capacity of the group to transform potential recruits. She described her ensuing experience.

> For two weeks I didn't know if I was a part of the world around me, whether my mind and body were connected; it was as if I were watching myself from the back row of a movie theater. I became so upset I couldn't sleep. One part of me was fighting for my sister, but the other began to wonder whether I might not be able to feel some relief by joining the Church. Soon I began to wonder whether the Church might not actually hold the truth for me. Then one day, I was with some brothers and sisters at the church house, and I was overwhelmed by an indescribable feeling. In a way it was an intense and physical feeling, of being torn between wanting to be part of the church and wanting to be separate. Then after a few minutes I could anticipate a feeling of warmth, of knowing that I would be doing the right thing in accepting the Divine Principle. Suddenly I knew I would join the church, and said that to the brothers and sisters right there.

A clinician might be inclined to draw on the psychiatric nomenclature to describe the experiences that preceded Annette's conversion. What she reported would meet the diagnostic criteria for a dissociative disorder—"a sudden, temporary alteration in the normally integrative functions of consciousness, identity, or motor behavior."[3] In particular, it represents depersonalization, which involves an alteration in the perception or experience of the self, so that one's usual sense of reality is temporarily disrupted. This can occur when a person cannot resolve an unmanageable and intense conflict, and, as with Annette, cannot integrate the conflicting forces of her own unconscious expectations with those thrust on her by circumstance.

Though Annette's destabilization might seem pathologic, from a systems viewpoint it may be understood as the means of producing compliance in a potential convert through the strong forces of transformation orchestrated by a charismatic group. These forces emerge naturally from members as they act in concert, once the group's direction has been set. And it is this conjoint action that makes the process so forceful. Each member encountered by the inductee contributes to the unquestioning affirmation of the verity of the group's position, thereby enhancing its ability to transform the recruit.

Annette's case demonstrates the potential of the transformation function in engendering neurotic symptoms, but this process can also have sufficient intensity to shatter the sanity of a potential convert, particularly in situations where it is carried out under intense social pressure, with little attention to selecting and protecting fragile individuals. Thus, the transformation function is prominent in the recruitment activities of est, a quasitherapeutic charismatic group that systematically structured its "training" procedures. est maintained that it trained people to free themselves from the seemingly paradoxical and confounding social demands of everyday life. It has been of considerable interest to the mental health community,[4] and the possibility of casualties occurring among those who participate has been studied. Glass, Kirsch, and associates[5] reported on a series of est trainees who experienced symptoms of major psychiatric disorders including paranoid delusions, hallucinations, and severe depression. Because of their unstinting commitment to the transformation process, est trainers apparently ignored psychiatric symptoms precipitated in their workshops.

One mother of three began to develop ideas of influence and to elaborate grandiose projects after the first of two est weekend workshops. She returned to the final workshop and was allowed to continue despite her patent derangement. There she behaved bizarrely, rolling on the floor and laughing uncontrollably. The psychiatric problems for which she later required professional treatment went unattended. Another woman became apathetic, depressed, and isolated after the training sequence. She broke off with friends, began gorging, and gained thirty pounds. In an attempt to ameliorate her severely depressed state, she decided to participate in a postgraduate est course, but rather than being buffered from further pressure in this experience, she was labeled by the trainer as a misfit because she could not "get it." The experience left her feeling even worse because of her inability to connect with the group's message, and she too sought professional help.

One might wonder how these problems could be allowed to unfold since est trainers have developed psychological sophistication and use many techniques drawn directly from the mental health field. How can a group that touted its capacity for improving emotional well-being ignore the emergence of major mental disturbances among those who came to join it?

Considering how the est movement functions as a system will help answer this question. A variety of devices are employed in this group to intensify the forces operating on potential converts. The "training" is carried out in protracted sessions where disagreement with the trainer is actively discouraged, often by harsh verbal abuse. Little respite is afforded from the intensity of the group experience, and the training setting includes as many as two hundred potential converts herded together in a large hall, with their behavior tightly controlled. The dynamism of the experience further heightens the potential for energetic group influence and emotional contagion, and altered consciousness is promoted by a variety of contextual cues and behavioral controls.

Conversion is in fact the primary task of est, conducted at the expense of almost all others. Casualties incurred may have to be ignored, and the problematic issues they raise, repressed; this is in line with the shared belief of devoted est followers, who see "getting it"—achieving personal freedom through the est formula—as a more important goal than attention to the specific conflicts or encumbrances of their day-to-day relationships.

Suppression of concerns that might detract from the primary task of an intensely committed social system is actually quite common. In time of battle, for example, an army may be mobilized to achieve its immediate military objectives, and its primary task is therefore the transformation of all personnel and material into a fighting force. The psychology of the troops is bent to this mission to the exclusion of all else since victory in battle is paramount. Concern for the needs of the wounded may be secondary, since this could detract from the thrust into battle. In a similar way, mobilization for the transformation process in the charismatic sect cannot be deflected by the difficulties experienced by individual converts because the usual constraints on exerting social pressure are suppressed.

Monitoring

To operate effectively, a system must transform input from the environment into a form that meets its needs, but must also observe and regulate the actions of its component parts, thereby assuring that their respective activities are properly carried out and coordinated. This constitutes its monitoring function. Such monitoring is essential to any system to assure the effective implementation of its primary task, whether that system is a living organism, a social organization, or a factory. The system must have an apparatus for monitoring its components. In the living organism, its nervous system serves this function, and in social organizations and factories it is some form of management structure.

An Illustration

A characteristic sequence of monitoring activities in a charismatic sect may begin with a specific plan undertaken by the leadership, which is implemented by proposing a suitable rationale to the members, which then is wholeheartedly adopted. A later shift in circumstances, however, may require a change in the group's agenda, and this in turn may necessitate a change in what is now a strongly held commitment of the members. Because such shifts are common, the system must have the means for observing and acting on the needed changes in attitude and behavior. The monitoring function will operate without undue need for communication or conflict resolution in an effective system. The system's components, the cult members, will respond automatically to the suggestions of the leadership, and the leadership will know how to observe and govern to stabilize the system.

An illustration of this sequence will help clarify the dramatic shifts of direction that often occur in charismatic groups. In 1982, over two thousand couples were married by Reverend Moon in a mass ceremony in New York. Shortly after these new couples had begun to settle down, Moon mounted a major recruitment drive. Mobile recruitment teams were activated across the country, and large numbers of recently married members were expected to leave the connubial status they had just established after more than three years of sexual abstinence. Despite this wrenching dislocation, the newly married members responded with enthusiasm, and many hundreds disrupted their living arrangements and moved to begin their work. Something of a religious crusade was at hand.

The undertaking soon proved unsuccessful, however, since the social climate of the country was becoming conservative in the 1980s, and young people had little interest in a movement that would require them to reject their familial values and disrupt their future plans. From the outset, very few youths approached in urban centers or college campuses considered joining, and no doubt it became clear in reports back to the leadership that potential converts were not to be had. Within a few weeks, the teams of recruiters who had been galvanized for action were deactivated, and had to drop their zealous goal. The situation was potentially tense, as much enthusiasm for the project had been generated.

Because of the effectiveness of monitoring within the sect, this major reversal in perspective was accepted without questioning. The shift away from the recruitment initiative was rationalized as being necessary to set up community-based family residences for individual couples, called "home churches." This change in policy was disseminated by the leadership and was accepted without question as to why the original initiative changed. Members applied themselves to the home church initiative with the same zeal as in the recruitment drive, and at no time did I hear any expressions of reservation about the viability of the initial undertaking or that there may have been a misjudgment by the church leadership about the potential for recruits. Whether consciously controlled or not, compliance with the group's announced perspective was complete.

To understand the means by which this charismatic group rapidly and effectively monitored the thinking and behavioral norms of its members, we must consider the psychological defense mechanisms employed by the group *as a whole*, which are not unlike those operating in individuals. These defenses are employed for the unconscious management of conflicting motives so that the group can function smoothly in the face of conflict. Although similar defenses may be observed in other social systems, the charismatic group responds in particular ways that distinguish it from less tightly knit groups, since the forces of group cohesiveness and shared beliefs in the charismatic group facilitate its operation as a functional whole.

These psychological defenses protect the group culture from unacceptable ideas, often "realities" produced by outdated initiatives or outside influences. Such realities may be ignored outright, by means of denial; forgotten through repression; or distorted through rationalization. In the shift from an active recruitment posture just described, the Unification Church leadership was able to rationalize its actions by maintaining that the same ends were to be accomplished by the home church movement, where members would recruit in their new neighborhoods. The apparent failure of the mobile recruitment teams was denied, as it could have exposed the leadership to question and caused demoralization. Members whom I spoke with gave no indication that the movement's momentum was in question because of the collapse of this recruitment initiative, or that an abrupt shift in attitude had occurred. In this regard, their views had been effectively manipulated to maintain the group's internal stability. *Identification* with the leadership's commitment to the home church movement completed the process.

Identification

In a social system, monitoring is most easily implemented when a voluntary collaboration exists between those in control and those being managed, since outright coercion necessitates undue expenditure of resources and detracts from cooperative efforts to carry out the system's primary task. It is best, in fact, if those monitored accept the leadership without conscious deliberation and, since the defense mechanism of identification operates in an unconscious fashion, those who adopt the attitudes of their leaders do so without deliberating over the wisdom of their actions.

Perhaps the most unusual type of identification takes place when the members' own safety and well-being are jeopardized by their leadership. An example of this is the Stockholm Syndrome, where individuals are cast together as hostages and their lives are threatened. Such captives may develop a positive bond toward the hostage-takers, not only complying with their expectations, but even defending them against people trying to secure the hostages' safety and release. A comparison between this situation and the monitoring process in the charismatic group is intriguing. In both settings the identification seems paradoxical to the outside observer, since those in the dependent position are actively participating with those in control in activities perceived by the outsider as directly conflicting with their own interests; yet they may maintain tenacious fidelity to the people who appear to be threatening their well-being.

Both the cult and hostage situation share the psychological pincer-like effect described previously: The agent inflicting distress on the dependent person is also perceived as the party who can provide relief. Thus, pressure is exerted on those experiencing distress to accommodate to the party who comes to be seen as the only one able to offer relief. The Stockholm Syndrome was first observed during an armed standoff lasting six days between a lone bank robber and the police in a bank in the Swedish capital city. After capturing the facility with an automatic weapon in an attempted holdup, the heavily armed gunman held four bank employees hostage for six days.[6] Reporters' contacts with the captives while they were still under threat of death revealed the startling fact that they had come to fear the police more than their captor, and even after being released the hostages could only puzzle as to why their sense of fealty toward their assailant persisted. For weeks after the incident, they were unable to dispel the feeling that he had been protecting them from the authorities, and could express little animosity toward him.[7]

It has been suggested that this phenomenon is an exaggerated expression of *identification with the aggressor,* a psychological defense mechanism originally described by Anna Freud.[8] Like all psychological defenses, this one represents an adaptive strategy whose purpose is to aid the individual in coping with unresolved mental conflict. In the Stockholm Syndrome, the hostage must avoid the threat of bodily danger but at the same time engage the support, or at least the benign neglect, of the very person who poses that threat. This can generate a conflict that is not easily resolved between the need to be cared for and an overriding hostility toward the person who can provide this care. The hostage, therefore, cannot readily act in a way that would engage the assailant unless the anger he or she naturally feels is not acknowledged and expressed. Once this repression is achieved, the victim may look to the captor for support and success. Victims implicitly hope that by means of fidelity and compliance, they may elicit the aggressor's protection. Like other psychological defenses, this one seems irrational at first glance, yet it may represent the best available means by which the person can respond to an emotionally untenable situation.

Identification with the aggressor is relevant here because it helps us better understand the monitoring process in charismatic groups. Members of these groups are often effectively under assault by their leaders. That is, in the consensual view of their surrounding society, they are pressed to participate in unpleasant activities, and are sometimes subjected to abuse. Members nonetheless have their own psychological need for maintaining affiliation with the leader and the group, since they are captives by virtue of the pincer effect, which makes their emotional well-being depend on involvement in the group that inflicts distress. In a sense, they have no choice but to unconsciously make peace with the potentially threatening agenda of the leadership and comply with its expectations to achieve emotional relief.

We saw this process in operation among the followers of Baba, who clung to their leader during the course of his protracted psychotic illness.[9] Baba became physically abusive and behaved in a highly erratic manner toward his devotees, inflicting them with adverse living circumstances and even sexual assault. Nonetheless, members remained faithful, using a series of rationalizations that, to the observer, were untenable. They claimed his madness was "divine," and said that he was "teaching them a lesson" with each bizarre demand.

Members who had become highly involved with the group, subject to its emotional pincer, found it necessary to identify with the leader-aggressor and sustain their dependency. The conflict between dependency needs and potential anger toward Baba was not unlike that observed in the Stockholm Syndrome.

SUPPRESSION OF AUTONOMY

Our discussion raises the question of how autonomy is suppressed in a charismatic group. Such suppression is vividly seen in the mobile street sales teams of the Unification Church. In these teams, members who had little acquaintance with each other rapidly adapted to living and working in very close quarters under considerable privation. They sometimes slept all together in cramped quarters and shared limited provisions of food. Often they would draw underwear from a common clothing pool, reflecting an unusual enforced intimacy established for economy. The religious injunctions for each team included "brotherly and sisterly" cooperation, typically rooted in citations from the Divine Principle, which offered the group's ideology as the basis for suppression of any deviant behavior.

Ex-members whom I interviewed said they had rarely experienced serious misgivings while on the mobile teams and certainly had not felt it appropriate to express reservations. Such hesitancy was born out of the guilt that disrupting the team's mission would have caused more than of fear of disapproval. Unlike army recruits, who might suffer similar privations, these sect members did not maintain a psychological distance from the leadership and did not complain or question the wisdom of the circumstances thrust on them, nor did they have consensual support from the broader society.

For a social system to regulate its functioning effectively, it must have the capacity to suppress members' deviation from its implicit or explicit goals. In charismatic groups, the penalty for those who deviate from norms is psychological distress; overt coercion usually is not necessary to induce compliance. How is this penalty exacted? We have seen that there is a decrease in psychological well-being among those who felt *less* closely associated with the group. Furthermore, members who were considering leaving the sect had attitudes most clearly at variance with those of the group, and their scores fell into the clinically depressed range.[10] Indeed, 36% of those who dropped out of the Unification Church reported the emergence of "serious emotional problems" in the period following their departure.[11]

These observations suggest that members may experience distress whenever they are inclined to think negatively about their affiliation. By recourse to learning theory, we may infer that attempts at achieving independence from the group's monitoring function would tend to be extinguished. One person suffering the penalty of distress was Allen, a young man who fell into conflict with the norms of a small neo-Christian cult. When I interviewed Allen he was sixteen years old and had just been hospitalized because of withdrawal from his peers at school, mounting disruptiveness in an aunt's home where he lived, and a two-week history of hallucinating Satan's voice. Allen had been a member of The Word of God cult for three years, but had left three months before his hospitalization. He had originally been introduced to the cult along with two siblings by his mother, who had been suffering from drug problems before she joined. The boy adapted fairly well to the group, but when he was caught smoking marijuana some members said he was tainted by the Devil. After this, he became a scapegoat of sorts, and his participation in the group's religious services was limited. By his own account and that of his aunt, he had previously experienced no psychiatric difficulties.

One of the group's leaders continued to harass Allen over his presumed satanic association, and it became clear that several cult members believed he was actually in communication with the Devil. As these views got back to him, the boy became increasingly frightened about the influence the leader would have on other members. He decided to escape the group and went to live in his aunt's house, but became anxious and depressed, ruminating over his possible diabolical taint, and after a few weeks began to hear the voice of the Devil on occasion accusing him of sinning in leaving the cult. He was soon admitted to the hospital, where he showed no other evidence of psychosis or thought disorder, but was preoccupied with the fear of the group's allegations of his relationship with the Devil.

In the hospital Allen was initially treated supportively, told he was free from supernatural taint, and led to understand the misfortune that had befallen him in being labeled as he was. His mother corroborated that his social adjustment had been adequate until the cult leader had seized on the episode of marijuana smoking as reason to question Allen's place in the group. During a one-month hospitalization, without medication, his symptoms abated and he was discharged.

Allen had fallen victim to the interpretation of the cult's ideology by one of its leaders, and was then made a scapegoat by members following this leader. In refusing to accept this role, he violated the group's monitoring functions and set up a conflict within himself. His departure from the group intensified this conflict and he began to manifest symptoms that meet the diagnostic criteria for a brief reactive psychosis.

Psychophysiologic reactions in such situations can be even more dramatic than the psychological consequences. The classical exposition of this phenomenon was made by the physiologist Walter B. Cannon in describing voodoo death. In the ritual of "boning," an Australian aboriginal may be rejected from the tribe, and when this happens the victim's

> cheeks blanch and his eyes become glassy and the expression of his face becomes horribly distorted. . . . He attempts to shriek but usually the sound chokes in his throat, and all that one might see is the froth at his mouth. His body begins to tremble and the muscles twist involuntarily. He sways backwards and falls to the ground, and after a short time appears to be in a swoon. . . . After awhile he becomes composed and crawls to his wurley

[hut]. From this time onwards he sickens and frets, refusing to eat and keeping aloof from the daily affairs of the tribe. Unless help is administered in the shape of a countercharm administered by the hands of the Nangarri, or medicine man, his death is only a matter of comparatively short time.[12]

Cannon's contribution was to suggest a physiologic mechanism underlying such events and support it with both clinical observations and animal experiments. In the voodoo death syndrome, he saw that the tribe has been the individual's protector so that ostracism precipitates an intense fear from which the separated member cannot flee, because of a deep and longstanding emotional bond. This crisis produces an excitation of the sympathetic nervous system and adrenergic release, followed in time by cardiovascular collapse. More recent studies have supported Cannon's views in demonstrating that the reaction to major environmental stress can precipitate ventricular fibrillation and death.[13]

Allen's case and the voodoo death syndrome both clearly reflect the remarkable potency of forces that may be mobilized *within* the group to monitor and regulate those who might be considered in violation of its norms. These complement the other facets of the monitoring function examined, namely benign identification and identification with the aggressor.

Feedback

Feedback is one way for a system to obtain information on how well it is carrying out its primary task. A portion of output is fed back into the system and this provides information for planning future operations. If a cult is trying to recruit, information on the relative response of potential members can be fed back to the cult leaders and guide them in improving the group's recruitment techniques.

Feedback may be either positive or negative. Positive feedback gives the system information that will increase the deviation of its output from the steady state, thereby yielding an enhanced or elaborated output. Negative feedback tends to diminish variations in the transformation function. When negative feedback ceases to be available, transformation activities may go unmoderated, the steady state can vanish, and the system's boundaries can be disrupted.[14] Consequently, the system must have unrestrained access to negative feedback to exercise a proper degree of self-regulation and not dissipate its energies.

This latter function is important in charismatic sects because they are prone to suppress negative feedback when it runs contrary to the group's internal stability. It is a special risk because of the highly effective monitoring function that allows the cult system to control the information made available to its members. Means of avoiding undue negative feedback are essential to charismatic groups because their ideology and practices often elicit hostility from the general society. If allowed to enter the system unobstructed, such negative feedback leads to suppression of the group's transcendent vision and a decline in members' morale.

Certain charismatic groups try hard to isolate their members from all negative feedback, but this can be dangerous as the group may lose information valuable to its own self-regulation. These groups usually are no longer actively recruiting and have little need for protracted contact with outsiders. We will see the potential for dire consequences of this phenomenon in Jonestown (Chapter 7). Other groups, however, rely on the successful recruitment of new members to provide them with positive feedback. Such successes are used to reinforce the merit of the group's own ideology and promote new initiatives that validate the group's chosen course. New converts give legitimacy to a group in the face of a hostile world and encourage members to carry the group's mission forward. Such feedback can be a useful tool for social regulation.

Successful conversion activities were widely publicized in the Unification Church. Overseas recruitment was also important, and here too reports of large numbers of converts were circulated. All this served to undermine the impact of the negative feedback from society at large. Accounts of the magnitude of converts were often exaggerated, betraying the leaders' motives. For example, members were consistently told of a very large enrollment in Japan, a sign of the movement's worldwide acceptance; one figure given to the press was 260,000.[15] When I visited the movement's headquarters in Japan, however, I was startled to find the figure of five million Japanese members in an English-language church publication. Such grandiose reports from Japan were apparently aimed at Americans and other English-speaking members. I spoke with American members in Japan in detail about the actual level of participation in the country and why the misleading brochures were produced. Soon it became clear that there were no more than a few thousand members in Tokyo and a similar number throughout the rest of the country. One member who was relatively at ease in discussing the issue was apologetic because he could not support figures used in the Church literature and explained that they represented a dubious count of signatories to a petition for world peace issued by the sect some years before.

In the United States, inflated figures were also regularly given to church members as evidence of its international impact. They were in effect counterfeit positive feedback.

Negative feedback assures that a system does not expend undue energy or embark on fruitless ventures. Because it can suppress initiatives needed to maintain commitment and group momentum, however, such feedback may engender conflict in a charismatic sect with an expansionist agenda, leading to its own suppression.

This occurred when Reverend Moon was first becoming known to the American public in 1976. He arranged for a large rally to be held in Yankee

Stadium in New York City, to summon up the faithful, attract potential members, and draw attention to the movement. The leadership assumed that this would elicit a positive response from the general public. Before the gathering, hundreds of church members, including large numbers of Oriental followers of Moon, most of whom had recently been brought in from overseas, were sent into the streets of New York City to clean up refuse. In wearing white work suits that were a startling contrast to the way other pedestrians were dressed, these Moonies gave the movement an odd and unappealing image and strengthened the widely held view that members were turned into automatons. Despite a modest turnout, church leaders pronounced the venture a success.

Here too, as with the incorrect membership figures, a realistic assessment of the situation would have carried with it an undue amount of negative feedback, and might have forced the membership to confront the sect's limitations. The public's bleak view of the group's Oriental affiliations and alleged dehumanizing qualities would then have implicitly discouraged the very initiatives the leaders were using to support the group's primary task at that time, namely zealous expansion to a world wide organization. So they suppressed the negative feedback.

Other examples of this can be found in a variety of commercial ventures on which the Unification Church embarked. These included sizable commercial fishing enterprises in New England and on the Gulf Coast, and the publication of newspapers—*Newsworld* and *Noticias del Mundo* in New York and the *Washington Times* in the nation's capital. These operations consistently showed a deficit, and from any rational business standpoint should have been closed early on.[16] But they promulgated the church's ideology and provided continued positive feedback. The fishing enterprises were an expression of a mystical commitment to maritime matters expressed by Reverend Moon, and the newspapers apparently reflected the church's desire for a platform to broadcast their view of public affairs, giving them credibility on national and world events. Such ventures were seen as evidence of the viability of the movement's ideology; to admit they had failed would have produced negative feedback that could have been destabilizing.

Boundary Control

As we have seen, an open system must carry out its transformation functions while maintaining internal stability by monitoring its own components and responding to feedback. These functions, however, can be disrupted by intrusions from outside. For this reason boundary control is a vital function of any system.

Boundary control protects social systems against dangerous outsiders. It includes not only the screening of people but also of information, since information is a potent determinant of behavior. If a charismatic group is to maintain a system of shared beliefs markedly at variance with that of the surrounding culture, members must sometimes be rigidly isolated from consensual information from the general society that would unsettle this belief system. During the initial phases of conversion to charismatic sects, novices may be regarded as vulnerable and actively discouraged from establishing contact with their families. After their integration into the group, when their beliefs have been consolidated, new members may be encouraged to reestablish ties with their families so as to promote a benign public image and perhaps make other conversions.

Two important facets of activity form the boundary of charismatic sects, each mirroring the other. The first is a set of behaviors and attitudes of members, often deviant, that is directed at outsiders. It reflects how the system focuses its social forces to protect its boundaries. The second is a reciprocal set of behaviors and attitudes of the surrounding society, often an aggressive response of outsiders to the group's members.

The System Raises Its Defenses

Any group that coalesces around a cause or function must soon establish a boundary to differentiate those who are participating from those who are not. One situation I witnessed illuminated the potency of such boundary control phenomena. It occurred at a Tavistock training institute for experiential learning in group behavior (see Chapter 2). These institutes are designed to stimulate the circumstances under which certain group forces emerge and thereby illustrate the nature of group interactions. Participants, generally mental health professionals, sometimes other interested parties, use this experiential exercise to acquire a firsthand acquaintance with the processes underlying group behavior.

In one exercise, members of the institute were asked to select rooms within the training center where they would establish small discussion groups and then, in these groups, define a common position in relation to a certain social issue. Assignments to groups were arbitrary, but members of each group were able to choose their common perspective within a relatively short time.

As a participant, I was struck by a particular sequence of events involving Paul, a mature psychiatrist well respected in the Washington D. C. community. He implemented the boundary control function for his group with undue zeal and aggressiveness, to the point that his behavior in retrospect seemed bizarre to him. Paul's group had shortly before begun to define its goals, and the members' mutuality was as yet uncertain, since they had only recently gotten together. A slight, elderly woman entered the room to observe this group as an emissary of her own, an undertaking that had been suggested in the instructions for the exercise. Paul, who had been assigned the role of screening outsiders, insisted that she not impinge on the group's territory and became quite curt. After an exchange in which the woman expressed little more than curiosity, he rushed over to her and tried to force her out the door, angrily throwing her to the floor and wrenching her leg in the process. He expressed no remorse, but instead admonished her for not knowing better than to intrude on a group deliberating among themselves.

The small group in which Paul was participating was involved in little more than a vaguely defined discussion of its "identity" and was created only for a day-long exercise. Nonetheless, it was beginning to delineate its borders. Paul felt it necessary to protect this perimeter, thereby assuring that the group's sense of purpose would be consolidated, without interference from outside. Paul had apparently become too closely identified with the system function he had been assigned, that of defending the system's boundary.

This episode illustrated in a small but chilling way the ardor that can flare up in those who defend a group, even a meaningless one, to which they belong. A month later I asked Paul what his thinking had been in accosting that defenseless woman. After saying with some embarrassment that he had located the woman the next day and apologized properly, he answered that

> The exercise was artificial, but somehow we were swept up in it. At the time, I knew that our small group was vulnerable and I was committed to see our unity preserved. She wasn't just an intruder on our space. She seemed like the beginning of the unraveling of our work. I wasn't really pushing her out. As far as I can recall, I was keeping out over a hundred other people in the institute exercise who would inevitably follow after her, leading to our group's dissolution.

The boundary behavior of cult members that has made the deepest impression on outsiders involves the glazed, withdrawn look and trance-like state that some find most unsettling. Although this may appear pathologic, it can help group membership by reducing the possibility of direct exchanges with outsiders—it has an insulating effect. Thus, the trance-like appearance protects the sect's boundary. It would be more likely to develop in settings that threaten the group's integrity, so that an observer who is perceived as an antagonist is more likely to see the behavior than one who is not. This may help explain the puzzling discrepancies among observers' reports on contemporary cults since they may approach the sects' "safe boundaries" in different ways. Some researchers, such as John Clark and Margaret Singer,[17] have had a great deal of contact with people leaving sects and have addressed at length the ill effects of membership. Their writings question the place of these groups in a society that protects the right to free and independent thought. They underscore the emotional constriction and stereotyped behavior sometimes associated with cult membership, implying that it is equivalent to psychopathology. Other observers, such as Thomas

Ungerleider and David Wellisch,[18] as well as my associates and I, established a positive working relationship with active cult members and tended to look at the more constructive aspects of membership. This second group has not found the same stereotyped behavior and emotional constriction. Sect members may thus respond to outsiders according to whether or not they appear to threaten the group's safe boundaries.

Fearfulness of outsiders, or xenophobia, a common characteristic of cults, is an important manifestation of boundary control. It holds groups together but it can reach the dimensions of outright paranoia. It represents a boundary control function carried to the extreme and is seen among those sect members pressed by family or strangers to give up their ties to the group. It is also evident in the way outsiders are often treated with a different standard of openness or honesty. (A "heavenly deception" is one perpetrated by a member of the Unification Church on a nonmember to further the Church's goals.)

At times, outright paranoia at the system's boundary may assume sufficient intensity to meet diagnostic criteria for a commonly held delusional system. Such a state is termed a shared paranoid disorder, wherein a delusional state is shared among two or more people so that the pathologic perspective of one person in the group is supported by that of the others. In a charismatic group, it can be characterized by persistent delusional thinking and occurs in the absence of other psychotic symptoms, since it springs from close association with others with a similar delusion rather than from innate psychiatric disability.

The Community Reacts

Defensiveness and paranoia associated with the boundary function of a charismatic sect elicit a complementary reaction from the surrounding community. This is seen in the animosity between family members of converts and the sects; in the breakdown in communication between sects and some religious groups; and in the hostility toward sects voiced by some former members.

Attempts at communication between parents and their children who have joined contemporary sects are often rife with misunderstanding and hostility. The convert often becomes an agent of the group's boundary control function and regards the relatives who make contact as attempting to disengage the person from the movement, whereas the parents, operating at the boundary of a highly cohesive group, frequently become preoccupied with the effort to dislodge the new member. Communications are often frozen at this level.

Two couples who came to me for consultation illustrate how these battles across the group's boundary take place. The first were parents of a young woman who had shortly before dropped out of college and gone to work as a waitress in a rural area. There she befriended an older woman who was a member of the Jehovah's Witnesses and who actively encouraged her to join the sect. When her parents heard of their daughter's growing interest, they drove to the town where she was living and approached her angrily, demanding to know why she was sacrificing her future for this "odd" group. In the absence of an acceptable reply, they consulted a psychiatrist who had treated their daughter for a transient problem while she was in high school. He suggested they adopt a more benign and accommodating attitude, but neither parent was able to respond in this fashion for fear of losing their daughter. Soon the girl made it clear to them that it was only through a more congenial attitude toward the group and its beliefs that they could gain the right to discuss the matter fully with her.

The parents felt their only choice if they were to "keep" their daughter was to either forcefully resist the girl's move or themselves accept the sect's views. They were torn between two compelling systems functions of the group: transformation, which demands compliance with the group's ideology, and boundary control, which rejects aliens and their views. Under these circumstances, it was almost impossible for them to establish viable communication with the girl.

Some parents continue their aggressive efforts to draw their children away from a charismatic sect long after they have become fully affiliated. Many sects want members to establish courteous relations with their families once the membership role has been consolidated, without compromising the members' own fidelity, and this gives parents an opening. But in their attempts to change their children's thinking, the parents may assault the group's boundaries and produce a breakdown in communication.

This was the case in a second unfortunate family that for eight years had been engaged in a tug of war with their son, who had joined the Hare Krishna movement. At first they sent their own local religious leaders as emissaries to encourage him to leave, but this only exacerbated his defensiveness. Subsequent encounters, which had become less frequent, were characterized by disputes revolving around the rituals of the sect in relation to diet, dress, and lifestyle.

Consultation with his family arose over their uncertainty as to whether to invite their convert son to the wedding of his older brother. At first, the parents were able to maintain a flexible posture in the exchange and their son agreed to attend. As further plans were made, however, they again began to express the hope that he would be sympathetic to the family's needs, a request perceived by the young man as suggesting their desire that he loosen his ties toward the sect. He then issued demands about the cultic food and dress he would bring to the ceremony and finally broke off communication, refusing to appear at the wedding. Conflicting demands on both sides of the boundary had not been surmounted.

The sect's boundary may also generate a reverse phenomenon in the form of an "anti-cult." This is seen most prominently among the members forced to leave these groups by deprogrammers. We may define deprogramming as the forcible indoctrination of a negative attitude toward the sect in an attempt to dislodge members from it. In our study of individuals who had left the Unification Church,[19] a striking contrast existed between members who had departed voluntarily and those who were deprogrammed. The first group had mixed feelings about their experience but expressed a relatively benign view of both their own involvement and the ongoing participation of their remaining compatriots. Most (62%) still felt strongly that they "cared for the ten members they knew best," and the large majority (89%) believed that they "got some positive things" out of membership. On the other hand, those who were deprogrammed had a much more negative attitude toward the sect and had apparently become more involved in a cohesive group of mutually committed persons attempting to deprogram other members.

These deprogrammed youths often became articulate and active critics of sects such as the Moonies and Hare Krishna, in contrast to the majority of ex-members who had left on their own initiative. In our own study, eight out of ten deprogrammed ex-members had participated in attempts to coerce other members to leave, whereas none of those who left voluntarily had done so. Their animosity toward the new religious movements in general paralleled the intensity of feeling found in the sects they opposed.

Members of a cult may be driven to behave as they do by forces that act within the social system to assure its stability and implement its primary task. On the other hand, the openness of each member to such influence can only be understood by recourse to one's biologically grounded responsiveness to group influence. We have considered the scope of both biological and systems perspectives. We can next look at more extensive examples of these perspectives in some representative charismatic groups.

III

CASE HISTORIES OF CHARISMATIC GROUPS

We will now examine three types of charismatic groups to demonstrate how the perspectives described so far can be reflected in different settings. The first is the cult that ends in disaster and immolation because of irreconcilable clashes at its boundary with the general society, with the Peoples Temple, the ill-fated followers of Jim Jones in Guyana, as a prime example. The second type of charismatic group is a religious sect whose activities did not lead it to disaster, but instead allowed for a measure of accommodation with the broader society. For this I will draw in depth on my own findings on the Unification Church.

The last group to be examined, one with direct relevance to the mental health field, is the zealous self-help organization, whose primary task is that of healing, to relieve the personal problems confronted by its members. Such groups can be remarkably effective in remedying deviant behavior and emotional distress. Alcoholics Anonymous will be considered as an example of such a movement. Although not reputed to have a divine mission as such, these groups generally become associated with a transcendent goal, usually one with a definitive assault on the medical problem they address.

7

TROUBLE AT
THE SYSTEM'S BOUNDARY

This chapter examines two examples of the disastrous outcomes that can take place in charismatic groups, and we will use the systems model to put the reported events into perspective. The first example is the Peoples Temple in Guyana, a cult that originated in a mainstream Protestant denomination but ended in the self-inflicted deaths of over nine hundred members. Although the events surrounding this episode are well documented, they still leave uncertainty as to how a group of relatively stable people might have evolved to the point that they so flagrantly abrogated the innate human drive for self-preservation.

A second example illustrates how aggressive actions taken by a cult-like group at its boundary can lead the society at large to embark on an uncontrolled assault designed to protect itself from a perceived threat from the group. In this case, members of the group called MOVE had been sequestered in a residential neighborhood in Philadelphia for several years and presented a highly provocative stance in attempting to foist their idiosyncratic views on their neighbors.

Jonestown

Events in an isolated village in South America gave the world a sudden shock in November 1978. In a mass suicide unprecedented for its magnitude in contemporary history, over nine hundred people died, mostly by poisoning. The casualties included almost the entire membership of the Peoples Temple, a cult composed of American-born religious converts residing in an agricultural commune deep in the jungle of Guyana, about 150 miles from the country's populated coast.

Background of the Group

The Peoples Temple was led by Jim Jones, a charismatic preacher whose religious activities had begun to take shape while he was an undergraduate at Indiana University. With a background in pastoral training in the Methodist Church, Jones eventually settled in San Francisco. There he pursued his interest in developing community service projects, such as a child-care center and a kitchen to feed the poor, and also worked in the political campaigns of a number of local and national figures in the 1960s.

By 1974, Jones had already begun to establish the Jonestown commune in Guyana, where he wanted to create a secluded haven for his followers. The Guyanese government had been eager to support this reputable group, which had a largely black membership, because Jones and his followers were willing to set up in a township in the country's remote interior where local blacks had refused to migrate, and because they were sympathetic to Jones' socialist philosophy. The commune also benefited from its religious status, which enabled it to import goods without paying customs to the Guyanese authorities.[1]

The situation began to unravel with the arrival of Leo Ryan, a U. S. Congressman from San Francisco. Ryan had come to investigate the reports of mistreatment of converts in this isolated setting and was accompanied by several journalists and relatives of Temple members who hoped to persuade their kin to leave. After meeting with Jones and visiting the colony for a day, Ryan's group was joined by four cult members who had opted to defect. The entourage was accosted as they were about to board their plane at the nearby landing strip and most, including Ryan, were shot dead. Within hours of the murder, Jones ordered a mass suicide of all his followers.

What happened then is known from a small number of eyewitnesses who succeeded in fleeing into the jungle and from audiotapes made of speeches during the carnage. A physician serving as medical officer for Jonestown prepared a large quantity of fruit punch laced with cyanide, and Jones ordered his people to drink this mixture, threatening that they would soon be under attack by the Central Intelligence Agency and that they had to prepare for a revolutionary death. Babies and children were first made to swallow the drink by the older members, and were then followed by the adults themselves. In the end, 914 persons died, including more than 216 children.[2]

The amount of force exerted to complete the mass suicide varied among the members. For most, no coercion was necessary; only a small minority acted under overt threats from Jones' henchmen, who were brandishing firearms. A survivor noted that when one member challenged Jones' demand that all present in the assemblage participate, "The crowd shouted her down."[3] If threats were used, they were typically warnings as to the fate any survivors would meet at the hands of the outside world. By all accounts, suicide was therefore a voluntary act for the large majority of the adults.

A Perspective

These bare facts are shocking. They tell of an entire social entity gone awry in a seemingly incomprehensible way. Although the group was driven by a deranged and paranoid leader, the course of events was played out through a complex social system.

While Jones and his group were still operating in San Francisco, the *transformation* function of this social system was directed at enlarging the sect's membership and bringing the broader community around to a favorable view of the group. Thus, it was estimated that during Jones' years in San Francisco between 50,000 and 100,000 people came to hear him speak, even though the actual membership of the Temple never exceeded 3,000.[4] This emphasis on transformation based on a zeal for conveying the group's message is quite common in the earlier phases of charismatic sects and is associated with the presumption that the leader's ideology is unassailable and infectious, a view untempered as yet by a lengthy history of rejection by potential converts or dissipation of the members' initial enthusiasm. When the Temple's committed members moved to Guyana, however, recruitment ceased to play a role in the movement's activities. Its energies now came to focus primarily on the close *monitoring* of its members. There were implicit demands for an intensification of commitment to Jones' idiosyncratic views, and increasingly bizarre beliefs came to be expected of these longstanding converts. Jones, for example, now claimed to be the reincarnation of Jesus, as well as Ikhnaton, Buddha, Lenin, and Father Divine.[5]

This monitoring function is illustrated in letters to "Dad," the confessionals of Jonestown residents to their leader.[6] They are quite revealing, in that they show the striking intensity of the group forces of shared belief and social cohesiveness. Expressions of commitment were laced with an intensified ideologic orientation, illustrating the system's growing control over the world view of its members. As one member wrote about his rejection of his prior views: "I am an elitist and an anarchist because I think back in the States when I wanted to do my own thing and did not want any situations for discipline. I didn't have the U. S. capitalism in me and I'm trying to get rid of it. Here I don't have any intention of becoming a traitor or going back to the U. S."

The letter of another member reflected the intensely cohesive force that was focused on Jones himself, and it foreshadowed the final act of commitment.

I will endure until I am dead. . . . I shall not let this movement down. I shall not beg for mercy either in that last moment. I shall proudly die for proud reason. You can count on *me* even if all desert you. I shall be by your side whether it be tangible or in spirit. If, suddenly, a U. S. vessel or plane will come to get us all to take us back with promises of all the luxury and benefits if we would sell you out, I would not go on board because I am attracted to your goodness as magnets attract one another. . . . Nothing will ever break your pull.

The theme of apocalyptic doom was part of the group's belief system from early on, originally reflecting Jones' fear of nuclear annihilation. In California, his preaching began to embody visions of CIA persecution and Nazi-like extermination of blacks,[7] but in Jonestown this theme of anticipated destruction soon became intertwined with the group's monitoring function. Because of their intense commitment, Jones' followers could be drawn deeply into this vortex of apocalyptic visions untempered by their independent judgment. Members were regularly scolded and punished by Jones; some were whipped or beaten before the entire community for "crimes" such as not conforming to prohibitions on smoking.[8] Others were punished perversely; in a typical incident, a woman accused of violating the rule of celibacy was forced to submit to intercourse with a man she disliked while the entire colony watched.[9]

On such occasions, an indistinct line existed between voluntary submission and coercion. On the one hand, members suffered a deluded identification with the leader-aggressor; on the other, they were realistically afraid of resisting his demands and too emotionally dependent to leave. This lack of clear distinction was evident in the words of one escapee.

The beatings were all over. . . . People would be humiliated in front of the crowd . . . and Jones would just sit there and just smile. You could never say anything about wanting to come back to the States, you couldn't say anything negative . . . a lot of people thought he had their minds controlled, he would tell them if they'd say anything negative that they in turn would get sick or something would happen to them.[10]

Acceptance of the leader's perspective is essential in assuring affiliation with a sect, and it meets the members' dependency needs. But if that perspective is irrational, conformity can be hazardous.

Needing to preserve their bond to the group in Jonestown, members were unable to reject Jones as an aggressor. As in the Stockholm Syndrome, they clung to him for security, coming more and more to accept his punishments. Jones precipitated members' problems, but as the mediator of group affiliation, he was also regarded by them as the only viable source of relief from their feelings of distress.

The "White Nights" Jones staged in Guyana laid the groundwork for the final mass suicide. These exercises began with states of emergency declared by Jones when the commune's population was awakened by blaring sirens to go through a rehearsal for death. An excerpt from the affidavit of one Temple survivor describes the experience. She wrote that in these situations Jones' deputies would

> arm themselves with rifles, move from cabin to cabin and make certain that all members were responding. A mass meeting would ensue. Frequently during these crises, we would be told that the jungle was swarming with mercenaries and that death could be expected at any minute. . . .
> We were given a small glass of red liquid to drink. We were told that the liquid contained poison and that we would die within 45 minutes. We all did as we were told. When the time came when we should have dropped dead, Reverend Jones explained that the poison was not real and that we had just been through a loyalty test.[11]

The fact that this bizarre ritual could be carried out at all reflects the strength of the members' commitment to Jones' demonic leadership. The absolute nature of his control must have countered Jones' fear of defections.

In Jonestown monitoring was not mediated by an intermediary level of personnel who could exercise independent judgment and temper Jones' exercise of power. The leader's psychology had become the template for the group's monitoring, and this made the members agents of his inclinations. With Jones (as with Baba) unbridled control over a cult generated grandiosity and even delusion as the leader came to believe in his own omnipotence. And, conversely, antecedent psychopathology in a leader may itself encourage him to seize absolute control to allay his deluded concerns. In either case, and both probably apply here, the monitoring process becomes embroiled in the leader's primitive mental defenses.

Such congruence between a single charismatic leader and the monitoring function is not true of all cults. The value of a "middle management" in moderating the role of a charismatic leader is evident in sects with a more influential administration operating between the leader and the membership body. In the Unification Church, for example, the impact of Reverend Moon's policy making was considerably tempered by a group of his close advisors, including the president of the church's American branch. Moon's initiatives generally passed through this group for implementation by a deliberative process that shaped the way those initiatives were articulated.

Feedback from the outside world can also be helpful in moderating a leader's deviant views. In the Peoples Temple, however, there was very little. Jones' seclusiveness clearly played a major role in constraining the group's access to feedback. The physical isolation, conceived by Jones as a means of protecting the group from assault, denied members access to the reactions of outsiders who might have raised questions about their bizarre beliefs and behavior. Outside views would have provided negative feedback for the system, and helped counter the leader's psychopathology. As noted in Chapter 6, access to negative feedback is essential to the continuing viability of an open system since it enables the system to assess its own effectiveness and change so as to eliminate maladaptive behavior. Thus, if the Peoples Temple had made active attempts at recruitment in Guyana, thereby engaging in an open interchange with the Guyanese society, potential recruits would have raised pointed questions with cult members about Jones' physical abuse of them.

Jones' growing paranoia and defensiveness were glaringly apparent in his drive to close all sources of feedback. He made a strenuous effort to avoid exposing the colony to the news media. In 1977, he successfully suppressed the attempt of a reporter from the *San Francisco Examiner* to prepare a series of articles on the sect. This involved a campaign of phone calls and letter writing balanced by the offer of a $4,000 contribution for a journalism scholarship to placate the paper's editors.[12] A month before the massacre, communication between Jonestown and the outside world was severed. Members were told that Los Angeles had been abandoned because of a severe drought and that the Ku Klux Klan was marching openly through the streets of San Francisco.[13]

The arrival of Congressman Ryan and his entourage portended the imminent disruption of the group's *control over its boundary*, and thereby precipitated the final events at Jonestown. For a leader and charismatic group of paranoid orientation, such vulnerability may be intolerable. Ryan's visit jeopardized the system's integrity. The fact that four cult members chose to leave with him posed a challenge to the group's monitoring of the membership. Moreover, an intrusion by the U. S. federal government meant that suppression of negative feedback could no longer be absolute. On both counts, it was reasonable for Jones to fear that the cult could no longer operate in total identification with his will. For Jones, already highly sensitized and paranoid, this was a severe threat. In deciding to assault the Congressman, he realized that, "They will try to destroy us."[14] Once it became apparent that his cult's boundary could no longer be secured, Jones chose to preserve its identity in spirit if not in living membership. At the last moment, this was underlined when he implied to the group that their deaths did not represent a failure, but rather a triumph of the group's ideology:

> So . . . you be kind to children and be kind to seniors, and take the potion like they used to in ancient Greece, and step over quietly; because we are not committing suicide—it's a revolutionary act.[15]

This commune was therefore to die in body. In terms of its spiritual mission, however, Jones was preserving its integrity and, in a perverse way, history may well serve to accomplish this end.

MOVE

Conflicts on the boundary of the charismatic group may unleash remarkably destructive behavior. We have seen how the Peoples Temple preserved its identity by surrendering the lives of its members when an incursion of its boundary was perceived to threaten its dissolution. In contrast, events may be precipitated by the general public itself in responding to a threatening charismatic group lodged in its midst. This happened with a cult called MOVE in 1985, in Philadelphia. The group had been responsible for a series of provocations at its boundary and the response by city authorities was overwhelming.

Background of the Group

MOVE was a small cult committed in an idiosyncratic way to a return to things natural and rejection of the accoutrements of industrialization. It occupied a modest row house on Osage Street in West Philadelphia. Members had a confrontation with authorities seven years before that left a police officer dead and nine members of the group in prison. They had now barricaded their current residence and were using it as a base to promote their ideas, often by railing angrily at neighbors through a loudspeaker.

A final breakdown in communications with authorities occurred when the sect's "defense minister," Conrad Africa, refused to negotiate with a city official regarding the group's disruptions unless the nine imprisoned MOVE members were released. Given this impasse, the group's hostility, and the possibility that members had arms in the house, the Mayor and police chief decided that an assault was necessary to dislodge the cult. The police then evacuated five hundred residents of the immediate area and began trying to flush the group out of the building. This task turned out to be much more difficult than anticipated, however, since members had turned their house into a virtual fortress, having boarded over the doors and windows and constructed a steel-reinforced bunker atop the building. What happened next was remarkable for the lack of restraint by local authorities.

The first step was to hose several hundred thousand gallons of water through high pressure jets at the bunker on top of the building. This proved ineffective and cult members responded by shooting at the police. Instead of waiting the situation out, the police then unleashed a storm of gunfire, almost exhausting their supply of more than 7,000 rounds of ammunition in an hour and a half.[16] At this point, several officers wearing helmets and body armor and carrying automatic weapons tried to penetrate the house through its cellar wall, but were fended off by members of the cult who opened fire.

It was then decided to "neutralize" the armored bunker atop the building by using an incendiary blasting agent actually designed for underground mining operations.[17] After making several passes over the street, a helicopter brought in for the task hovered sixty feet above the building and dropped its makeshift bomb. A fire erupted within minutes, but the fire department, present in force with its high-power hoses, did not respond for a full forty minutes as the flames spread. Firefighters were apparently planning to let the fire burn through the building so that its occupants would be forced out or killed.

This violation of firefighting standards was a tragic error, as flames soon engulfed the aging structure and spread rapidly to nearby homes. Sixty-one homes were destroyed in the blaze, leaving two hundred and fifty residents of the neighborhood homeless. Eleven MOVE members who had been in the house at the time, including four children, were killed before they could escape the fire; only two were known to survive.

In the aftermath, it was not clear why such a cataclysm had to happen. A four-day search through the rubble uncovered one rifle, two shotguns, and three pistols. None of the automatic or semiautomatic weapons, the underground tunnels, or hidden caches of explosives rumored to have been there were found.[18]

How could this assault have been launched at the children and adults in the building at a time when they were innocent before the law? How could a major American municipality, in an attempt to respond to the needs of a residential neighborhood, drop explosives on that locality and bring about its destruction? An attempt to answer these questions requires some background on the cult itself.

MOVE emerged in the early 1970s under the leadership of Vincent Leaphart, a charismatic black third-grade drop-out who made his living as a handyman. Leaphart preached an ill-defined blend of primitivism and anarchy. His group was confined to Philadelphia, with a membership that never exceeded one hundred. The impact of the group's intense cohesiveness and its commitment to its ideology, however ill-defined, soon became evident. Both served to fuel the group's *monitoring* function, which removed members from the influence of common social norms of behavior. To demonstrate their unity and common identity, the members all adopted the surname Africa. Their belief system also came to serve as the basis for a variety of idiosyncratic activities. At first they staged a series of little-noticed protests against a wide range of social institutions, from the public education system to the ill-treatment of animals in pet shops. To act on these views, the members did strange things, such as constructing a makeshift shelter for stray animals, thereby obstructing public facilities adjacent to their house; allowing their children to roam naked, eat out of garbage cans, and steal from neighbors; and throwing large quantities of refuse into their front yard.

During the years preceding the final confrontation with Philadelphia authorities, the group stopped recruiting actively, and the small coterie of members remained stable in number, drawing in more around a paranoid center. As with the Peoples Temple in Guyana, its energies were channeled into monitoring its own members. Also like the Jonestown cult, the group increasingly cut back on the feedback it would accept from the surrounding community, shielding its members from opposing views. Jones enhanced this isolation by moving to a faraway jungle; MOVE secured its boundaries by boarding up windows and doors, refusing to listen to the complaints of its neighbors, and mounting a public address system on the front of its building. Through the loudspeaker they issued angry tirades and obscenities related to the group's ideology, while allowing no response from the community. The decline in conversion efforts coupled with the restriction of community input increasingly isolated the group and prevented negative feedback that would have undercut its activities.

In its final stage, the group contributed to its own tragic fate by aggressive management of its *boundary control* function. The group was the victim of its tenacious insistence on preserving its membership and its provocative fending off of outside authority. In refusing to accept the state's prerogatives to jail its members, the group had extended its own boundary into the proper domain of civil authorities. Vulnerability at their boundary made the cult members fearful and tense, obstructive in responding to the attempt of city authorities to negotiate. MOVE members could not exercise any flexibility for they, like Jonestown cult members, had good reason to fear that an intrusion on their boundaries would bring dissolution of their bizarre social system.

It is quite common for aggression to be directed at the boundary of the charismatic group by the surrounding community, but in the case of MOVE this resulted in unbridled assault. Tensions had risen for some time, and a theme of animosity had developed between MOVE and the police, precipitated in large part by the killing of one of the police seven years before. This animosity was reflective of the society's need to protect its own boundary from deviant subgroups. Furthermore, local community groups had been protesting the presence of MOVE in their neighborhood for many months before the assault since the cult members were unwilling to respond to issues of legitimate community concern. The degree to which MOVE had set itself apart as a threatening alien group was evident in reports that the Mayor's office had been developing plans for an assault on the house for eighteen months before the actual event, while police were secretly testing explosives for eventual use.[19]

Views expressed after the assault also reflected the animosity a charismatic sect can arouse when it engages in aggression across its boundary. When the Philadelphia fire commissioner was asked why his department had not responded to the raging flames at the house for a full forty minutes, even though ample equipment was in place, he replied cynically, "We're firefighters, not infantrymen."[20] Not only did city officials respond angrily, but public opinion was also rallied against the cult on the day after the assault.[21]

MOVE and the Peoples Temple show how a hostile confrontation can ensue at the boundary between a charismatic group and the surrounding community. Protective functions on both sides of the group's boundary may become intensified, leading to mutual provocation and paranoia. If neither party takes steps to defuse the situation, grave consequences can result. This vulnerability to escalating destructiveness across the boundary of charismatic groups should not go unnoticed in dealing with terrorists and nations that have turned to religious fundamentalism with a vengeance. Here, too, failed attempts to neutralize the threat they pose may only fuel their anger and their tenacious pursuit of idiosyncratic goals.

8

A RELIGIOUS SECT
THE UNIFICATION CHURCH

The Unification Church was established in the United States early in the course of its evolution as a religious sect, at a time when intense conversion experiences and fervent commitment were reflected in the way new members were engaged. Because of this, studies of the church during this period of expansion and active recruitment offer insight into the nature of the zealous feelings that can emerge in the early stages of such sects. The church provides examples of the idiosyncracies of a religious sect, yet it also illustrates the underlying principles governing behavior in those charismatic groups that reach some form of accommodation with the society around them.

A History of the Sect

The Reverend Sun Myung Moon, self-styled head of his own neo-Christian religion, arrived in the United States from Korea in 1972, a year after the guru Maharaj Ji had come from India. Whereas Maharaj Ji eventually relaxed his hold over his followers, Moon was tenaciously committed to maintaining close and lasting ties between his devotees and the church he founded. Because of this stance, as well as his aggressive political and financial activities, Moon became perhaps the most notorious and heavily investigated religious leader of this period.

Moon's background is partly obscured by a lack of objective sources. He was born in North Korea in 1920 and maintained that, "From childhood I was clairvoyant. I could see through people, see their spirits."[1] He told his followers that as a youth, while he was praying on a mountainside one Easter morning, Jesus appeared in a vision and called on him to carry out His unfinished task, and that he later met and conversed with Moses and Buddha. Moon further avowed that during these years he discovered the "process and meaning of history, the inner meanings of the parables and symbols of the Bible and the purpose of all religions." But it is also known that Moon, as a young man, was arrested on three occasions, with reports differing about the nature of the charges. His followers insist he was being persecuted by the Communist regime for his religious commitments, while early acquaintances, as well as some of his detractors, maintain that the arrests were made for acts of promiscuity and bigamy.[2]

By the age of thirty-four, Moon, now a self-ordained minister, had moved from North to South Korea and had taken out a charter for his newly formed religious sect, the Holy Spirit Association for the Unification of World Christianity. As this group grew, Moon made the acquaintance of the authoritarian leader of South Korea, General Park Chung Hee, and although the regime imprisoned hundreds of critics during this period, including many independent clergymen, Moon's fervid anti-Communism and support for the government's policies resulted in a good working relationship with Park. Moon's business activities also began to grow, and he became board chairman of South Korean concerns as diverse as a pharmaceutical company specializing in ginseng tea and a corporation that manufactured shotguns.

This successful minister and industrialist soon considered the possibility of overseas expansion of his sect and moved first to establish a branch in Japan, where he had initial success in recruitment, particularly among political conservatives. In 1959, Moon sent missionaries to the United States. Under Young Oon Kim, an English-speaking former university professor, semiautonomous state satellites were established, and a young Princeton graduate, W. Farley Jones, named national president. The following decade, however, brought relatively little success in America. The five hundred members scattered across the country were poorly responsive to a central national leadership and the American branch of the church often operated at a deficit.

Moon himself came to the United States in late 1971 to take charge of his American Church. Unlike Japan, where his movement faced considerable political and religious opposition, and Korea, where it was at the mercy of an autocratic central government, the United States offered a relative measure of security because of the First Amendment. Neil Salonen, an articulate and active man, became president of the Unification Church in the United States at age twenty-eight and was successful in establishing a firm leadership and expanding the sect's membership.

Rather generously, Salonen reported more than 25,000 American members in 1974 and more than a million members each in Korea and Japan.[3] My discussions with church officials and a review of church records with the staff at the national headquarters in America and Japan around this time could verify no more than about 7,500 American members and not many more in Japan. The American members were similar in background to those of the Divine Light Mission. Most were unmarried (91%), white (89%) young adults in their mid-twenties. Protestants (56%) and Catholics (36%) predominated, although members of Jewish extraction constituted only 8% of the group, one-third their representation in the Divine Light Mission. This disparity in figures between the two sects probably reflected the absence of a history of conflict between Judaism and Hinduism.

Changes in members' lifestyle were evident in their embrace of new sexual and marital standards. Sexual contacts among converts were prohibited, and marital choices were generally arranged at the discretion of Reverend Moon, most dramatically in two mass ceremonies.[4]

Recruits to the Unification Church were offered a fairly elaborate theology, in contrast to the ill-defined views of the Divine Light Mission and many other new religious movements. Because these beliefs differed on crucial points from Christian theology, they alienated the group from mainstream denominations to the point that reconciliation with American Christianity was impossible. The sect's religious beliefs were spelled out in the *Divine Principle,* its principal religious document, which presented an interpretation of the New and Old Testaments based on Moon's revelations.

Although members of the Unification Church do not publicly claim Moon to be the new Messiah prefigured in his doctrine, this is clearly suggested by both Moon himself and other leaders of his church. Interestingly, it was alluded to in a federal court when Moon was called to testify in a lawsuit following the attempted deprogramming of one church member. In response to questioning, he acknowledged that his followers "believe" in him, and then avowed that "I have the possibility of becoming the real messiah."[5]

In addition to promoting his distinctive religious beliefs, Moon's anti-Communism was adopted as part of the sect's reinterpretation of Christian doctrine. Moon himself entered directly into the political arena. During the Watergate investigations, he organized a media campaign to support the beleaguered President, investing $72,000 in the effort.[6] His position, as announced in his newspaper advertisements, was that "at this moment in history, God had chosen Richard Nixon to be President of the United States."[7] As the Watergate crisis was mounting, Moon brought 1,500 followers to demonstrate in Lafayette Square across from the White House. Nixon's daughter Tricia Cox and her husband mingled with the group to express their appreciation, and Moon was invited to meet with the President the next day. It was later revealed that the church had committed other resources to political activities, creating a quasiautonomous group called the Freedom Leadership Foundation to promote public relations and conservative political causes. Such political activities, however, compromised the movement's protection under the First Amendment.

Moon's overseas political ties also caused concern. It was suggested that his church had links to the Korean government through certain members, such as Moon's translator, Colonel Pak, a fourteen-year veteran of the Korean army who served as a Korean military attache in Washington during his early days in the church. In response to rumors of a relationship between the church and the Korean CIA, a congressional investigation was undertaken by Donald Fraser, chairman of the House Sub-Committee on Internal Organizations. Although no judicial action resulted, the investigation clearly put Moon in a bad light.

Public relations became increasingly important to the church since a good public image might facilitate recruitment and minimize persecution by community groups beginning to mount campaigns against its activities. To improve its image, the church conducted a number of large-scale public events. A widely publicized rally was held in Madison Square Garden in 1974 and another two years later in Yankee Stadium to celebrate the American Bicentennial. Both drew less than anticipated attendance.[8] For another demonstration at the foot of the Washington monument, the church spent nearly $1.5 million on the event itself and its advance publicity, but this too fell short of projected numbers. An annual conference on the Unity of the Sciences was begun in 1972, and attracted at least 25 Nobel Prize winners in the following twelve years.[9] In this venture, the sect was successful in obtaining positive press coverage while expending relatively little capital, since speakers and attendees were attracted by the leading scholars who had agreed to participate.

The sect's finances garnered considerable public attention, and whatever it gained from its public relations activities it no doubt lost through publicity over its fund raising. Mobile fund raising teams traveled throughout the country and raised money in public places from the sale of small specialty items such as flowers or ginseng tea. It was reported that each of hundreds of members brought in from one to five hundred dollars on an average day, usually not revealing their affiliation.[10] The church also made sizable real estate acquisitions that were heavily mortgaged and served as long-term investments. Properties such as Moon's own residence on the Hudson River, a twenty-five acre estate purchased for $556,000, and the New Yorker Hotel in mid-Manhattan, bought for $5.6 million and used to house followers, were widely perceived as lavish acquisitions made with funds earned by impressed labor.[11]

Ultimately, public concern had to leave its mark on the movement. The Jonestown tragedy in 1978 raised questions whether Moon's group might itself pose a similar danger. Moon was the most visible of the remaining sect leaders, and further congressional inquiry into his group was undertaken. A report by the House Sub-Committee on International Organizations stated that it "had found evidence that Reverend Moon's international organization had systematically violated the United States tax, immigration, banking, currency, and foreign-agent registration laws, as well as state and local laws on charity fraud."

In 1981, Moon was indicted for filing false tax refunds. The charges stated that he had failed to report more than $150,000 of his income in a three-year period. Before indictment, Moon had apparently deposited $1.6 million in New York bank accounts in his own name and failed to report almost all the interest.[12] During the trial, Unification Church officials, with support from several mainstream religious leaders, maintained that Moon had fallen victim to religious persecution and was being charged on grounds that might have applied to other religious figures. But Moon was convicted and after an unsuccessful appeal spent eleven months in a minimum-security federal prison.[13] Even after his release in 1985, the church placed newspaper advertisements insisting that in his handling of his tax liabilities Moon was no more culpable than many other leading public figures.[14] Throughout his period of confinement, I saw no decline in commitment among long-term group members. Toward the end of this period, some church members began publishing a periodical, *The Roundtable,* that aimed for more independence of thought within the movement. This clearly reflected a weakening in the church's monolithic system of social controls, but at the same time allowed for the expression of dissent by members who were interested in reform yet committed to their church.[15]

Induction

In the Unification Church recruitment occurred in two different ways. One was open, the other was by deception. The choice in a given area usually depended on the experience of those who had assumed control over the local program. In the San Francisco Bay area, for example, a major source of recruits for the sect, the process was generally surreptitious. Potential members were approached under the guise of introducing them to an innocuous socially oriented group and only when the potential recruits became fully involved in the group were they made aware of its association with the church. On the other hand, induction workshops that I studied in the northeast and in southern California were generally labeled clearly as activities of the church and the young people who became involved were well aware of their developing association with this sect.[16]

Two Entry Routes

During the late 1960s and early 1970s the church operated actively in the Berkeley area since the campus was a magnet for estranged youths seeking an alternative set of values during a period of considerable social turmoil.

The church concealed itself under a wide variety of names and causes capitalizing on this situation. Youths might be presented with the opportunity to join a "Creative Community Workshop" in which they were introduced to an ideology more palatable than that of the Moonies. Ecology, world peace, improved race relations were all put to use in recruitment drives.

The outside world naturally took a dim view of such deceptive practice. One father contacted me for a consultation after his son became a Moonie in this way. After completing his second year at an eastern college the young man went with a classmate to California intending to work in Yosemite Valley for the summer. On arriving by bus in Berkeley, they were met by two young women who invited them to participate in a "New Educational Development System" conducted at a house not far from the university campus. A short while later, the son called his father to say that he and his friend planned to take a three-day workshop in Berkeley for which each would pay $20. The boy was not clear in describing the purpose of the workshop or the issues that would be discussed there, and added to his father's suspicions when he avoided specifying its exact location. In a second call two weeks later, the boy said that he did not plan to return to college, but would not provide details on the group with which he decided to spend his year. His parents were deeply concerned but were unable to gain further access to either of the two youths.

The next contact with the family occurred after six weeks, when the young man revealed that he had just become aware that the group he was joining was in fact the Unification Church. With prodding from his parents, he acknowledged that he might have been reluctant to get involved had he known this. But its philosophy now made unassailable sense to him and he was pleased that he had been introduced to it under circumstances where his suspicions had not been aroused. When his parents asked to meet him to discuss the matter further, he declined by saying that he had to devote his time to gaining a fuller understanding of the church's religious doctrines and did not want to be disturbed while pursuing that goal. He told them that he would be leaving for a camp in the nearby Napa Valley and asked that they respect his wish and not contact him.

Some members I interviewed mentioned similar experiences. They described a situation where close attention and concern had been focused on them, a process the group's detractors called "love-bombing."[17] This elicited commitments from many young people, but revelations about the approach figured prominently in criticism of the sect. The remarkable ease with which some recruits adopted a vaguely defined philosophy in these workshops attests to how readily individuals can be made to attribute meaning to any credible, or even incredible, line of reasoning in times of uncertainty if the context is highly supportive.

Induction by subterfuge was often used to attract young people casting around for new ideas. In these cases, the appeal of a fad might be the starting point for subsequent indoctrination. Bennett, for example, was doing well as a third-year college student when he attended a two-day workshop on extrasensory perception. His previous interest in the issue had been casual, based only on the whimsical notion that "there might be some way in which people can sense each other's feelings, even without talking." Bennett did acknowledge to me several years later that he had felt a certain lack of meaning in his life at the time, and furthermore said that he could not "raise the interest" to choose a major or plan for a career.

As it turned out, the workshop was actually sponsored by the Unification Church, and the woman who spoke there related the possibilities for extra-corporeal communication to opportunities for a deeper sense of religious commitment, although she gave no clue as to the nature of that commitment. As Bennett listened, he began to get a sense of the speaker's wisdom and was attracted to the "ultimate truths" the group seemed to offer. As the meeting closed, it was apparent that a number of the people there knew the speaker well, and as Bennett asked further questions, they took a strong interest in his own willingness to discuss more thoroughly the topics raised and expressed support and affection he had not felt for some time.

This modest example of "love-bombing" was not without effect, as he readily accepted an invitation to come back for dinner the next evening. But not until three or four weeks later, after his involvement in the group had become secure, did the members tell him that they were affiliated with the Unification Church. At this point, he had already accepted the group unconditionally and saw the details of dogma they now revealed as no more than a sensible way to help him gain a better understanding of their philosophy.

These covert recruitment techniques had both advantages and disadvantages for the Unification Church. Since the sect had been widely criticized in the press as practicing "mind control" on its members, leaders were reluctant to announce the group's identity to potential recruits for fear of putting them off. In this way, the need to operate surreptitiously perpetuated itself, and certainly outraged the families of young people who joined in this way.

Officials in the church public relations office in New York, and leaders in California and Boston whose workshops were carried out in a more forthright manner, expressed considerable uneasiness to me about the impact of this approach on the public. Although they sometimes voiced concern to their superiors, they had to acknowledge reluctantly that the techniques had proven effective in recruitment. Discussions with church members from different parts of the country indicated that during the peak recruitment years of the early 1970s about half of the new members were brought into the sect by deceptive procedures like those just described. The rest came in through encounters where the group and its workshop site were clearly identified.

The open format had its own problems. Most youths approached straight-forwardly refused to listen to recruiters. Furthermore, parents were gener-ally informed of the induction earlier on and might intercede before their children became fully engaged. At the time of the Jonestown debacle, I was observing this induction procedure in anticipation of a more elaborate study. Parents of five youths attending one workshop drove a long distance to the retreat where it was held and demanded that their children return home with them. One couple brought a police officer. Although none of the par-ticipants were minors, the church leaders felt obliged to accede to the par-ents' demands.

The potential converts in the open workshops were young people ap-proached in the street or on a college campus and invited to visit the church headquarters for an informal discussion or a lecture. Those who did go were next offered the opportunity to participate in a two-day program in a nearby rural setting. Their motivation was usually modest, since their familiarity with the sect was generally based on no more than a few encounters. Their understanding of the church's creed was also quite modest since it was not presented in detail until the residential workshop, but they were aware of the identity of the sect and willing to be exposed to its philosophy.

Those who participated in the two-day workshop were usually driven in a group to a secluded site on a Friday evening. A van or two would arrive at the workshop center each weekend carrying potential recruits along with the members responsible for their "witnessing," or recruitment. Other re-cruiters were already present along with the workshop staff. In the con-trolled study that I conducted, the urban headquarters were located in west Los Angeles, and the workshop center was in the San Bernardino Moun-tains, some seventy-five miles away. The setting was informal, but comfort-able accommodations and a full complement of meals were provided.

The program for the weekend ran from eight in the morning to eleven at night. The main component was a series of ninety-minute lectures, each concentrating on major points from the Divine Principle, followed by a half hour of small group discussion that explored the meaning of these religious principles relative to the individual participants' lives. Although a certain measure of emotional involvement was expected, intense, cathartic experi-ences were not encouraged. The discussions tended to be intellectually ori-ented, as church members felt that their religious doctrine had considerable intellectual content and could serve as a major source of attraction on this count alone.

Communication was regulated in subtle but nonetheless effective ways by workshop leaders. For example, recreational activities such as singing, sports, and skits were interspersed with the lectures and discussions, but these seemingly casual functions were well structured and provided a context in which information-sharing and communication about the church took place. Conversations and ideas that did not bear on the themes under discussion were discouraged in a congenial but firm manner.

The balance between active members and nonmember recruits during the small group discussions also assured control by the leaders over the context of communication. Most exchanges took place in groups of four recruits, the four members who had invited them to join the workshop, and the designated group leader. Thus, the majority were committed to supporting the church's philosophy through either overt or covert management of communication. Under these circumstances, it was possible to suppress deviant points of view, often before they were expressed. Potential converts were therefore engaged throughout the two days in an organized agenda determined by the leadership, and designed to discourage ideas contrary to the group's perspective.

The following exchange illustrates how communications were managed in one group, although the transcription itself cannot convey the many nonverbal cues, such as a glance or frown, by which important communications were often made. The setting is a small group discussion at the workshop involving a leader, four potential recruits, and the four members who had shepherded these recruits through the initial stages of their involvement with the sect. The group had been examining a fundamental element of church doctrine that God had intended Adam and Eve to marry and bear perfect children and thereby perpetuate the "Kingdom of God on Earth." According to the Divine Principle, Eve was literally seduced by Satan and, thus tainted, brought Adam to sin as well, which made Satan a spiritual parent for all humanity. This sequence is what the church views as the original sin that led God to cast the first family out of Eden. The doctrine is difficult for a contemporary youth to accept because of its very literal interpretation of the Adam and Eve story. Furthermore, the church's retelling alters its outlines in the Bible, so that it is incompatible with the traditional Christian view. The discussion that took place after this theology lesson reflected these difficulties and showed how the church dealt with them.

One of the workshop guests, a fairly headstrong young man named Steve, expressed doubts about the literal nature of the material presented, and appeared uncomfortable, saying, "I don't understand. How can you say that the Devil actually existed and literally seduced someone?"

One church member turned to him and said, "I had trouble understanding that too. It took me quite a while to catch on, but if we don't understand the literal meaning of the Principle, well then it's just another book." By saying this, the member supported Steve in having to deal with uncertainty, but at the same time conveyed the view that his doubts were actually unfounded.

Because this member had informally played the role of an "assistant leader," over the course of the discussion, Ellen, another workshop guest, now turned to him as if he were an authority who might help her to clarify her thinking and asked, "But is it literally true?"

A second member then turned to Ellen and said, "Yes, this all becomes

clearer when you understand how evil and misunderstanding are felt every-
where in the world. It's little surprise how many people have died in senseless wars over the course of history, even though people have tried to prevent them." At this point, another member added, "We lose out when we
treat the Bible as a relative thing, as something that can be made into just
a story." By underlining the views of the first member, these two members
have therefore relieved him of the burden of arguing alone for church doctrine. The voices of three church members together have greater credibility
than one, and they seem to take on the quality of a consensus. Since none
of these three was the formal leader of the group, they also carried the
credibility of peers rather than imposing authority as a leader. Ellen was
reluctant to contradict their statements and simply said, "Oh, I see" in
response.

It was probably not coincidental that the focus of the exchange had shifted
to Ellen, since the church members could sense that Steve was more forceful in presenting his doubts and thus more likely to take issue with them if
pressed to acquiesce to their position. The leader now looked around the
group as if the issue had been resolved and turned to Ellen saying, "So you
can see how it's hard to accept this bit of history at first. But later on we
will see how it's a base we can build on."

In fact, Steve's doubts were later addressed by the group, but in a way
more suitable to him and that avoided confrontation. He was showered with
support and affection, making it less likely that he would want to press his
reservations further. The church members in his group complimented him
profusely for his insight into the Divine Principle and his ability to pick up
on the hardest issues to understand. In this way, a more argumentative
guest such as Steve could be won over to compliance without thrashing out
points of doctrine on their merits.

By Sunday night of the first weekend in these workshops, the talk turned
to the choice open to those who participated. Did they wish to stay on for
another workshop that would run through to the end of the next weekend
or would they return home? Members were free to choose; those who left
were reminded that they could come back at some other time, and many of
those who left were in fact contacted again. Usually, only a minority of
participants agreed to continue, but this is hardly surprising since the church
had presented an unusual set of views along with the suggestion of further
involvement.

In the week-long workshop lectures and discussions were longer, with a
three-hour session each morning. This was followed by an afternoon of sports,
hiking, and maintenance work at the induction center. In the early evenings
there were further discourses and after dinner, further sharing among the
workshop guests and members.

Guests also kept "reflection notebooks" so that they could write down
their feelings about the week, sharing their thoughts with other recruits

before bedtime. During these late evening discussions, emphasis was placed by group leaders on the importance of dreams, and guests often found that they could recall their dreams much better than usual, not unlike psychoanalytic patients who are also in a setting where such recall is encouraged. The very vagueness of the dream material lent itself to interpretation by the workshop group, usually directed to support a participant's deepening commitment.

One member recalled having the following dream after four days in a workshop.

> I had fallen and hurt myself while rushing to get to my college class. There was a strange man nearby who said he would help me, but I felt I couldn't trust him because he reminded me of a neighbor I had been afraid of as a child. I decided to run on, hoping to find help, but was frightened because my arms and legs were bruised. I came to a large building and was given directions. I had made it to safety.

The members of the group interpreted the threatening man to be the dreamer's past sins, and the large building symbolic of the safety of the workshop center. They were no doubt trying to persuade this young recruit that the center and hence the church were a safe haven from the distress in his life. They did not speculate that the dream might have been interpreted otherwise, to represent the dreamer's fear of a disrupted life if he succumbed to the views of Reverend Moon (the stranger) and his need to escape the workshops and return to the large house in which he lived.

In any case, several members reported dreams that were seen as leading to an acceptance of the views proposed by the church. It was not uncommon for a member to say that such a dream had helped crystallize a decision to become more deeply involved.

After the second weekend of the extended workshop another decision point was reached. The remaining guests now had the option of participating in a final workshop, which meant spending two more weeks with the group. Recruits who stayed on were brought into activities that resembled those of regular members. One week was devoted to full-time recruiting and the other to fund raising; both were usually spent in the urban center the recruits had come from.

The daily schedule during these two weeks was quite rigorous. Recruits slept in modest communal settings in the city, rising at six in the morning and spending most of the day promoting the church. Early in the morning, at midday, and late in the evening, time was set aside for prayer and lectures, as well as notebook entries.

One striking aspect of this two-week segment is the adversity faced by the recruits as they spent long hours toiling for the church. Street-corner recruiting was regularly punctuated by the derision and hostility of pedestrians and the potential recruits they approached. Fund raising required long hours of streetside peddling. Typically, these fledgling recruits experienced very limited success or return for the effort they invested.

Because so many people whom they now encountered ridiculed the views they had just come to espouse, these recruits were forced to argue in the face of considerable opposition. Yet this seemed to enhance their emerging commitment to the sect. As we have seen, there is experimental support for the contention that argument against opposition can bind a person more closely to his or her viewpoint, even when the person had taken the position only because asked by someone else to do so.[18] In any case, participants generally agreed that the two weeks of labor for the church contributed materially toward strengthening their ties to the group.

At the end of the workshop series, the remaining participants were given the option to choose whether they would formally join the Unification Church. Those who did—only a small fraction of the initial number—were made full members, and their names given to the U. S. national headquarters in New York. They were soon assigned to a church center or mobile team at whatever location they were needed, generally at a site hundreds of miles from where they had encountered the church.

A Study of Induction Workshops

Whatever the relative political consequences of the two recruitment settings, the open workshop sequence offered a structured format whose operation and effectiveness might be studied. The church used a standard format that was systematically reproduced in a number of metropolitan areas across the country. The site for our study was the Southern California Workshop Center, because the number of "guests" there would enable me to obtain a sizable sample in a relatively short period. A new workshop sequence began each week, and all guests who entered the center over a two-month period would be evaluated. Eight workshop sequences were studied in all, including 104 guests.[19]

In framing the study I hoped to ascertain the differences between those workshop participants who joined and those who did not, and to use the relative roles of group cohesiveness, shared beliefs, and psychological well-being to distinguish between them. Questionnaires about these and other factors were administered on five separate occasions so that members' views could be monitored over the course of the workshop sequence. They were filled out anonymously, but each participant marked all five questionnaires with an individual code so that they could be grouped together at the end of the study.

The responses revealed no difference between the background of these recruits and the members studied previously. The workshop guests were predominantly single (94%) and white (77%), with an average age of 22. Perhaps the most interesting findings about the workshop experience were

Table 8-1. *How Far into the Workshop Sequence Did the 104 Participants Continue?*

Subgroup	Stayed for	Percent of Participants	General Well-being Score
Early dropouts	1–2 days only	71%	74.7
Stayed beyond the first weekend	More than 2 days	29	67.2
Stayed beyond the first week	More than 9 days	17	—
Actually joined	More than 21 days	9	61.9
Control group	Community residents, nonmembers	—	83.4

the number who actually agreed to continue in the sequence at each juncture, and how many actually joined (Table 8-1). These findings are quite similar to those reported by Eileen Barker, a sociologist who studied a large sample of people who participated in similarly structured workshops in London the following year.[20]

After the first weekend, almost a third of the participants agreed to continue. Of this group, a majority stayed through the first arduous week.

As noted, participants had the option of joining the church after the full three weeks of workshop sequence. There could be little doubt that this was a major step, reflecting a commitment to enter into the uncompromising communal living situation the group offered. Nonetheless, half of those who had embarked on the final two weeks decided to join.

I was able to ascertain the status of all nine individuals who joined four months after their entry into the sect. By that time, three had already left the group. One had returned to his family overseas; another was reported to have been abducted by relatives while visiting his aunt's home on the way to another church center, and the third was said by those who knew him to have been "not serious" in his original commitment. The remaining six were still active in the church.

Altogether, after four months this sect had retained as members a total of 6% of the sample of potential recruits who had agreed to participate in the initial two-day workshop. Although this was a modest portion of those attending, it represented a considerable potential for recruitment when the times were ripe for initial engagement in the streets. Furthermore, a larger number had been more strongly influenced than they had anticipated when they volunteered for the two-day workshop and might reconsider joining at a later date.

The next step was to characterize the workshop participants who went on to join the sect. Two issues turned out to be most important in this regard: their relative emotional distress and the alienation they felt before entering. Table 8-1 shows that the psychological well-being scores of those recruits who dropped out early were considerably below those of the general population, and that the recruits who stayed longer in the induction period scored even lower. The scores of those who decided to join were lower still—actually in the clinically distressed range—confirming that the sect tended to attract people who were experiencing distress. This is all the more notable since the workshop leaders themselves screened out recruits who seemed unlikely to be able to withstand the rigors of membership for emotional reasons. Three workshop participants were asked to leave for this reason. Clearly, the Unification Church did not want to be a haven for people who would draw their own psychological stability from it without contributing much in return.

In addition to psychological distress, affiliativeness to the sect was an important discriminator between those who joined and those who did not. Recruits' feelings of social cohesiveness were measured by means of the scale described on pages 33–34. Shared beliefs were assessed with a series of items related to church creed such as "Some of the problems I see around me began with an immature use of love by the first human ancestors," and "My understanding of Jesus' mission to restore God's ideal of Creation will lead to a more meaningful life for me." Both the cohesiveness and the creed scales were completed on each of five separate occasions in the first nine days of the workshop series.

Some telling results emerged when the responses were categorized in three groups: the *early dropouts*—the 29% of the participants who left by the end of the first weekend; the *late dropouts*—the 20% who stayed after the weekend and chose not to join; and finally the 9% who *joined* at the end of three weeks. The early dropouts scored lowest on both cohesiveness toward the workshop participants and on the creed items. But no significant difference was found between the joiners and late dropouts in their scores on these items. Not only did they seem equivalent in their enthusiasm for the sect, but they developed this attachment equally early in the workshop sequence, as reflected by their scores on the repeated questionnaires.[21]

How were the late dropouts distinguished from those who finally did join? The dropouts scored significantly lower on the scale for cohesiveness toward persons *outside* the sect.[22] Lacking strong ties, they would not as readily be drawn back into the community. Those likely to join the Unification Church were unhappy young adults with limited feelings of affiliation toward friends or family who were sufficiently responsive to the group to become strongly engaged early on in the workshop sequence.

Another way of evaluating the induction experience is to see how members assessed it in retrospect. Relevant information had been solicited during our initial study of longstanding church members. Most of these active members recalled their conversion period in a positive way. As noted previously, when asked to assess their feelings on a scale of psychological distress, the overwhelming majority (91%) indicated a decline from the period before joining to the one after joining,[23] and more often than not they "felt an appreciation of the reality of God very much" (76%). Some, however, did allude to the psychological disruption of the experience, and indicated that they had encountered much more than usual conflict or unhappiness (18%) or disruption in eating (22%) and sleeping (21%). Only a few felt that they were "under someone else's influence" during the experience (12%)—a surprisingly small number, and quite telling in light of the considerable degree of group pressure actually applied during the recruitment process.

Transcendental experiences were not uncommon during conversion and many respondents reported that they had experienced the following "pretty clearly": "a special unfamiliar feeling in my body (45%)," "time passing slower or faster than usual in a very special way (39%)," and "the presence of someone important to me, even though most people couldn't have seen him" (35%). These items, however, capture only a part of the alterations in consciousness experienced during the protracted and intense group encounters included in the various conversion formats. Thus, it was not uncommon for workshop members to report the return in waking hours of dream images they had written about in their reflection notebooks. Sometimes they would perceive the presence of persons important to their religious thinking, such as Reverend Moon himself, while they participated in workshop activities.

A statement from one young woman reveals her intense feeling during the induction experience. She described the point at which her decision to join crystallized.

> I had just begun witnessing, and made the mistake of approaching a disagreeable, matronly woman who glared at me after I told her why I was speaking with her. She said, "Get away from me you little fool." I was crushed by the thought that she could dismiss everything that I wanted to express without even listening, and with a feeling of hatred at that. But my mind flashed back right then to what the workshop leader had told us just before: that we had to expect people's anger, and that this was the beginning of a path that we'd follow in God's steps. I hadn't really understood that at that time, but suddenly I knew that it was literally true, and I felt warmed by an intense feeling of faith throughout my body. Suddenly I knew I was literally in the company of Jesus and Reverend Moon themselves, carrying God's mission forward. I didn't dare to turn around to look. It was a remarkable feeling of not being alone; they could have spoken to me if they chose to. I knew at the time that my commitment would hold fast, whatever might follow.

Family and Marital Structure

The mass engagement and marriage ceremonies of the Unification Church created some of the most memorable images of the new religious movements.

In 1979 over the course of two days, 1,410 members were matched to their future spouses in a ritual engagement held in the church's World Mission Headquarters in New York. Mates had been selected by the Reverend Moon in a seemingly random fashion and appeared to have little doubt that they had indeed been provided an ideal choice of spouse. They were apparently pleased to wait patiently and endured a protracted period of engagement. Three years later, in a widely publicized ceremony, over 4,000 members were wed en masse in New York's Madison Square Garden. These events left the public incredulous over how this social rite could be so profoundly altered yet remain acceptable to young people who had grown up in the American mainstream.

I examined this process in some depth because it dramatically illustrated the way a charismatic group is knit together as a social system that regulates its members. Through it Reverend Moon was placing his own stamp on the lives of his American members and shaping their participation in the church for years to come. He could do this, however, because the marriage rituals in the Unification Church were deeply embedded in the group's ideology and its command structure. They epitomized the lockstep coordination of members within a charismatic group, who, as a rule, adopt the attitudes prescribed for them without question.

The Engagement Experience

The announcement by Reverend Moon of his plans to carry out a mass engagement was greeted with enthusiasm by church members. By this time, many of Moon's American converts had been devout followers for a decade or more and had been of an age suitable for marriage for some time. In particular, many women felt they would soon be rather old to begin a family. There was also a precedent in the movement for this unusual ritual, as mass marriages had been held by the church in Korea and in Europe.

Because of the large dimensions of the project, members applied for engagement to a church Blessing Committee; the Blessing referred to Moon's sacred wedding rituals. The requisite forms asked for very little: name, age, term of relationship. In addition, applicants were also asked whether they had been divorced before joining the sect and whether they had committed any sexual indiscretions during their term of membership. The Blessing Committee was composed of senior female members of the church, including Neil Salonen's wife. Although appropriateness for marriage was reviewed by the Committee, final decisions about some postponements were left to Salonen.

After the Committee made its decisions on eligibility, the members approved for engagement eagerly awaited notice of the matching ceremony, knowing that Reverend Moon would designate their future spouses at that time. The proclamation that Reverend Moon had decided to begin a two-day matching ceremony was made only a day or two before the event. Eligible members from around the country were told to appear at the church's World Mission Center, located in the New Yorker Hotel, a church-owned facility in midtown Manhattan. Its large ballroom could accommodate the entire eligible group at one time, if crowded together.

Moon began "matching" his assembled flock by designating several small subgroups among the applicants. He first called the black members and asked them whether they wanted to be married to persons of their own race; few of them did, since a commitment to racial integration was strongly emphasized by the movement. Moon then proceeded to match members who had volunteered to marry blacks and did the same with Orientals.

Two additional groups of members, students at the church's religious seminary and high administrative figures, were next asked if they wanted to have mates chosen within their respective subgroups or from the full body of those assembled. Finally, Moon made selections for those who were previously divorced and others over thirty-five years of age. The remainder of the crowd, the large majority of those assembled, was paired off without any designation of subgroups, in seemingly random fashion, with the assumption that the matches reflected a divine choice. Although Moon was accompanied by a member or two of the Blessing Committee in his rounds of the hall, he made all matches himself. Only a very small number of those present were paired off with someone they had known from a relationship predating the ceremony.

Those matched were allowed to speak with each other for fifteen minutes to see whether there was any reason why they might decide against becoming engaged, but needless to say, some potential spouses had problems that were not evident in the brief encounter. To remedy this, subsequent matching ceremonies were arranged so that persons with specific anomalies could be labeled as such. On later occasions, for example, members actually wore tags to this effect: "unable to bear children," "taking medications for mental illness," or "problems with homosexuality."

The following accounts of members' experiences with the engagement are quite typical, each reflecting different aspects of the psychological impact of the ritual. Nicole had joined the Unification Church twelve years before the matching ceremony at the same time as her boyfriend. The couple parted ways, since unmarried members were to abstain from all sexual relationships. When the engagement plans were announced, she had been witnessing in Boston. Along with other eligible members on her team, she made arrangements to fly to New York immediately. Within a few hours, she found herself in the hotel grand ballroom sitting toward the back of a large throng, wondering when she would be matched. Suddenly she heard Reverend Moon ask for those who had been divorced to stand up as a group, and she did so since she had been married for a short time several years before joining.

Only now did Nicole fully realize that her turn to be matched was approaching. She had consciously avoided thinking about who her fiancé might be since she felt that it would be a violation of the character of the occasion to second guess her leader. Soon she was taken by surprise as she heard her name called. She walked calmly up to the front of the ballroom to stand next to Reverend Moon. There were so many faces in front of her that she could not distinguish them. She felt a bit dazed, and hoped only to follow Moon's wishes. As he had done many times that day, Moon turned to the audience, pointed to a man across the large room, and said, "You."

Nicole later described her initial response to her fiancé-to-be.

> I looked at him and it was like looking at my own brother, someone in my own family. Our relationship was immediately special. I sensed that he could really love. . . . It was like love at first sight. I had tested myself so much that I could accept anyone in my relations with church members. I would always find the points that I liked when I developed relationships with people in the church. . . . I'm pleased to accept what the church had offered me, and see only a happy future. I could never have doubted the choice that Reverend Moon made.

Immediately after they were matched, Nicole and her fiancé-to-be stepped aside to talk for about ten minutes and felt no reservations about each other.

The next day a ceremony was held to consecrate all the engagements. Members' callings had to be pursued, though, and since intimacy or cohabitation were not permitted during the engagement period all fiancés returned to their respective work sites, however great the separation between them might be. Thus, Nicole drove to Boston and her future husband flew to the West Coast.

Although Nicole was profoundly content, even beatific, while she described her matching to me, she still seemed to convey the specifics of her experience with reasonable accuracy. Some other members embroidered the experience, adding miraculous events to the recollections of the two days. Wally, for example, was a sensible young man who supervised repairs at the World Mission Center. I had met him on several occasions while making preparations for the Unification Church studies. He reported neither transcendental experiences nor psychiatric difficulties before joining the Unification Church, but his description of the matching included supernatural events.

Wally told me about a dream he had three days before the announcement of the matching ceremony in which he saw Reverend Moon introducing him to a young woman whose identity and even general appearance he was unable to ascertain. But he awakened the next morning "fully aware" that the ceremony was imminent. He said that the dream presaged Reverend Moon's making the best choice for him. There was no doubt for him that a divine hand led him to this premonition.

Wally recalled his experience in the ballroom while Reverend Moon was selecting a financé for one young woman who was standing in front of the assembled throng. Wally did not recognize her at first, but soon remembered that they had worked together briefly on a mobile fund-raising team, and that he had found her an earnest and likable person. He laughed to himself quietly, surprised at knowing her, but then perceived that the recognition was a divine signal that he would be chosen for her. Slowly, Reverend Moon looked around the auditorium and settled on Wally as the woman's mate.

Wally concluded that two divine interventions had taken place in relation to his engagement. He did not see either event as coincidental or a retrospective distortion. Such reports of presumed supernatural experiences, no doubt precipitated by the sharp sense of anticipation among members, were quite common. They illustrate the plasticity of perception and recall in the highly charged situations created by charismatic groups.

Nicole and Wally experienced the engagement somewhat differently. Nicole seemed content to be a passive recipient of a divinely inspired act, and was filled with joy by her new status. Whatever the church offered, she could accommodate. Wally, on the other hand, believed that he had predicted both the ceremony's occurrence and the identity of his spouse and hence saw himself playing a more active role in the selection process. Apparently, he took comfort from having a hand in the course of events. Both engaged members, however, shared the belief that their leader would select a satisfactory partner and did no more than adapt psychologically in their own ways to the church's expectations.

This kind of unfailing faith in Reverend Moon's choice was expressed most clearly in what members came to call the "Kodak matches," a format probably initiated because of a modest excess of male members in the United States. For these pairings, Reverend Moon matched an American man with a woman who was born in Japan or Korea and still resided there. As an aid to selection he would rely on photographs of the young women and men, since none of the participants were present. This arrangement was announced before the actual matching ceremony, and the American volunteers who were allowed to participate regarded themselves as a fortunate cadre chosen to articulate the church's goals. After Moon made the matches, the financées from overseas usually did not appear in the United States for months.

Six months after his Kodak match had been completed, one young man tried to explain why an engagement under these circumstances was such a good opportunity.

> I had been involved in three relationships before joining and was glad to be rid of that looseness. Not one of them had any real meaning to it beyond worldly interests. Now it was like being a pioneer and starting out anew in a new world. So I knew that this relationship would be a pure and lifelong commitment. . . .
> Since I joined I'd always felt that the Korean women had a very special

quality about them. Most of all, they had been church members since early in their lives and could bring to a marriage the real seriousness of religious commitment. This was the right person to start out a spiritual family modeled after Reverend Moon's.

He then took a photograph of a church-sponsored Korean dance troupe from his pocket, and proudly pointed to one of the twenty women, saying that she was his bride-to-be.

He had met her two months after the engagement when the troupe toured the United States; the couple now exchanged letters every week or two. The engagement perplexed his parents at first, but they were well disposed toward his membership since his life had improved after his conversion, when he stopped moving from city to city and using drugs heavily.

The way Reverend Moon was able to make this highly personal choice for his members cries out for explanation. In one sense, it can be seen as an expression of the church's religious creed. In another, as an articulation of the group's needs as a social system. In fact, doctrine and social function coincided in this case.

According to its theology, the Unification Church is the vanguard of a universal brotherhood that will form once its word has spread throughout the world. The church will herald the Second Coming. For this reason, the recruitment of new members, or "spiritual children," is essential to the growth of the United Family and hence to Moon's divine mission. After a new member becomes committed, he or she eventually attains the role of a perfect child in Moon's United Family. In time this "child" may qualify to join in the "sacrament" of establishing a family in the church. His own family is then modeled after Reverend Moon's perfect family, and thus brings salvation closer. This religious concept also contributes to the complete acceptance of Moon's authority over the United Family, justifying authoritarian regulation of members' lives by him and his agents.

On theologic grounds, nuclear families must be consecrated to embody Moon's messianic vision, which is much more important than any personal gratification a family may offer a couple. With regard to monitoring the membership, each couple must mesh well with the system of central figures. A couple's autonomy must not compromise the exercise of social control in any way. As sociologist Arthur Parsons has pointed out, members do not protest this unlimited power held by Moon; instead, they find repugnant any restrictions on his personal authority precisely because such limitation would pose an unwanted ambiguity.[24] In the end, the marriage is part of a tightly woven web that they must be sure to protect.

The engagements therefore draw on the forces of the charismatic group in shaping members' behavior. An intense social cohesiveness was evident in the members' pleasure in responding to Reverend Moon's call for the matching ceremony, and the virtual interchangeability of members as potential spouses demonstrated a remarkable merging of identities within the group.

Their beliefs allowed them to make the leap of faith for relinquishing traditional aspects of mate selection, and to believe that their leader's choice was divinely inspired.

A Study of Engaged Members

To clarify how this sect carried out mass coupling, I wanted to undertake a study that would examine the details of the engagement ritual and its underlying psychology.[25] Permission to carry out this study was given by Dr. Mose Durst, then the sect's newly designated American President.

I began with extensive interviews of engaged members and planned to administer a structured questionnaire one year after the engagement. Four test sites would be used: two centers in New York City, one in Boston, and one in upstate New York (which included the church's religious seminary). Because church members frequently moved between cities, these centers drew on a population representative of engaged members across the country.

A number of scales from previous studies were included in the questionnaire and others were introduced. The questionnaires were completed at the end of one of the meetings required of the betrothed members, held for the purpose of discussing the engagement and planning for their future marital lives. In all, 321 of the 1,410 members matched in 1979 were studied a year after engagement.

Almost three-quarters (72%) of these participants were born in America, while 10% were Europeans and 9% Japanese, a breakdown representative of the population of the Unification Church in America at that time. Their mean age was twenty-nine and they had been members for an average of nine years. Almost all had at least some college experience (81%) and quite a few (15%) completed graduate or professional training. In summary, they were largely American-born, middle-class, educated young adults with a longstanding commitment to the church.

Respondents and their fiancés had had very little contact during the year after the engagement ceremony—a sign of the sect's effectiveness in abrogating conventional norms of engagement behavior. Only a small minority (16%) lived within a mile of their future mates, and many (42%) were separated by more than five hundred miles. Over a third (38%) had not seen their partners during the previous two months. Sexual contact between fiancés was strictly forbidden, an injunction scrupulously observed according to all reports.

Most salient in the disruption of conventional engagement practices, however, was how members experienced the elimination of their independent choice in mate selection, since Reverend Moon had determined all matches on his own. Almost a third of the men (30%) had been paired in the Kodak matches to Japanese and Koreans, and a large majority (87%) of the respondents indicated that they had felt no preference at all for a particular individual before the matching ceremony. This fit in well with the attitudes expected by the leadership, and reflected the ability of the church to suppress the natural curiosity and personal desires of the members.

A modest remaining number reported they had felt some preference for a specific mate before they were matched. Of those who did, a minority (4% of the total) said they *had* been matched to the person they hoped for. Most of these had probably petitioned the Blessing Committee to allow Reverend Moon to match them with a particular member, but it is also possible that some decided after the fact that the financés chosen for them were indeed the ones they always wanted. The remainder (9% of the total) also reported that they had actually felt a preference for a particular financé, but had not been paired with the one they preferred.

The general well-being scores of the members who had Kodak matches (30% of the men) and of those who did not get their preferred choice were not different from the scores of other respondents.[26]

A small number (3%) indicated that they were contemplating ending their engagement. These members about to break a major commitment made through the church had lower well-being scores than the balance of the group, falling within the range of clinically significant distress.[27] Clearly, they were not unaffected by the psychological consequence of disrupting the engagement, though their ties to their financés must have been minimal.

Current sociologic thinking about mate selection emphasizes traits that individuals consider desirable in a spouse. Marital choices are believed to be determined by a market economy of sorts, a tacit decision-making process in which the marketable assets of potential husbands and wives are entered into a calculus of relative desirability.[28]

In line with this, I included seven traits commonly felt to be important in a prospective partner, such as "sufficiently intelligent for you," and "looks attractive to people." Seven additional spouse traits related to the values of the church were also included, such as "can convey the church's spiritual values to your children" and "is profoundly committed to the Divine Principle." Each of the fourteen spouse traits was scored by the respondent in terms of how the person saw its relative importance in a potential spouse. Remarkably, *all* the Unification Church items were ranked higher than the "secular" traits. The members had moved far away from the value system of the general public in their thinking about marriage. Their responses suggest that they would be fairly content with Moon's selection, and they raise the question of what mechanism might underlie such pervasive conformity.

To answer this question, I tested two hypotheses by means of scales included in the questionnaire. The first one drew on observations made in the general population, namely, that a person's psychological well-being is adversely affected by disruptive life events such as moving or losing a job. I hypothesized that the engaged church members were similarly vulnerable to disruptive life events, including those relative to their life in the church.

Second, I hypothesized that the emotional distress caused by such events in the life of the sect member would be muted by the relief effect operating in charismatic sects. That is, the distress caused by these events would be countered by emotional support derived from a member's commitment to the sect: the more closely the person felt affiliated, the more he or she could place disruptive experiences in the perspective of the sect's beliefs and thereby avoid a sense of hopelessness and despair.

One scale developed by Thomas Holmes and Richard Rahe[29] has been widely used to assess the incidence of forty common disruptive events in a person's life; it was a convenient measure for my study. Typical items are "experienced a major personal injury or illness" and "began or ceased formal schooling." I tailored the scale to the experiences of church members by adding thirteen additional events such as "a major change in your method of witnessing," and "attended a church workshop."[30]

Altogether, members experienced about the same number of disruptive life events as a normative population, but the *relationship* between these events and the group experience was most revealing. My first analysis revealed that these disruptive life events predicted a small portion (15%) of the variability in members' well-being scores; thus, church members reacted like other population groups in their vulnerability to the psychological effects of disruptive life experiences. A second analysis, on the other hand, included items reflecting members' feelings of affiliativeness toward the church (cohesiveness and shared beliefs) as predictors of emotional well-being in an attempt to assess the degree to which attachment to the church affected members' general well-being. The life events and affiliation items together predicted an appreciable portion (31%) of the variability in members' well-being scores.[31] This supported the notion that sect affiliation acts as a buffer against the effects of disruptive life events: disruptive life events detracted from members' well-being while affiliative feelings enhanced it. Members not only experienced psychological well-being in direct proportion to the intensity of their affiliative feelings for the church, but they also enjoyed a corresponding relief from the depressive effects of those disruptive events.

From studies on operant conditioning we learn that such emotional rewards (or reinforcement) lead animals and people to persist in the behavior that brought about the reward. The emotional support they receive in unsettling circumstances reinforces members in their commitment to the sect and obedience to its authority.

Members' compliance with the engagement ritual parallels their malleability in all other areas of conduct. They accept what they are told because they have been conditioned to stay closely affiliated with the church. A long history of operant reenforcement of compliance prepares the members for accepting or rationalizing whatever is asked of them by the leadership. In this case they discarded their conventional views of marriage and rationalized their acceptance of Reverend Moon's choice.

Other models of group conformity are relevant in understanding the impact of the church on long-established behavior patterns such as marital engagement rites. One compelling example is found in studies on obedience to authority. Stanley Milgram[32] has shown that in certain settings people can easily be induced by an authority figure to perform acts that conflict with their usual values, even to the point of harming innocent people. Milgram solicited volunteers for what were actually sham experiments, carried out in a seemingly legitimate psychology laboratory. Typically, the volunteer was instructed by the "researcher" to help condition a second subject played by an actor by administering electric shocks in a study on learning. As the experiment progressed, the volunteer was expected to give the learner subject increasingly strong electric shocks—the volunteer was not aware that the shock was simulated. Most volunteers inflicted the shock without questioning the propriety of the undertaking, even when it appeared to cause considerable pain to the learner subjects. These were ordinary people, yet they followed the rules set down by the experimenter's authority without being constrained by the values they presumably held.

Milgram's sham experiment illustrated the degree to which individuals will comply with authority when its role in the management of a situation is assumed to be unimpeachable. His experimental setting was similar to the engagement ceremony in that both were managed by an authority figure who was sanctioned to set standards of behavior.

Cognitive dissonance theory is another body of research that can contribute to our understanding of the Moonie engagement. This theory has shown how individuals cannot easily dismiss a belief or attitude they hold, even when the attitude is directly contradicted by evidence or events. People will sooner adopt farfetched ideas to explain events than relinquish their preconceptions.[33] In so doing, they avoid having to face the dissonance between what they see and what they have long believed. The dismissal of plain reality can happen when people are confronted by challenges to their ingrained patriotism, their prejudices, or their religious values. Under these circumstances, they may ignore cruelty, hypocrisy, or incompetence, or create elaborate rationalizations rather than challenge the principles espoused by their leaders. Thus, church members not only accepted the validity of Moon's deviant method of engagement, but also developed rationalizations to sustain it. For example, they took its peculiar nature as evidence of the divine inspiration of their leader, rather than as a reason to question his judgment. To have questioned it would have shaken the foundations of their religious beliefs.

The Marriage

After the mass engagement, time passed with no announcement of a marriage ceremony—with no clear reason announced. Three full years elapsed until Reverend Moon finally announced the ceremony that would bring together in a lifelong matrimony most of his American members. Madison Square Garden in New York was the site for the event. Thirteen hundred members who did not yet have fiancés but had been members for the requisite three years were brought together a week before the wedding ceremony and matched off by Moon. One hundred fifty Japanese women were flown in just days before the wedding to balance the number of mates in this group.[34]

When the day of the ceremony arrived, members who were to be married dressed in identical outfits, as if to flaunt their conformity before those who insisted that the church made automatons of its members. The 2,075 brides all wore Simplicity Pattern #8392 with the neckline raised two inches to preserve their modesty; the grooms wore dark blue suits and maroon ties.[35] In addition, 6,000 parents, friends, and guests were gathered in the vast auditorium to witness the ceremony. These people displayed a wide variety of attitudes: some smiled, some were bewildered, others were in tears. The assembled relatives were far from unanimous in their approval. A sister of one of the brides said of the wedding, "That man has caused more heartache in my family and everybody else's than anybody I can think of. My mother can't even talk about it without crying."[36]

Strains of Mendelssohn's "Wedding March" played serenely during the ceremony, and a triumphant note was struck at its close when participants linked their arms together after the Reverend's blessing and shouted, "Mansei!" (eternal victory). In ironic contrast to his role of heavenly matchmaker at this event, Moon had been convicted for tax fraud in federal court only six weeks before, and was facing sentencing in two weeks. The marriage epitomized many contradictions inherent in the rise of this new religious movement, but in terms of the sect's religious doctrine, it symbolized the fruition of Moon's messianic mission.

As the ceremony came to a close, members began a "separation period" during which sexual relationships were still not allowed, a period that would end a half year later, and then only if each spouse had brought into the church three new members. For most of those engaged in the original matching ceremony whom I had studied, the end of the separation was "only" six months away. For others matched later, it would continue for years. Yet most members adapted to the whole experience with relatively little difficulty, as the following examples indicate.

Ed was born in the Midwest and was thirty-seven years old when I interviewed him a year after his marriage. He had joined the Unification Church twelve years before while in graduate school at a large state university. Noreko, nine years his junior, was the woman he married. She had come to the United States several years ago from her native Japan at the behest of the church, having joined the sect while working in a factory owned by one of its Japanese members.

At the matching ceremony Ed volunteered to be paired off with an Oriental member because he felt they best embodied the principles of the church; he recalled being "immediately fully pleased" with his fiancé when she was selected by Reverend Moon. The couple was separated right after the ceremony, however, as their church missions were located several hundred miles apart. They wrote to each other frequently, but only visited each other several times before the blessing. Ed did not find this unusual and stressed that he had busied himself with the work of the church during this period.

Ed's parents refused to speak to him when he first joined the sect, but after he had been a member for three years, they initiated some contacts, and there were more exchanges after the marriage. Ed explained:

> They were very negative when I joined and saw me as the black sheep in the family, as if I would amount to nothing, never working at a regular job, never giving them any grandchildren. My sister and brother, on the other hand, had done nicely for themselves as far as my parents were concerned, and had all settled down not far from home. . . . My marriage softened my parents up. They seemed to think that maybe I will "do something" for myself now and become a family man. They didn't even seem to mind that my wife wasn't an American; I think they were just relieved.

The improvement in his family's response could be attributed in part to his participation in the sect's home church movement. After the separation period, several hundred members who volunteered for this movement began to live together, each couple in its own separate dwelling, generally not far from church centers. These couples would regularly touch base with the movement by attending church services and religious meetings, but were responsible for the management of their households. It was hoped that each of these families by way of example would interest nonmembers from their community in the church.

These members acquired a certain amount of autonomy in managing their affairs; nonetheless, the home church carried with it the monitoring function of the larger sect since important decisions were always made in close consultation with the couple's "central figure," the local religious leader who coordinated their religious and secular pursuits. A central figure would usually be the leader in a work setting, such as a fund-raising team, an administrative office, or a business establishment. Married couples were usually placed jointly under the leadership of the same central figure so that their mutual needs could be aligned with those of the church.

When Ed and Noreko turned to their central figure for consultation on the appropriateness of moving into a home church, there was an extended discussion of their ability to deal with the responsibilities they would have to assume. For the first time in more than a decade they would need to maintain an independent bank account, manage a budget for rent and groceries, and organize all their household duties. Ed admitted to a certain trepidation about leaving the fold, while at the same time expressing optimism about this new challenge.

Noreko, who spoke English well, described her reaction to this major transition, which entailed moving out of the church headquarters in mid-Manhattan.

> We were so happy at first to move into the World Mission Center after the separation period, and have our own home together. We had one room with a bath. It used to be a hotel room. We ate all our meals in the main dining room with the other brothers and sisters, but six months ago we asked our central figure if it would be wise to plan on moving into a home church, and he said we were ready. After we all discussed this, he suggested I take a job that would help Ed and me save for our own apartment and I began to work as a secretary. At first, I felt like a stranger at work because I was separated from my brothers and sisters all day, but this way Ed and I could save the money I earned to set up our own apartment.
>
> We just now took a place on Staten Island about an hour from the Center, and we're trying to juggle the bills, relying on my salary and the small amount of money that Ed gets from the church for his work at the printing plant. It isn't easy, but our home is not just an apartment; it is a sacred part of the church. Our marriage there gives us a chance to belong to the perfect family. It is a very beautiful place for us both.

In this case, the expectations of the church and the natural inclinations of its members operated in concert. Both Ed and Noreko were comfortable with the mythology underlying the sect's marital ritual and also had no material difficulty adjusting to their marital relationship. Because of this, and because they saw their central figure understanding their needs, the structure binding them to the sect operated smoothly.

The home church movement represented one phase of the sect's evolution, reflecting a change in perspective on the part of Reverend Moon. During the period preceding the mass marriage, the church had become somewhat looser in its management of individual members, and tight coordination of daily habits became less common. Members living in the same residence no longer awakened each other for morning communal prayers; some began to keep their own checking accounts and acquire modest personal effects. The home church movement was part of this transition in which Moon was pressing members to complete their schooling or acquire a trade so that they might advance themselves. Many members were now trying to complete their college courses or continue the graduate training they had abandoned before joining.

Several months after the wedding ceremony, though, Reverend Moon announced a project for recruitment of new members, the International One-World Crusade (IOWC). Although such initiative had been mounted before, this one was to be conducted on a massive scale. Participants in previous campaigns were organized into teams of 25 for each state; in this new crusade 250 teams were formed, each with eight members, for a total of 2,000 participants, nearly twice as many as before. More than a third of the members married in the Madison Square Garden ritual joined the teams.

A call was made by Reverend Moon for all members to participate in the IOWC; those who complied were extolled for their commitment, while those who refused were expected by their central figures to have an acceptable excuse. The IOWC was mounted with great publicity among the membership, with articles in successive issues of *Unification News,* the church's nationwide newspaper for its members. Maps showing where mobile teams were located at any given time were published with updated reports on their activities. It soon became obvious that the numbers of new recruits hoped for in the campaign were not forthcoming, most likely because the country's youth, in a period of conservative good feeling and self-interest, were no longer so inclined to depart from the mainstream. The teams were redirected to fund-raising activities in the streets, and many were later sent back to their old locales and expected to begin work and family life anew.

The entire undertaking was highly disruptive for the sect, and complaints were acknowledged even by the church. In the *Unification News,* descriptions of the IOWC written for other members by recruiters in the field reflected this.

> Have you ever experienced a situation that could only be described in accurate terms as "Hell"? The state of total absence of God's love, a place of secret enemies or complete dislike of another person? I am now confessing that I have had all these experiences during my time on IOWC.

This course of events was highly distressing to the members because they were dislodged from residential or marital arrangements they had earned, so to speak, by their long and faithful years of service to the church. They also had to accept a major upheaval in their occupational roles to solicit funds in the mobile teams. For those who had become ensconced in more comfortable positions, this was a difficult and embarrassing shift to make after years of advancement in the church hierarchy. Several married members became disillusioned and even left the church. The large majority, however, managed to regroup their energies of zealous commitment. Open criticism of the church itself was rarely expressed.

Sarah, a married IOWC participant with whom I spoke around this time, revealed the strength of the monitoring structure in resuscitating members' ebbing devotion.

> What was hardest about going on the IOWC was that I began to mistrust my husband, and even the sanctity of our marriage. I felt that he was rejecting me when he let me go off at the time. I ruminated about it for weeks as our team moved from city to city, at first recruiting, and later selling flowers on street corners. And it was hard to feel comfortable and secure, but when I came back, luckily we had an understanding central

figure who was able to speak with Larry and me about my confusion. Over a few months he pointed out how my own problems in accepting my mission should not interfere with my understanding of the marriage as a sacred ritual, and not a secular project.

Sarah's counseling experience also suggests a similarity between the role of the sect's central figures and that of the mental health professional in stabilizing members' social adaptation. Both caregivers must interpret social values to troubled individuals, and both to some degree are given the prerogative of adapting these values to the individual's needs. When Sarah's central figure pointed out the way she must accommodate her feelings to the marital and fund-raising practices of the church, he wore the mantle of someone presumed to understand the broader social and religious issues underlying the needs of a troubled person. In like fashion, the contemporary mental health practitioner is perceived by clients as understanding general principles whose application will help resolve their own psychological conflicts. Faith healers, of course, are also accorded such roles within their cultures.

The central figure's importance in resolving conflicts related to the Moonie marriage is clear-cut in the case of Calvin, a member who was beginning to acknowledge his homosexual orientation before he joined at the age of twenty-three. His inclinations were morally unacceptable to the sect, and he ultimately adapted to the church's marital ritual.

When I spoke with him nine years later, Calvin said that his decision to join the church was prompted by the "idealism it offered, and the alternative it provided people to a constant obsession with sex." But it also appeared to offer him a release from conflicts over his own sexual orientation.

Calvin had not dated members of the opposite sex before joining but had been regularly preoccupied with homosexual fantasies. In addition, he had initiated several homosexual encounters with strangers, and recalled with distress that he knew he was "sure to move into a gay life, sooner, or later." When he first met members of the church, he was living in a neighborhood largely populated by single people whom he felt were more socially active than he. He was moderately depressed, and neither able to relate to the heterosexual community nor accept a gay identity. The anxiety caused by this conflict abated after his conversion because, as he said, "Faith in Reverend Moon and the support of my brothers and sisters relieved me of these sinful ideas."

After several years of membership, Calvin had only occasional homosexual ideation. But then he experienced one distinct episode of attraction to a male church member, which made him anxious again. For solace and guidance, he turned to his central figure, discussed his concerns in depth, and accepted his mentor's religious homilies.

When the opportunity arose for members to apply for the matching, Calvin "decided not to worry" about the problems that might be raised by his history of sexual confusion, telling himself that Reverend Moon's involvement in the choice of his financé would help resolve this problem. He felt that the "strength of the church" would be bestowed on him through the blessing ceremony, thereby allowing him to live according to its creed.

The separation period that followed the engagement placed little pressure on Calvin with regard to a heterosexual relationship since his spouse was living several hundred miles away, but when the time came for the consummation of their marriage four months later, Calvin demurred, explaining that he felt the time for physical intimacy was not yet at hand. In fact, such requests were not uncommon among the newly married couples because a variety of interpersonal issues often had to be worked out before couples felt comfortable with each other. But Calvin was frightened by the thought of sexual relations with his wife, even though he felt quite warmly toward her, and was very enthusiastic about the marriage as a Unification Church sacrament.

He turned to his central figure several times over the next three months and on his advice moved into a room with his wife and began to share his bed with her. He recalled the experience a year later.

> It's not that I didn't want sexual relations, but the idea made me very uneasy. After I spoke with [my central figure], I learned to keep my mind on the church's idea that our union is part of our faith, and not a matter of outright sex, and soon the fear lessened. I think it worked out because I knew that we were part of a sacred family and not just partners in the flesh.

Calvin spoke of successfully completing sexual intercourse on several occasions in the following months, and added with pride that the couple's prayers for a pregnancy were soon met. He denied having any homosexual preoccupations since the time of the matching, over four years before.

Through the close collaboration between Calvin and his central figure, this charismatic group was able to produce a long-term change in behavior in someone whose natural sexual inclinations ran counter to church doctrine. Calvin's central figure shaped his individual needs, initially deviant in the church subculture, into a sexual adaptation that was acceptable to him and to the group. This change in sexual behavior is a striking example of the power of focused social influence.

Calvin's case highlights the difference between voluntary compliance in a charismatic group and coerced conformity in an authoritarian context. If Calvin had not been fully committed to the group's value system, his overt behavior might have been controlled but his fantasies and desires would likely have remained as before. The forces of intense cohesiveness and shared belief, rather than the overt threat of an authoritarian regimen, allow for such effective shaping of individuals' behavior within a cult.

Table 8-2. *The Original Sample of Engaged Members,*
Four Years Later

Documented active in the church	93%
Married to a fellow member 85%	
Never married 1%	
Married and broke up 6%	
Dropped Out	4%
Not located by mail, church records, or contacts	3%

Married Members: A Follow-up Study

The opportunity for a follow-up study of the engaged church members was extraordinary. For the social scientist, the entire sequence of engagement to strangers, waiting period, and marriage had the quality of a grand experiment of nature, as if a remarkable research manipulation had been carried out on thousands of unsuspecting subjects. An extensive questionnaire was mailed to all the original subjects who could be located four years after the original engagement survey and a year after the mass marriage. These members' responses provided further evidence of their tenacious commitment to the church: almost all were still active, and the large majority were currently married to a fellow church member (Table 8-2). Only a small number were either breaking up their marriages or had never been married at all.

Members' commitment to the church view of the marriage was still staunchly upheld. They were asked to evaluate the relative importance of fourteen assets in a fiancé, the same ones used in the original study. Again, the seven traits related to the church's religious values all ranked higher than the others that mirrored values held important in the common culture. Traits in a spouse such as "willingness to sacrifice personal needs and comfort for the church" still ranked higher than practical ones such as the ability to "contribute successfully to your economic support or to skilled homemaking."

The deviant nature of the marriage, evident in the couples' cohabitation practices, may help explain this finding. Most respondents (65%) were still in the ritual separation period, and had yet to have sexual relations. In fact, many (38%) lived as far as five hundred miles away from their spouses, and less than half (48%) reported that they had spent a single night in the past two weeks in the same building as their spouses.

Not surprisingly, the role of the church was prominent in shaping members' plans for childbearing. Conception was encouraged among all those who had completed the separation period, and at the time of the follow-up a sizable number of couples already had a pregnancy or birth (24%). Since the separation period continues until both spouses have converted three new members, however, most remaining members (45% of the respondents) could not plan for children because they had not yet brought in a sufficient number of recruits.

The questionnaire had also been constructed to assess the impact of the church's control over members' psychological state. To this end, it included a list of experiences related to the marriage, all initiated by the church leadership. Typical experiences were "leaving your spouse for more than a week on church business," and "establishing a home church."[37] To assess the impact of these events on members' general well-being, the questionnaire asked if they had experienced any in a disagreeable manner. The questions were so framed because of recent evidence that life events with a perceived negative impact have a pathogenic effect on individuals' mental health.[38]

Did marital events determined by the church, if viewed negatively by members, also have a deleterious impact on their well-being? Furthermore, would members' affiliative feelings for the church mute this negative impact? An analysis of their responses revealed that an appreciable portion of the variance in their general well-being could, in fact, be predicted by the extent that they perceived church-related marital events as being undesirable (14% of the variance), and even more could be predicted by the combination of affiliative feelings and life event scores (32%).[39]

These statistical results suggested that specific life experiences engineered by this sect could produce a diminished sense of psychological well-being. Significantly, though, the members' commitment to the church buffers this distress by enhancing their well-being. Thus, one member of a newlywed couple might be sent off to a remote point on a fund-raising mission. The couple's faith in the church, however, buffers them from this church-imposed stressful event. These two phenomena, the creation of distress and its buffering, together create a *pincer effect* in the following way: The members implicitly sense that relief from distress is provided by their bond to the sect, and turn to the sect for solace when faced with disruptive life experiences. Ironically, their resulting compliance with the sect's dictates leads them to further conformity to its potentially disruptive demands. The sect thereby creates distress at the same time it relieves it—and at the price of further compliance.

Leaving the Sect

The way members leave a charismatic group can be as revealing as how they join. In a sect where the need to remain bonded is so compelling, departure entails rejection of the transcendent mission ascribed to the leader and carries a burden of soul-searching and guilt. As with induction, the full force of the charismatic group may be brought to bear on individuals.

Members left the Unification Church in two different ways: voluntary separations and deprogramming. Most people who left reached the decision over a period of time while continuing to live within the fold of the church. Deprogramming, or forcible removal, was much less common but received much more publicity.

Voluntary Dropping Out

A member's decision to leave the Unification Church reflects malfunction in the monitoring role of the church, as the member's disillusionment arises from the inability of member and sect to sustain mutual understanding. The members' experiences illustrate the complex circumstances that can lead to such a "failure" in the system's operation.

One member's ostensible motive for leaving was his loss of faith in the church and his own mission, but it can be seen how the monitoring system of the sect failed to sustain his commitment. Armand had been working for two years as a copy editor at *Newsworld*, a general circulation New York newspaper operated by the church, and had taken great pride in his contributions to the sect's impact on the media, since he believed that the paper was doing an important job in conveying both the news and Reverend Moon's message. As frequently happened in the church, Armand was transferred to a new work setting, and stationed several hundred miles from *Newsworld* headquarters. The young man eagerly immersed himself in his new assignment of witnessing, since he felt that bringing new members into the church was also of utmost value. The recruitment methods practiced in this region were open; potential converts were informed from the outset that they were being introduced to the Unification Church. Within a few months, though, a new central figure, a native Japanese, was appointed to the team, and its mission changed from recruitment to fund raising. Armand found that this new leader was less open in his dealings with the public, as was common for Oriental-born church functionaries. Unlike previous central figures, he was a person Armand could not fully respect. Furthermore, "heavenly deception" was now a prominent theme in conducting the team's affairs, wherein it was acceptable, even laudable, to mislead nonmenbers when necessary to promote the church's goals.

Armand soon found himself quarreling with the team's leader about matters of strategy. He insisted that the degree of deception practiced ran contrary to the principles of the religion to which he was committed, and that a straightforward approach would be more effective in raising funds. In particular, he balked at not revealing fund raisers' identification with the Unification Church and their aggressive door-to-door sales techniques.

On one occasion Armand went so far as to telephone the central figure to whom he had reported while working at *Newsworld* and voice his reservations about the team's operation, hoping for a sympathetic hearing. Much to his mortification he was told that it was not for him to question the principles of the church.

Armand recalled:

> I was made to feel like a bad person for speaking honestly. He even said that God would not be with me, and here I had trusted him and was sure he would understand. But I wasn't about to go on sneaking into stores, lying about the permits we were supposed to have, and believing that the ends justify the means. . . . I was angry and hurt, but I also began to feel very guilty, as if I were abandoning the church. I began losing sleep, not caring what happened.

A month after the telephone exchange with his former mentor, Armand, in a state of disillusionment, moved out of a church center where the group was temporarily staying and returned to his parents' home, which he had left five years before when he had joined the sect. Ironically, he had ignored numerous pleas made by his parents that he leave the church because of its alleged abuse of its members.

Armand's parents spoke with me at this point and reported with distress that he was now removing himself from social contact and spending all his time in his room, lying in bed. Furthermore, they said that he had lost much weight in the few weeks since his return, that his mind was "always somewhere else," and his gaze "vacant." They feared he would not be able to manage on his own and thought he might best go to a hospital. Armand, however, refused, although he did agree to one psychiatric consultation with me.

A year later Armand called and asked to come by. He had begun to resume an active life and appeared in good spirits. He was working full time as a sales representative and had moved into an apartment with two friends, one of whom had also left the sect. His feelings about the movement were ambivalent.

> As for myself, I still respect the Reverend Moon and the *Divine Principle;* he is a very important religious teacher. On the other hand, how could I have continued to place my faith in a group that preached God's word but could also mislead people at the same time? The contradiction was more than I could live with when I left.

The moral dilemma Armand had faced and the ensuing soul-searching and depression were quite common; it was reported by about half those interviewed. In Armand's case, we may use systems theory to clarify how circumstances coalesced to shake his faith. All religious groups confront contradictions when their members are forced to live in a community where contrary values are espoused and must then rely on protective operations at the system's boundary. For a small charismatic religious group, the resulting conflicts are more intense because contact with the surrounding society forces the group to deal regularly with an inhospitable, even hostile, world. Unpleasant collisions with this world highlight the differences between the two ideologic systems. Often members must dismiss the society's broader values by systematically denying the humanity of outsiders and even subjecting them to abuse. In the case of the Unification Church, this aspect of boundary control often took the form of "heavenly deception." Armand, however, found himself unable to do this.

In his work at *Newsworld*, Armand was exposed to the values of the broader society, but only when transferred to the IOWC did he experience difficulties in assuming the necessary protective stance. In this setting, he was ill prepared to assume the defensive posture of the group since he had been wrenched from a relatively protected position at the *Newsworld* and placed into direct confrontation with a hostile public. His daily face-to-face contacts at the newspaper were nothing like his dealings with the targets of the group's "heavenly deceptions." Armand also came into conflict with the monitoring personnel of the sect, both his original and his new central figure, and this occurred as he experienced an unexpected loss of autonomy and decline in status.

These difficulties loosened the ties binding Armand to the system. He began to relinquish his grip on the church's shared belief system, its model of right and wrong, and adopt the values espoused by the general society. At this point, he was no longer effectively maintained within the group's boundary and ceased to be a component of the system.

Although Armand said he left the church because of a loss in commitment to the values it espoused, many members expressed their reasons for departure in more mundane terms. Doris, for example, was a temperamental young woman who had been a vocalist with a professional singing group sponsored by the church. She described her departure in terms of disappointed love. Her story shows that no matter how strong the hold of a charismatic sect on its members, it cannot fully expunge the romantic feelings some may feel, however great their desire to live up to the standards of their adopted religion.

Two years after leaving, Doris related her experience with a measure of bitterness, and acknowledged that even during her later years in the church she felt less positively about it than most members and was often unhappy about her circumstances. In discussing the mass engagement, she pointed out that she and other longstanding members were "strung along for five or ten years with the carrot of the [eventual] matching dangled in front of us." She said that members were constantly told an engagement and marriage would soon be forthcoming, only to find it repeatedly deferred. She sometimes wondered whether the requirement that members enlist more recruits was not a form of blackmail they had to pay for a marriage. Doris rarely hinted at her feelings and then only to a few trusted friends who were not sympathetic to such misgivings.

Doris also admitted to being attracted to a co-worker during her years at

the performing arts department of the church, another sign of her alienation. In time, this attraction became a grave problem for her since she
secretly hoped that he and she might be matched. Under unusual circumstances, some members would be considered by the blessing committee for
a prearranged match, but Doris had no precise notion as to how such a
pairing might be granted. The church disapproved of the discussion of any
romantic interest between members, which made it inappropriate for her to
make such a request based on her own attachment.

As the matching date approached, Doris hoped that her secret affection
for her co-worker might somehow be requited, and also assumed that his
apparent friendliness actually reflected his desire to be her spouse. After
Reverend Moon called for volunteers to be assigned by photograph to Korean
and Japanese women, however, this co-worker turned to her one day at work
and said that he hoped to participate in a Kodak match, since he saw these
Oriental women as the finest in the church. Doris became deeply resentful
over what she regarded as a rejection and also grew anxious, fearing that
Moon would assign her to someone with whom she would not be happy.
Only after she had been out of the sect for a year, however, did she realize
that her expectations of being matched to her co-worker had been ill founded,
as was her assumption that he had wanted to be her mate.

At the matching ceremony, the young man whom Moon selected for Doris
seem personable enough, but Doris was not comfortable accepting him as
her spouse. She now became obsessed with the fear that she could no longer
find a satisfying marriage in the church, and discussed the matter at length
with her central figure, an older Korean woman with whom she previously
had a good working relationship. Doris was assured by the woman that she
could break off the engagement if she wished, but she came to feel that any
match at all within the church would end up being problematic. Unlike
other demanding church edicts she had agreed to accept in her eight years
of membership, this one was threatening and unpalatable.

Doris hoped to gain support through proximity to her family, which had
previously been accepting of her membership, and sought permission through
her central figure to take a new work assignment in the city where she had
grown up. Her request was granted and while there she met a man she had
known who had left the church only a year before. Within a few weeks, a
romantic relationship developed, one that Doris felt could be permanent. He
told her he would rejoin the church for her sake, but only if she would
present their union as a fait accompli since he believed it would otherwise
be abrogated by the church elders.

Doris agreed to his terms but feared that the entire situation would be
unacceptable to the church. Once again, she turned to her trusted central
figure at the performing arts department since the woman was well connected in the higher echelons of the church. The woman was distressed to
hear the story, but agreed to intercede on Doris' behalf with a senior church

figure. She returned, however, saying that Doris would have to reject her new lover immediately to remain in the church. Doris had not wanted to leave the sect, but now felt she had no alternative. She established a home with her new mate outside the church and got a job.

The matching and wedding produced real difficulties for several members, but through its monitoring function the church was able to draw on their strong commitment to help them get through the situation. With a major disruption like the matching, however, it is not surprising that some loss in members did result, as in Doris's case.

Other members left the church after realizing that they could no longer sustain its arduous lifestyle. A great amount of work was expected of them. Respondents to my initial survey, for example, reported devoting an average of 67 hours a week to tasks that would have been recompensed by wages outside the sect. The members rarely questioned this expenditure of time and effort; and there were unusual occasions when a combination of circumstances might put the work in a less favorable light and even undermine a member's commitment. This sometimes happened when there was a sudden shift in work assignment.

Alec, for example, had been working in one of the church's semi-independent businesses, a Korean restaurant, for two years when he was transferred to a mobile fund-raising team. He later told me he had probably become "spoiled" by having his own room and schedule during that period. Furthermore, in his office job of overseeing a small work force, he viewed himself as a manager rather than a line worker.

Initially, Alec had hoped that his efforts in his new position would give him something of a spiritual renewal. He had served on a fund-raising team for two years after first joining the church, and generally had not minded the work. At this point in his career, though, it turned out that Alec could not help feeling the activity was beneath him, an indignity; he could hardly suppress his feelings of dissatisfaction as his team worked from early morning until late night peddling flowers on city streets.

What Alec found least tolerable was the faceless anonymity imposed on members of the team. They were herded about in a van as they traveled through their territory and spent their nights bedded down in sleeping bags in cramped quarters, "lined up like a bunch of sardines." To save time and energy, clothing was pooled and team members got back different garments after each washing.

Soon Alec began to feel confused and rebellious. To retain "a shred of identity," he acquired a small suitcase and began to launder his own underwear and other clothing, his first abrogation of church standards. As he later made clear, this was a sign of doubt about his place in the church.

> Nothing was my own. I had no space. Even the clothing I wore was a challenge to my identity. I asked myself, "If you need to keep these few shirts away from your brothers in the church and don't really want to go

along with this terrible schedule, then what are you doing here?" I started asking myself this and couldn't come up with enough of an answer to keep it up. Then I got frightened that I didn't have what it takes to support the others who were on the mission with me. Maybe I thought I was letting them down.

Alec's disillusionment slipped into depression and anger at himself. He consulted with his team leader who, after realizing that Alec's concerns could not be resolved in his present setting, suggested a change of place. In his new position, Alec worked on special assignments for one of the church leaders, but still could not recapture the sense of commitment he once felt. His disaffection from the church was sharpened when he found to his surprise that the leader's wife was herself disheartened because the church hierarchy was pressing her to keep her toddlers in a full-time communal nursery. Alec sympathized with her and began to see the church as an oppressor. He also started to think seriously of leaving the church, having decided that its lifestyle no longer "made sense" to him. For days he was tearful and ruminated over what seemed to be an inevitable rift between himself and the principal commitment he had made in life. The leader's wife became his confidante and tactily encouraged him. One day he bade her farewell and set off for the town where he had gone to college, his last link with the world outside the sect. After his turmoil, he felt relief in leaving.

Whatever their reasons for leaving, members who departed voluntarily prepared for this task in deliberating over their choice; they felt the decision was essentially their own. In contrast to those abducted and forced out of the group, they thought through their own rationales for leaving and somehow reconciled them with a remaining affection for the group. For those who were deprogrammed, however, the experience was quite different.

Forced Departure

Deprogramming refers to the use of physical restraint by a family or its representatives in an attempt to dislodge a member from one of these zealous groups. The degree of coercion exercised varies from parental observation of a child in the family home to physical abuse by strangers behind locked doors in remote settings, and the legalities involved in such interventions are complex. Deprogrammers generally draw on state conservatorship laws that allow a family to intervene when one of its members is judged mentally incompetent, but their practices were often found to violate members' First Amendment rights of free speech and free religion. Conflicting views of deprogramming were held by different legal authorities. Richard Delgado, for example, pointed out that a meaningful distinction should be drawn between the constitutionally protected right of traditional religious practice and the affiliative ties arising from coercive induction into certain cults. He asserted that "religious cults expose their indoctrinees to a greater variety of classic brainwashing techniques and with greater intensity," and therefore, "two essentials of informed consent—knowledge and capacity—are not present simultaneously."[40] This position served as the basis for curtailing the autonomy of certain adult cult members.

In contrast, the American Civil Liberties Union, in a number of cases, defended the rights of cult members to maintain their affiliations and espouse whatever beliefs they held, pointing out that absolute free choice and even risk are inherent in the privileges associated with the First Amendment. Jeremiah Gutman, president of the New York Civil Liberties Union, expressed this view in saying that "all religions are equally good or bad. That's what the First Amendment says."[41] Many a heated argument involved these distinctions, in court and outside.

The courts generally upheld the rights of sect members to resist the forcible incursions arranged by their families[42] and well-known, normally "professional" deprogrammers such as Ted Patrick and Galen Kelly lost crucial legal battles in cases where they had forcibly intervened. Even though "professional" deprogramming procedures left their practitioners vulnerable to legal charges, families of some cult members still sequestered relatives in an attempt to reverse their conversions.

In examining the psychology of these circumstances, we will consider two types of forced departure from the Unification Church: one "professionally" organized and one family directed. Both cases also demonstrate different ways in which a mental health professional can be drawn into these forcible removals.

In the first case, a representative of the Unification Church asked me to assess the mental competency of Michelle, a twenty-five year old who joined the sect five years before, had been abducted by deprogrammers, but then escaped and returned to the sect. A conservatorship had been issued alleging that she was not mentally competent to care for herself.

Three weeks after Michelle returned to the church she appeared in my office. She was accompanied by a husky male church member, as she and the sect's officials were fearful of another abduction. My interviews with Michelle, as well as a full battery of psychological testing, were conducted in private and the results were confidential. The evaluation showed that her mental competency was unassailable, and I gave her attorneys a brief statement to that effect.

Michelle gave me a revealing account of her failed deprogramming. Eight weeks before, she and three other church members were returning to their headquarters from a recruitment meeting when their car was stopped by three unmarked vehicles. A police officer stepped out of one of them, demanding the driver's license of the church member who was driving, and Michelle's brother stepped out of another car and identified her to the police. At this point the parties present, some in police uniforms and others in civilian clothes, asked that she leave her car, as they wished to serve a conservatorship on her. Michelle became frightened and refused, but was then dragged out and forced into one of the police cars. Once inside, she was handcuffed and brought screaming to the local police station where her father had been waiting. From there, she was driven to a nearby motel and placed in a room by two uniformed guards.

During the next week, Michelle was kept in seclusion with the door of her room locked and shades drawn. Her watch was removed and she soon had little idea of what time of day it was. She became fearful that she might be physically tortured or even raped, despite being reassured by her captors, strangers to her, that this would not take place.

All exchanges during that week were intended to turn her against the sect. The only visitor with whom she spoke at any length was an apparently experienced deprogrammer who repeatedly told her that the Unification Church was violating the rights and liberties of its members, and then pressed her to agree that the church's activities were ill conceived. He repeatedly played recordings of persons who had allegedly left the Unification Church and segments from television shows on unsavory aspects of the sect. The deprogrammer told her over and over that she had been brainwashed by the church, but she felt that it was only now that this was happening.

After about three days of this treatment, Michelle concluded that it would be to her advantage to act as if she accepted the deprogrammer's point of view, so she started speaking as if she had begun to agree with the endless tirades against the sect. Toward the end of a week, as she estimated the time, her brother appeared and took her for a walk outside her room, perhaps, she surmised, to test her acceptance of the deprogramming procedure and to see if she would try to escape. Michelle decided that running away from him was not feasible, since the deprogrammers apparently had the cooperation of the local police. She had heard stories of other members being taken to mental institutions after attempting to flee. Her brother now told her that she would be flown that night to another city to stay at a different center, and that evening he accompanied her to the airport along with the deprogrammer and other persons involved in the undertaking.

The new center, where she stayed for a month, was housed in a converted motel with a staff of a dozen or so people. At any given time, about eight "residents" were undergoing deprogramming from a variety of groups, including the Unification Church, Hare Krishna, and some lesser known religious sects. Here Michelle was subjected to repeated questioning and extensive defamatory talks on the Unification Church. She commented on their imposition on her strong religious feelings.

> First, all of my moral convictions and feelings about the Bible and the [Divine] Principle and just about everything in life were open to discussion. There was always pressure for me to conform to their way of thinking, and what they presented was considered proper morality. Then the

pressure was always intense to decide that if you're righteous, you will get on the bandwagon of deprogrammed people and see the Reverend Moon as the Devil. But it was easier for *them* to talk about being righteous than it was for *me* to get to church; that didn't seem to be something they liked. After I insisted, though, I was able to attend church only once out of five Sundays, even though I was taken out half a dozen times to bars and dance halls.

Along with the other residents at the deprogramming center, Michelle was expected to review both scholarly and popular material on brainwashing, on the assumption that she would realize the mistreatment she had undergone in the church and would turn away from her beliefs. The imposition of these ideas was ironic according to Michelle, since she was subjected to verbal assaults and implied threats of coercion in a way she had never experienced while in the Unification Church.

Despite the overt oppression she was exposed to, there were limits on the demands made on Michelle. Staff at the center accepted her refusal to give the names of her church associates, and they did not use physical force to keep her and others at the center, as far as she could see. But she did think they would pursue her if she tried to escape. As in the charismatic groups themselves, the line between voluntary compliance and coercion was not always clear. In any case, Michelle reported that after a month at the center, she was asked to speak with a reporter writing about the deprogramming practices there and told him that she wanted to reestablish contact with the Unification Church. According to Michelle, he helped her by providing her with an excuse to leave the compound, and she successfully escaped.

In a series of interviews, Michelle revealed a modest psychological residue from the deprogramming experience. She initially spoke of the great fears she had experienced when she was first abducted, but acknowledged that she was generally comfortable while at the deprogramming center. On returning to the church, she was tense and had trouble sleeping at first but then attended a two-day workshop that apparently constituted the sect's attempt to "re-program" her. She spent a lot of time preparing the defense for her conservatorship hearing. Michelle stayed in the company of church members at all times and insisted that she had no qualms about remaining affiliated with the church. She seemed to be stabilized by these activities and by the close support she received. When I met with her, however, she still felt uneasy about her own safety and was anxious sometimes while alone at night.

As a victim of forced departure tactics, Michelle had been dragged across the boundary of a sect's social system and was then able to return. This provoked strong feelings and perhaps distorted perceptions. So it is wise to refrain from drawing definite conclusions about Michelle's experience during the five weeks she was held for deprogramming. For instance, she may have been more swayed by her captors for a time than she could admit to herself after she returned to the sect. Nonetheless, based on my own psychiatric evaluation and on independent psychological testing, she was clearly mentally competent at the time of the interviews and capable of deciding for herself whether to stay in the sect or leave. She seemed a calm, deliberate, and thoughtful young woman.

Reasons for exercising caution in drawing conclusions about events at the border of a charismatic group become more evident in the case of Kim, a relatively unstable young woman of twenty-one who was removed from the Unification Church by her parents. Details of what happened to her were obtained from multiple sources, including the young woman herself, her family and, later, from an active member of the Unification Church. It became clear that none of these sources could have independently provided a full and coherent reconstruction of what had taken place.

For four months, Kim attended workshops and social activities of the Unification Church on an intermittent basis, while living with her parents. During this time, she had led her parents to believe that she was involved with a mainstream Protestant sect, and only after she moved into a Unification Church residence did they become aware that she had entered a cult-like group. After two months of uncertainty and distress, Kim's parents contacted Dennis, a young man who had been in the church for several months the year before and was removed by his parents. With some advice from him, they planned to take their daughter back and sequester her at home. They hoped she could be persuaded to abandon the church with assistance from both Dennis and Kim's recently estranged boyfriend.

The father now managed to get a phone call through to Kim at the church residence and convinced her to meet him outside the building, whereupon he, along with her mother and boyfriend, urged her to come into their car for a moment and then sped away with her. Kim spent the next week at home. She later told me she had not wanted to stay, but was also reluctant to resist the demands of her parents, whom she still cared for. Dennis, the family's youthful consultant, came to visit her for an hour every day or two. Kim was hesitant to speak with him, but they did discuss her views on the church as he tried to point out to her its pernicious influence.

After several days, Kim told her parents of nightmares in which church members, in the form of ghost-like figures, came to menace her. She also began to fear abduction by church members in roving vans when she went out for short walks with her parents, but could give no examples of such abductions having been carried out on other ex-members when I later asked her about this. She was unable to fall asleep unless in the company of one of her parents or her former boyfriend. When her parents were no longer able to leave Kim alone at night at all, they contacted me for a consultation. I explained that I could address her symptoms but was not prepared to pressure her into staying out of the church.

Kim was quite defensive when I spoke with her, and did not want to discuss in any depth her feelings about being a church member or leaving. Although she expressed anxiety over her nightmares, she discussed them only briefly. She was probably fearful that an extensive examination of her conflicts would threaten her fragile adjustment. A week later, Kim began to go out for an hour or two a day with her boyfriend. She was now able to fall asleep without someone nearby and complained less of nightmares. She also expressed a desire to stay out of the church but was still unwilling to examine her feelings about the entire affair.

Kim appeared to be a histrionic and rather dependent young woman who had entered the church in part because she did not want to continue living with her parents and working in the family business, but had trepidation about an independent existence. Also important was her rocky relationship with her boyfriend. The sect provided an alternative object for her dependency needs and a way of coping with her disinclination to set out on her own. She showed no evidence of disordered thinking and had no prior history of paranoia, so her fears of abduction were probably no more than a situational reaction.

After she was spirited away from the church, Kim became involved with her parents again and regressed to the point of needing someone by her side at night for fear of nightmares. But her emotional state was improving. A month after my contact with the family, Kim's mother called to say that her daughter had been on the phone with people she feared were acquaintances from the Unification Church. By now, Kim was spending a good deal of time by herself and was supposed to be looking for full-time work, but she displayed little interest in that, exacerbating her mother's concerns about what might happen to her over the long term.

A month after her mother's call, Kim left the family's apartment one morning and did not return. Her parents notified the police who issued a missing persons bulletin. I tried to reassure the parents that Kim was no doubt physically safe, but must have found her way back to her friends in the church. Since her parents had no idea how they might reach her, they were understandably frightened. The police contacted me and, at the parents' request, I gave them a description of Kim's psychological state.

Two weeks later Kim's parents received a call from the police in a nearby city informing them that their daughter had appeared in a stationhouse saying that she had no money and wanted to return home. They had put her on a bus and expected her to arrive home shortly. When Kim did arrive, she explained that she had been kidnapped by a church member driving a van and had been held by the sect for the last two weeks until she was able to escape. The story did not ring true since no such abductions had been reported before, and any action of this kind could have serious grave legal consequences for the sect. I suggested to her parents that they support her apparent desire to leave the church.

The parents themselves placed little stock in their daughter's tale of abduction, but since they were willing to accept Kim on any terms, they went along with what she said. Dennis, the ex-member, on the other hand, began to press the family to secure the services of a private investigator to look into the supposed abduction, and was soon drawing Kim into a project of retribution against her "kidnappers." The parents now became worried that Dennis was a destablizing force who would only encourage her to persist in the confabulated tale. Increasingly, they saw him as an irritant and finally told him that his assistance was no longer welcome.

I did not meet with Kim again until several months after her reappearance, although her parents spoke with me intermittently. She now seemed committed to staying with her family and had returned to her situation before joining the church by involving herself once again in the family business and resuming the relationship with her boyfriend. She was still reluctant to give details about the period during which she had disappeared, but did not depart from her original story.

As common with events occurring at the boundary of a charismatic group, several questions remain unanswered. Had Kim indeed returned voluntarily to the church after being at home for three months? If so, how long had she been harboring plans for this during her stay at home? Was she lying intentionally about this, or could her behavior be attributed to an unconsciously mediated denial of reality? Some time later I found that a Unification Church member whom I knew well also knew Kim. He told me that she had returned willingly to the church from her parents' house and, with her agreement, was then brought to a center for the management of disturbed members in another city. Within two weeks, however, she began to express misgivings about remaining with the group and vanished from where she was staying, much as she had left her family two weeks before.

Kim's experience is a variation in the theme of conflict for individuals torn between a charismatic sect and a close-knit family. Often such conflicts cannot be resolved smoothly, and the troubled person is compelled to create a credible enough tale to repress the conflicting motives. Like others who cannot reconcile their divided feelings, many who leave the church come to believe their own stories and cling to them because they provide respite from unmanageable conflict.

A *Study of the Departed Members*

It is difficult to obtain objective observations on the psychiatric status of ex-members, given the heavily biased information provided by participants, especially while they are still enmeshed in the immediate circumstances of the departure. In an attempt to arrive at a balanced view of the dropout phenomenon, I sent structured questionnaires to those who had left the Unification Church some time before.

There were two sources for this study: the follow-up on the Moonies who had been engaged and married and a separate survey of dropouts contacted after they had left the church. Both groups provided valuable insights.

The engaged members were followed up after three years, one year after they were to be married. Of this sizable number (314), three subgroups are relevant here. The first consists of engaged members who *had left the church* by the time of the follow-up study (14). The initial questionnaire allowed me to examine what their attitudes had been three years before. On measures of psychological well-being, affiliativeness toward the church, and satisfaction with their fiancés, they had not differed from other members at that time.[43] When they completed the first questionnaire, these members had indicated no dissatisfaction with the church that would have predicted their eventual flight.[44]

A second subgroup (9 persons) *were considering leaving the church at the time of the first survey* and in contrast had shown significant psychological distress then. Surprisingly, only one of them actually dropped out in the subsequent three years, and the scores of the rest were not different at follow up from those of the other respondents with regard to either psychological well-being or affiliative feelings toward the membership. Clearly, the desire to leave can be transient, albeit accompanied by considerable distress.

A third subgroup of respondents (14) indicated *at the time of the follow up* that they were thinking of leaving the church. None of them had expressed this inclination three years before. These members now had much lower affiliative feelings toward the church and diminished psychological well-being relative to the balance of the group.

In light of these findings, little relationship seems to exist between a member's actual dissatisfaction at a random point and the person's eventual departure from the sect. Members who contemplate departure at a given time are clearly depressed, probably at the thought of severing ties with the church and reestablishing a new identity. In the end, however, few actually leave. Apparently, certain relatively acute circumstances lead persons to leave these groups, ones not necessarily evident a considerable time beforehand. The expression of a strong inclination to leave is likely measured in weeks, or months at most, rather than years.

The unreliability in predicting possible dropouts in this population prompted me to study dropouts who had clearly committed themselves to leaving. My previous work with Unification Church members offered the chance to make contact with several people in different parts of the country who for varying reasons had chosen to leave the sect. Eight former members agreed to cooperate as a project team for the study, largely out of a desire to assure that both the public and they themselves get a clear picture of the consequences of departure. Many felt that everyone who had ever joined the Moonies was viewed in a stereotypical way, as if permanently altered by the experience.

This core group gave me lists of all the ex-members whose locations they knew. Altogether, the project team contacted sixty persons, and all but two agreed to take part in the study, yielding a sample of sixty-six who lived in twenty-one different states. All answered a structured questionnaire anonymously and sent their responses to me for computer coding. These participants had left the church after an average of four years and were evenly divided among men and women. Their average age was twenty-nine, almost all were white (96%), and half were college graduates.

On the whole, they had adapted well in their respective communities according to standard measures of social adjustment. For example, only three had been married before leaving the church, but most (52%) were married now, and none was living with parents or relatives. In addition, the large majority (79%) were either full-time students or engaged in salaried work. Only a few members (6%), all of them married women, were not employed at all. Furthermore, their level of emotional adjustment appeared to be good. The general well-being scores for this group were no different from those of the general population.

Nonetheless, the experience of departure was difficult. Over a third of the respondents (36%) reported that they had experienced "serious emotional problems" after leaving. An appreciable number (24%) had "sought out professional help" for these problems and two had been hospitalized.[45]

Comparisons could be drawn with the responses of active members to determine what changes had come about in the dropouts' psychological adjustment and views on the church. Although some years had passed since respondents had left the church, they still indicated a surprising degree of positive feelings toward the members who had *not* dropped out. Thus, the majority (62%) still "cared strongly" for "the ten members they knew best," a figure not so different from the portion (89%) of active members who had answered the same way in our previous survey. These affiliative feelings were not necessarily confined to the persons they knew best in the sect. A small but notable portion of the respondents (20%) indicated that they still "cared strongly" for "all church members the world over," compared with 38% of active members who had answered this way.

The religious beliefs that persisted among the dropouts were also similar to those of active members. Thus, a large portion of ex-members maintained that they still strongly felt "a close connection with God" (40%), albeit less than the portion of active members who felt the same way (76%), and almost half the ex-members (41%) still avowed a strong acceptance of specific church tenets such as, "The kingdom of Heaven can be established on earth if all other people fulfill God's desire for man."

A large majority of the ex-members agreed either moderately or strongly that they "got some positive things" out of membership (89%). Yet this sign of a relatively benign disposition toward the church was balanced by the response of a majority (53%) who felt that "current members should leave the Unification Church."

In examining these findings further, a telling distinction emerged. Differences in perceptions of the church rested in large part on the way members had left the group: those who had been coerced expressed a much more negative view toward the church. To learn more about the role of coercion in relation to members' attitudes, I arranged to have the project team designate which respondents had been deprogrammed, based on their knowledge of each one. Ten of the sixty-six dropouts were identified, and the deprogramming was corroborated by their own reports.[46]

The deprogrammed former members showed a greater alienation from the church, scoring lower on loyalty toward the members they knew best and on their relative acceptance of church creed.[47] Significantly, all eight respondents who later participated in deprogramming other church members had themselves been deprogrammed. Thus the process did have a lasting effect in sustaining animosity toward the sect.[48] This latter finding was most revealing, because it showed how influential boundary phenomena are in generating aggression between a cult and the general society. The battle for a member's allegiance may come to represent the group's survival to both those inside and those outside. This applies not only to continuing efforts at deprogramming, but also to the protective response to any assault on the group. We have seen the profound consequences of this with Jonestown and MOVE.

9

CHARISMATIC
HEALING GROUPS
THE AA EXAMPLE

A contemporary charismatic healing group such as Alcoholics Anonymous provides a model of an effective, inexpensive social instrument that can be used to treat certain psychological problems, and the operation of this group can be understood by comparing it with charismatic religious sects. Members of AA healing groups are highly cohesive; they maintain a system of shared beliefs and their behavior is strongly influenced by the group. Despite these points of similarity to religious sects, however, important differences emerge. For example, the behavioral demands of such a healing group relate only to the recovery from illness, not to unrelated aspects of their members' lives such as the occupation they should pursue or how they should manage their family relations. Religious sects generally have a universalist philosophy and a code of behavior touching on all aspects of the lives of their adherents.

The two types of groups also differ in the target of their efforts. The healing group directs its emphasis primarily at change in its own members, while the religious groups promote an ideology ostensibly intended to transform the world. Insofar as AA does not impinge on the values of the broader society, it is less likely than religious sects to generate conflicts at its boundary. Indeed, its ideology is compatible with mainstream attitudes and often gets support and encouragement from nonmembers.

Alcoholics Anonymous (AA), founded in 1935, is an excellent illustration of how a charismatic healing group can develop from its origins in intense personal leadership through to its establishment as a stable, albeit zealous, institution. Although AA is now a worldwide organization with over one million members and a stable administrative structure, new recruits still

176

recapitulate the zealous experience of its founder in some fashion as they become engaged into the group. We will consider the evolution of AA in three stages, each with counterparts in the development of other charismatic groups whose success has allowed them to follow a path of maturation—using a model originally developed by Max Weber.[1]

The Charismatic Gift of Alcoholics Anonymous

Alcoholics Anonymous had its origin in the transcendent religious experience of its principal founder, Bill W., whose tale, like those of so many other leaders of charismatic groups, was one of protracted distress—in this case from alcoholism. He is referred to by his first name only, in accordance with the AA tradition of anonymity, but his history is well known.[2] He was born in East Dorset, Vermont, in 1895, into a middle-class family. Bill began studies in electrical engineering while in reserve officer training in college, but also began drinking heavily. He recalled later that he used liquor to override the inhibitions he felt in dealing with people, particularly his "social betters." By the time of the Great Depression, Bill was drinking gin around the clock, while living off his wife's meager income.

In the course of Bill's deterioration, an old drinking friend named Ebby came by to visit him, and described his own experience in the Oxford Group, a zealous religious sect. Ebby averred that his involvement in this sect allowed him to overcome his problem with alcohol and achieve sobriety. Meetings of the Oxford Group were characterized by open confessions and guidance from the members in the assembled group.

At the time of this encounter, Bill's situation was grave—he had been hospitalized for detoxification four times during the past year. Wearied and shaken by his drinking, he was struck by his friend's good grooming and attractive appearance and by the influence that might be exerted when one alcoholic shared with another his own struggles to control his drinking. Not long after he had a revelatory experience.

> All at once I found myself crying out, "If there is a God, let Him show himself! I am ready to do anything, anything!"
>
> Suddenly the room lit up with a great white light. I was caught up on an ecstasy which there are no words to describe. It seemed to me in my mind's eye, that I was on a mountain and that a wind not of air but of spirit was blowing. And then it burst upon me that I was a free man. Slowly the ecstasy subsided. I lay there on the bed, but now for a time I was in another world, a new world of consciousness . . . and I thought to myself, "So this is the God of the preachers!" A great peace stole over me.[3]

The very intensity of this transcendent experience made the episode a turning point in his achieving sobriety and Bill began preaching to alcoholics at the hospital where he had been admitted many times.

But this in itself had little impact. So, influenced by the Oxford group, he established a network of mutual aid and discovered the effectiveness of social support when there is a commitment to a common goal. By 1937 Bill and a co-founder could count forty alcoholics with whom they had struggled, who had themselves experienced the intensity of spiritual recovery and its attendant abstinence.[4] Within two more years their group had grown to one hundred, and they published the book *Alcoholics Anonymous,* which was to become the movement's bible. From the start, AA displayed characteristics of a charismatic sect: strongly felt shared belief, intense cohesiveness, experiences of altered consciousness, and a potent influence on members' behavior. New adherents also pursued an apostolic mission of converting despairing alcoholics, imbued with the charistmatic zeal and proselytizing urge of its founder Bill W.

The Routinization of Charisma

The sociologist Max Weber defined the role of the charismatic leader in terms of the ability to galvanize people into pursuing a transcendent mission, but he pointed out that such a leader could only be successful in the long run if he created a structured social order and an attendant body of tradition. Alcoholics Anonymous has indeed evolved from the zealous ideal of its founder into an effectively managed organization. By the time of its fiftieth anniversary in 1985 it had 58,576 chapters in over ninety countries with more than one million members.[5] Harrison Trice,[6] who has closely followed AA's evolution, suggested that its expansion illustrates the manner in which it conforms to Weber's conception of the routinization of charisma. Through historical study, Weber observed that the powers of a charismatic leader persist as they become invested in a successors' organizational roles and the ritual trappings of their movement.

THE DEVELOPMENT OF RITUAL

The transcendent mission of a routinized charismatic group is expressed in its rites and rituals. Using these behavioral prescriptions, the group establishes standards of how its members should conduct themselves in their own lives and in their joint activities, in conformity with the group's mission. Although few rites and rituals are rigidly defined by AA, members across the globe adhere carefully and zealously to the ones that are.

As in the Oxford Group, AA meetings exhibited from the outset ritualized open confessions of prior transgressions and the acceptance of a "Higher Power" for guidance. Of the Twelve Steps of Alcoholics Anonymous, ten are based on the creed of the Oxford Group. The other two, the open acknowledgment of helplessness before alcohol and carrying the message to other alcoholics, are unique to AA.

A central ritual in membership is the regular attendance of AA chapter meetings. Inductees are expected to come to "ninety meetings in ninety days" when they first join, so as to bolster their abstinence and commitment to the group and after this they attend meetings at least once or twice a week, often daily. The meetings vary in format only slightly in different chapters, and their rites are therefore immediately recognizeable in settings separated by thousands of miles. For example, all who speak at a meeting begin by saying "My name is ____, and I am an alcoholic," symbolizing their rejection of the denial of their illness typical of alcoholics. Such well-known sayings as "One day at a time" and "Easy does it," drawn from the writings of Bill W., are part of the verbal exchanges. They appear on posters and signs at meetings, and are even popular as bumper stickers. This ritualized use of language binds people together and reinforces the conformity requisite to committed membership. It represents an acceptance of myth-building and the "loading" of language with the group's own connotations.[7]

Specific meetings are also given their own ritualized meaning, such as those celebrating members' achieving ninety days and then a year of sobriety. On these occasions, the celebrants relate the story of their alcoholism and recovery to date. Each typically portrays the descent into alcoholism, his or her abject state during that period, and eventual transformation by means of engagement with Alcoholics Anonymous. The litany of sin and redemption by each speaker, heard in different variations many times over, is compelling for the sincerity and weight of personal testimony. Even the casual observer cannot help being swept up by the intense commitment of the speakers. One patient whom I referred to an AA meeting was skeptical before going but returned enthusiastic.

> I can't tell you how remarkable it was. I sat quietly in back, almost hiding from anyone who would acknowledge my presence, but each speaker drew me in. There was a magnetism and passion in their tales, and I felt moved by them as people who had just then become important to me. It was personal in a way I never expected.

As in most charismatic groups, the pursuit of new members is an important component of ritual. It supports members' commitment by underlining the credibility of the movement, since the testimony of new members provides further validation of the group's ideals. The mutual assistance inherent in the induction process also helps established members sustain their sobriety, as they themselves identify with the struggle of new members to overcome the denial of their illness and withstand their craving for alcohol.

Emphasis on induction has been an essential theme running through the group's evolution. It was a central aspect of Bill W.'s charismatic mission, from the time he began to preach to hospitalized alcoholics. His subsequent work with Dr. Bob, the next convert to Bill's emerging model, was prototypical of the later ritual of "Twelfth-Step" recruitment activities carried out between a member and a new recruit. This role has been transmitted in an apostolic manner to subsequent generations of members; all inductees are expected to establish a formalized relationship with a long-term member who can serve as their sponsor in the arduous process of recovery.

The sponsorship ritual illustrates the value of the formalized induction format within the charismatic group, as the fledgling member chooses a mentor from longstanding members. The relationship is a rather demanding one for both parties, and entails daily confessional communications from inductee to sponsor for many months. Members are thus introduced to many of the group's practices, such as the Twelve Steps, and engaged in a continuing dependency. These roles have their counterparts in most other routinized charismatic groups, such as the central figures of the Unification Church.

One study of the exchanges between sponsors and inductees revealed the evolving relationship between the two.[8] As the recruits' length of sobriety increased, a shift occurred away from morale building and specific instructions for achieving abstinence toward personal change and spiritual growth. As in other charismatic movements, the new member first picks up the rudiments of conformity and later moves on to a deeper restructuring of psychological adaptation.

The sponsorship ritual is important to the sobriety of the sponsor who derives strength from providing advice and serving as a model. One study of a sample of AA members revealed that a majority (66%) of those who successfully achieved abstinence had served as sponsors, while only a minority (19%) of unsuccessful members had played this role.[9]

As in all other charismatic groups, involvement in newfound rituals creates conflict in the member's preexisting relationships, since major changes in commitment and lifestyle do not come without a disruptive effect. The nature of induction to AA and the conflicts it may raise can be seen in a patient I treated for alcoholism and referred to AA. Harry consulted me because of increasing difficulties at work. As an executive in a large corporation he was under the scrutiny of his superiors because of several episodes of intoxication on the job, particularly while on business trips. When he and I reached an understanding that his problems were caused by alcoholism, we agreed that his treatment plan would include attending Alcoholics Anonymous and taking disulfiram (Antabuse), a medication that deters the alcoholic from drinking since it precipitates physical discomfort when alcohol is consumed.

Harry did well at first, but his commitment to AA was modest and on two business trips he skipped his disulfiram and drank immoderately. With my encouragement, he sought out a sponsor and began speaking with him each day. Despite reservations, Harry became increasingly involved with his sponsor and started to attend meetings on a daily basis. His "conversion," as it were, became evident in one of our psychotherapy sessions when I asked him how he felt about some problems he had been having at work. He responded with a look of calm determination that "I know now that everything will be all right as long as I follow the program because the alcoholic in me isn't speaking any more. I take it one day at a time." The program was *the* program, AA, and "one day at a time" was one of its unmistakable catch phrases.

Harry and his fellowship had connected. He decided to follow the AA regimen and maintain sobriety, and continued to use AA catchwords and interpret many of his problems in terms of AA rhetoric. Actually, the language of AA served him reasonably well in expressing himself in therapy and probably in daily life.

Harry's strong bond to AA caused two problems in his ongoing relationships. His wife did not have the same enthusiasm for the fellowship, and his frequent absences from home while he attended meetings made her feel isolated and resentful. Despite Harry's attempts to convince her to attend Al-Anon, AA's counterpart organization for family members, she was uninterested in this group. As with members of charismatic religious groups, he had trouble empathizing with the reservations of a reluctant family member. Indeed, like those groups, AA instructs its members to cut off a spouse, sibling, or parent if they jeopardize one's commitment to the goals of membership. Harry was applying a ritualized AA solution to a family problem: send the spouse to Al-Anon. But it wasn't working.

Another conflict arose over Harry's taking disulfiram. Like many AA members, his sponsor was opposed to all psychiatric medications, viewing them as "crutches" whose use detracted from a full recovery through AA. Like other zealous groups, AA tends to see the world in black and white and sometimes eschews professional and scientific thinking alien to its ideology.

Both of Harry's conflicts demanded resolution. I met with him and his wife several times to aid her adjustment to his commitment to AA and help them work out some issues in their relationship. With Harry himself, I dealt only gingerly with the issue of disulfiram and AA, not wishing to come into direct conflict with the group. After a while, Harry saw less of his sponsor and continued taking the disulfiram in large part because he had chosen to avoid a conflict with me. But his commitment to AA remained strong. When discussing his problems in organizing a division of the corporation where he worked, he commented about a competitor at work:

> I was going to get into a grand confrontation with Carter but you can't afford resentments if you're an alcoholic [an AA catch phrase]. I thought of Bill W. and of his setting up the General Service Board to succeed him. If he could work that miracle, I could certainly handle this problem of mine without a battle.

Harry was integrating the amorphous philosophy of the group as well as the experiences of its founder into his everyday life.

THE DEVELOPMENT OF WRITTEN AND ORAL TRADITIONS

A second component of the routinization of charisma is the emergence of traditions in which the sanctity ascribed to the original leader and the group is invested in fixed codes of behavior. The Twelve Steps, a written tradition, have a hallowed position in AA literature and are repeatedly reviewed and studied by members as they become more deeply involved in the movement; they are the group's Ten Commandments. Much of the success of AA is attributable to how the Steps deal specifically with alcoholism and do not form a general code for behavior. They are therefore applicable to diverse segments of society with very different lifestyles. Their narrow focus also serves to undercut the abuse of members for financial or personal gain, and minimizes the fears of new recruits that their lifestyles will be materially compromised by membership.

Consider the role of the first three Steps in supporting an abstinent lifestyle.

1. We admitted we were powerless over alcohol—that our lives had become unmanageable.
2. Came to believe that a Power greater than ourselves could restore us to sanity.
3. Made a Decision to turn our will and our lives over to the care of God, *as we understood Him.*[10]

In the Fourth Step, initiates are asked to undertake a protracted confession that, in Lifton's terms, acts to heighten their self-surrender.[11] In AA this is called a "fearless moral inventory," in which the member reviews individual failings and attempts to make amends. One other vital tradition, that of prosyletizing, is embodied in the Twelfth and final Step, in the words, "We tried to carry the message to alcoholics." The Twelve Steps therefore serve as written guidelines for the personal conduct of members themselves.

THE ESTABLISHMENT OF AN ADMINISTRATIVE STRUCTURE

For a social system to sustain itself over time, it must have an internal organization that creates new initiatives, keeps order, and resolves everyday conflicts. Thus, a final component of the routinization of charisma is the development of an administrative apparatus to assure that the leadership functions are carried out over time. Here too Bill W. may be credited for having passed on his mantle of inspired leadership to a stable and effective organization, and the success of this accomplishment alone may well warrant the praise that Aldous Huxley gave him as "the greatest social architect of the century."[12] The well-organized but democratic hierarchy of AA bears his influence. While tradition is preserved by this organization, numerous devices prevent an ossification of leadership ranks and allow for the lively expression of the group's original charismatic mission.

Consider the ritual of sponsorship, the first rung in the group's leadership ladder. A sponsor is chosen by each new recruit and is then responsible for inculcating the new member in the lore of AA and helping the person follow through on the Twelve Steps. Because the choice of sponsor is essentially a free one, the institution prevents rigidity in this important managerial stratum.

At the next level of administration, in the chapters, formal and informal discussions define the proper relationships between members, and deliberations among chapter officers provide governance over local administrative issues. Chapters elect their officers at meetings open to all members and conduct their business by parliamentary procedure.

The Twelve Traditions define norms for behavior at higher administrative levels in a way that assures both the preservation of the group's charismatic role and the disavowal of personal gain or profit. They stipulate that members "need always maintain personal anonymity at the level of press, radio and films," thereby preventing the use of the affiliation for personal gain. They state further that "each group has but one primary purpose—to carry its message to the alcoholic who still suffers. . . . The name of AA ought never be drawn into public controversy," thereby preventing the development of offshoot causes and enterprises that could vitiate the group's function. Feminist issues, for example, have attracted considerable attention among AA members in recent years, but they did not become established as institutional prerogatives because of this constraint.

In her study of utopian communities, Rosabeth Kanter observed that those communes that achieved stability for the long term had succeeded in dispersing charisma throughout the corporate group.[13] The establishment of the General Service Board of Alcoholics Anonymous, which Bill W. had designated as the permanent successor to the fellowship's founders, made this possible for AA too. Operating through an annual General Services conference attended by elected delegates from ninety-one geographic areas, the Board promulgates guidelines on issues of concern or controversy.

One further characteristic of the group's administrative function is dictated by the Traditions' injunction against accruing assets and power within the organization. Members pay no dues, but instead make small contributions of no more than a few dollars at each meeting. Even at the national level, large donations are not accepted, and no contributions at all are accepted from nonalcoholics. The fellowship's central offices are manned by a volunteer staff. The wisdom of this policy becomes apparent when comparisons are made to other charismatic groups in which leaders have been able to take advantage of members for their own financial advantage.

The Fully Evolved Healing Group

Alcoholics Anonymous is a good example of an institutionalized charismatic group with a narrowly defined goal. To learn more about such well-delineated groups, we will consider first AA's strengths and weaknesses, and then look at how some related groups, offshoots of AA, have fared. A comparison between certain aspects of AA and charismatic religious groups will highlight how the format of the charismatic group may be adapted to specific focal goals.

AA's Success in the Community

In a careful review of studies on the outcome of AA participation, Chad Emrick and his associates concluded that drinking problems abated in about two-thirds of AA members during their period of participation; they consumed either less alcohol or none at all.[14] Almost half of those who improved remained abstinent for a year. On the whole, AA proved superior to professional treatment in helping alcoholics maintain total abstinence, although organized professional care without AA membership was somewhat more effective than AA in helping alcoholics to reduce their drinking without total abstinence. AA therefore compares very favorably in outcome with more elaborate and costly professional management for those who turn to it for aid.

How did AA achieve success when there was little public appreciation of the needs of the alcoholic? In answering this question, we must examine the social context in which AA arose and then its psychology as a charismatic group. As a social movement, AA had a considerable advantage in gaining acceptance. Unlike the charismatic religious sects, no changes of the broader society were necessary to achieve its goals. Cooperation was expected only from its own participants, and they themselves were forewarned that they should anticipate little help from those close to them. The family and friends of AA recruits usually were pleased to be relieved of their burdens of so many years now that these alcoholics were attempting to help each other.

Response to AA in the press was quite positive too: reports heralding its success appeared soon after its inception. One early article in the Cleveland *Plain Dealer,* for example, led to a growth in the membership of its local chapter from fifty to three hundred in only twelve weeks. Another in the *Saturday Evening Post* brought 6,000 letters of inquiry from readers who wanted help.[15]

Alcoholics Anonymous also succeeded in developing a good working relationship with the medical community. Many hospitals now host AA chapter meetings, and AA inter-group offices maintain working relations with detoxification centers, thereby assuring ready access to medical care for both new recruits and relapsed members. In fact, few if any medical facilities designated for alcoholism treatment in the United States today do not have on-site meetings integrated into their programs. Furthermore, the American Medical Society on Alcoholism and Other Drug Dependencies, the principal medical organization in this field, actively supports AA as a primary form of treatment. Indeed, the Society counts among its members a good number of recovering alcoholic physicians who recovered through AA. When it is successful, the battle that AA fights against an inner opponent, the craving to drink, enhances the beliefs of new members and draws them into close ties with their fellow members, strengthening their commitment to the group and its mission. AA members are very much bound together by their struggle against a common enemy.

AA Psychology

The psychology of AA as a charismatic group is of course central to its success. Alcoholics are most likely to turn to AA when they have "bottomed out," or reached a nadir of despair, which opens them to alternatives. In this they resemble recruits to religious sects, who tend to be distressed as well as alienated from those closest to them at the time of their induction.[16]

Recruitment into AA occurs in a psychological context that allows communication to be closely controlled, so as to assure that the group's ideology will be sustained in the face of uncommitted active drinkers. As in the Unification Church workshops, most of those attending AA chapter meetings are deeply involved in the group ethos, and the expression of views opposed to the group's model of treatment is subtly or expressly discouraged. A good example is the fellowship's response to the concept of controlled drinking, an approach to alcholism treatment based on limiting alcohol intake rather than totally abstaining. Some investigators and clinicians have reported success with this alternative to treatment.[17] The approach, however, is unacceptable within the AA tradition, and the option is therefore anathema to active members. It is rarely brought up by speakers at meetings and suppressed when it is raised. As an inductee becomes involved in the group, the sponsor monitors the person's views carefully, assuring that the recruit adheres to the perspective into which the sponsor was drawn; any hint of an interest in controlled drinking is discouraged. Similar constraints would be applied if a recruit questioned the importance of any of the Steps or the need to attend meetings regularly.

The issue here is not the relative merit of controlled drinking: in the United States it is not a viable treatment approach for the large majority of alcohol-dependent people. Rather, it is the way communications are managed in AA. As a charismatic group, AA is able to suppress attitudes that could undermine its traditions. Indeed, deviance from the abstinence norm is regarded as a serious "slip." As David Rudy points out, by rigidly defining the limits of acceptable behavior, the group strengthens and reaffirms its own boundaries.[18]

AA generates an intense personal involvement in the group, one comparable to the members' previous dependency on alcohol, and thus provides them with "an alternative dependency." Over 80% of members invite fellow members to their homes, outside the meeting format.[19] In his studies of the life histories of alcoholics, George Vaillant has found that recovery from alcoholism most commonly happens when an alternative dependency is substituted.[20]

The emotional impact of this dependency on AA is apparent in the experience of many members whose equanimity is closely tied to their stable relationship to the group. One of my patients, a successful lawyer who regularly attended AA meetings, spoke of his irritability in dealing with his wife and partners after returning from a long business trip.

> Missing meetings while I was away was a big problem. I didn't get to one
> for five days last week and I just couldn't take to that old "button-pushing."
> I kept barking at Jennie and was unpleasant at work. I knew something
> was unsteady inside of me that was making me more irritable at every turn.
> But getting back to a meeting made me feel like my old self again. I'll have
> to make a meeting every day on the next trip.

Charismatic groups tend to divide the world into the good within their groups and the evil lodged in their enemies. AA also relies on this psychological defense of projecting outside themselves the evil that members fear from within. It personifies unacceptable evil in the form of alcohol itself and the alcoholic disease process. This breeds the typical Manichaean outlook in which the world is divided into good and evil. It leads members to avoid all persons who may again entrap them in drinking and affiliate even more strongly with others in the fellowship. As Margaret Bean points out,[21] the initiate is usually encouraged to give up social contacts outside AA, for the express reason that the person is endangered by these people, since they are the ones amongst whom he or she fell prey to alcoholism in the first place. This strategy works well in promoting the alcoholic's recovery at the cost of some friendships.

For a few potential members, AA's appeal is limited by its sectarianism, recently reflected in more elaborated dogma.[22] Agnostics and atheists may react aversely to chapter meetings, which are often begun with the Lord's Prayer and may dwell on the idea of a Higher Power. In Eastern cultures, the Christian orientation of the group also presents problems for recruitment. On a visit to Thailand I found that attempts to establish AA chapters had met with success among Western-born Christians, but were poorly received by the Buddhist majority. More acceptable variants have emerged in Japan.[23]

Another point of doctrinal rigidity that can cause recruitment problems is controlled drinking. Because of its origins as a charismatic group, AA relies on received knowledge rather than experimental research. While experiments with controlled drinking have raised interest among some American social and medical scientists, they have been rejected by AA. This is not unlike battles over dogma that charismatic groups have fought—and in this case won: in the United States today, AA has set the tone for treatment across the country.

The possibility of being co-opted by other institutions within the treatment mainstream also makes AA vulnerable. Many AA members have become therapists in hospital-based rehabilitation programs for alcoholism and their commitments to the AA approach have softened. Increasingly, new AA members are being referred from professional settings; over a third of new members now come from institutional rehabilitation programs.[24] In time, AA may be seen by its members as one option among many, rather than as the definitive vehicle for their rehabilitation. Indeed, over 40% of one recent sample of AA members turned to professional help *after* joining, and most reported that such help played an "important part" in their recovery.[25]

There is a lesson is this; the fellowship struggled for years to have alcoholism find its place in the mainstream, and AA's relative influence might now decline because of its own success. Charismatic groups sometimes retain their integrity better when persecuted than when embraced by the broader society. The charismatic group may succeed on a broader scale, however, when its message becomes part of the cultural mainstream.

In conclusion, we find that AA serves as a good example of a fully evolved charismatic healing movement. Its strengths are drawn from the psychology of the charismatic group: in its proselytizing, its control over members' communications, and its Manichaean outlook. At the same time, it has the vulnerabilities of charismatic groups, and is subject to the dissipation of its founders' zeal as it achieves organizational success.

AA Offshoots and Synanon

Self-help movements vary considerably in their structure and format. Some collaborate closely with institutional caregivers, while others stand apart, making little contact with established organizations or professionals. I have studied three zealous, cohesive groups oriented toward healing in some detail. One, the Federation of Parents for Drug-Free Youth, is a national anti-drug movement that draws on parents' concern for their children's welfare.[26] The other is Recovery, a long-established self-help movement for the psychiatrically disabled.[27] And the third is a self-help program for alcoholism developed in my own hospital, closely integrated into hospital-based institutional treatment.[28] While each offers a useful perspective on the adaptability of certain aspects of the charismatic group, it will be most instructive to focus on groups that evolved most directly from AA.

Many groups have been modeled closely and successfully after AA. Over a dozen "Anonymous" groups draw specifically on the AA Twelve-Step format. These deal with issues ranging from drug dependency, like Pills Anonymous and Cocaine Anonymous, to gambling and obesity. The admission of helplessness before one's problems and the bonding together with those similarly afflicted appears to work well as a self-help formula for many compulsive behaviors.

Furthest along the scale of addictive behavior lies dependence on the opiate drugs, such as heroin and morphine. For treatment of this marginally manageable problem a more profound group commitment is required, one that can take place in a residential therapeutic community. In this setting, all aspects of a member's life become engaged in the charismatic healing program, and residence is required for many months. The residential therapeutic community is used less frequently in the treatment of heroin addiction than is methadone maintenance (opiate replacement therapy) and these communities illustrate the limitations of a charismatic healing approach. Less than a fifth of all patients under treatment for opiate addiction in one state, for example, were in therapeutic communities, while the remainder were on methadone.[29] Nonetheless, certain charismatically oriented therapeutic communities such as Phoenix House and Daytop Village have gained wide acceptance because of their thoughtful use of group therapy techniques, openness to independent follow up, and collaboration with other community agencies.

Synanon, the first of the drug-free therapeutic communities, symbolizes many of the failings of charismatic healing groups. This movement was founded in 1958 by Charles Dederich in California. A recovered alcoholic who had achieved sobriety in AA, Dederich attempted to adopt the fellowship's techniques for narcotic addicts. Principal among the changes he instituted were the shift to a residential setting and—at the outset, at least—elimination of a religious orientation. When most successful, in the early 1970s, the movement had 1,350 members, mainly in southern California. Although the majority had entered for the treatment of drug addiction or alcoholism, about a quarter had joined to address their own problems of personal adjustment.[30] Many prominent figures, from the psychologist Abraham Maslow[31] to senior federal drug officials, were impressed by the group in its earlier days.

The Synanon experience began with inductees severing all ties with outsiders for three months, after which they lived in isolated settings and worked in Synanon-operated businesses, all designed to remove them from influences in the general community that might rekindle their craving for heroin. Strict compliance with the group's practices and standards for behavior was required from the time of entry, and enforcement was carried out by intense group encounters called "games." Members spent an average of thirty hours a month in the games, which were characterized by very harsh exchanges. The games served a number of functions, some explicit and some not. Their overt purpose was to convert the addict to a new style of living. They also acted as a safety valve for the strong feelings and animosities aroused in the communal setting. On another level, as described by Richard Ofshe,[32] they assured members' compliance with all demands of the group, and thereby secured the leaders' firm control over the community.

The group soon became increasingly self-sufficient by employing its members and monitoring them closely. By the mid-1970s members were drawn by Dederich into sexually perverse acts, defectors from the group were harassed, and critics of the movement subjected to violence. An initially enthusiastic public and professional community wondered how the group had gone awry.

From the outset, Synanon fell victim to the inflated role of Charles Dederich, its charismatic leader. In contrast to Bill W., Dederich was arrogant and controlling, and in time even designated Synanon as a religion, granting himself a transcendent role far beyond that appropriate to the director of a drug treatment program. Unbridled power leads to feelings of grandiosity that may be difficult to withstand, so the outcome of this group depended on the establishment of a rational administrative structure. Unlike AA, however, Synanon did not develop a stable organization or a democratic community. Instead, power was concentrated in the hands of a single individual who proved ill fit to manage it.

Whereas AA addresses a highly circumscribed aspect of members' lives, alcohol use alone, Synanon impinged on all aspects of social adaptation. No doubt, the magnitude of the addiction being addressed by Synanon was thought to justify such controls.

Dederich separated Synanon members from the economic life of the broader community by putting them to work in light manufacturing and retail sales in small businesses owned by the group. He thereby lay the groundwork for concentrating the group's economic assets in his hands. Dederich later acknowledged in court that his own family had received $2 million of the organization's funds over a four-year period.[33] Such pecuniary gain, of course, stands in sharp contrast to the traditional limitation on the acquisition of assets with AA, and the disavowal of all personal benefits by the founder.

In time Dederich's personal role became more bizarre, as he compelled married members to change partners at his bidding.[34] His grandiosity and increasingly unstable mental state is clear in the following statement he made in one court deposition in the later years of his rule.

> I am more famous than Santa Claus. We had enormous amounts of publicity. We had all the big ones—*Life, Look,* everything but *Reader's Digest.* More people knew about me than knew about World War II, according to various surveys we made.[35]

The splitting of good and evil and the projection of evil onto outsiders was an aspect of the aggressive paranoia of this deranged leader. When an attorney brought a case against Dederich on behalf of a disenchanted ex-member, Dederich told some of his aides:

> We're not going to mess with the old time "turn the other cheek" posture. Don't mess with us—it could get you killed dead—that's our interpretation of what a religious posture should be. I want an ear in a glass of alcohol.[36]

In response to this, three members of Dederich's armed "Imperial Guard" placed a rattlesnake in the attorney's mailbox, nearly killing him. The episode resulted in Dederich's being fined $5,000 and placed on five years' probation, with an injuction against participating further in running his cultic group.[37] Clearly, an open system of governance, as established in AA, would have mitigated against such a turn of events.

Recommendations

The contrast between Synanon and Alcoholics Anonymous suggests measures that would prevent abuse of power in a charismatic healing group. In particular, it is important to avoid improper concentrations of power and stifling contact with the outside world.

1. A charismatic healing group should have a broad-based administrative structure and establish written traditions for preventing the emergence of autocratic leadership. A democratic electoral process is one option.
2. Clear limits on incursions into members' social lives should be defined to avoid their being manipulated more than necessary for their own recovery.
3. Large contributions of money and other resources should be discouraged; staff functions should be carried out by volunteers.
4. Independent sources of information and open exchanges with the society at large should not be suppressed. They serve to minimize the dangers of excessive reliance on the group's own idiosyncratic beliefs and internally generated values. They can also facilitate valuable collaboration with outside professionals.

Ironically, these very steps toward temperance can also undermine the group's charismatic zeal. Herein lies the challenge in establishing and continuing such zealous healing groups.

EPILOGUE

This book closes with a cautionary note about charismatic groups, in describing the ways they can spawn violent behavior. Aggression sometimes flows from the zeal of charismatic religious sects and domestic political movements gone awry; this combination has fueled the growth of international terrorism. Indeed, xenophobia may develop in any charismatic group, and with it a loosening of restraints on aggressive behavior. We may see only too clearly that defensiveness can become paranoia, which together can lead to violence.

Violence and Religious Sects

We have already considered how religious cults may turn to violence *against their own members* under a deranged leader. The most glaring example of this is of course the mass suicide of members of the People's Temple at Jonestown. Violence may also be directed *outward,* as in the murders committed in 1969 by Charles Manson's quasireligious cult in southern California. These eight killings, including a pregnant woman, were done in a brutal, bizarre way, with multiple stabbings and ritual positioning of the victim's remains.

Subsequent investigations revealed that Manson was able to promote these actions by a variety of devices. He was highly selective in choosing followers; only those fully compliant with his demands could stay with his small group. He also relied heavily on eliciting altered states of consciousness in his followers, regularly plying them with psychoactive drugs, LSD in particular. Outsiders were viewed as "aliens." By ascribing to himself the roles of both

191

Jesus and Satan, Manson could be seen to embody both good and evil. His cult was physically and socially isolated in the California desert, and outside information—often including clocks—was prohibited.[1] Manson's personal appeal is in large part a mystery. It is probable that cultic leaders like him become grandiose and demanding as they interact with their members. They find their vanity and inadequacies addressed by adoring followers and are shrewd enough to manipulate their flock effectively. I doubt whether they have clear-cut personality traits in common *before* they become absorbed in their roles as leaders. Indeed, charisma can arise from many sources: from the engaging charm of a psychopath, the intense commitment of an ideologue, the zeal of a desperate alcoholic, the boldness of a warrior, or the belief of the paranoid in his distorted view of the world. Each of these traits can catapult a seemingly unremarkable individual from anonymity to adulation given the right combination of circumstances.

Small, violent, autistic religious cults such as Manson's crop up unexpectedly, and in their explosive actions usually precipitate their own demise. Another that met a cataclysmic ending in Memphis, Tennessee, in 1983 was an even smaller quasi-Christian cult. Its membership consisted of six black men and their deranged leader Lindberg Sanders, who proclaimed himself the "Black Jesus." The group had come to believe that an imminent lunar eclipse would lead to an Armageddon, and they acted on this deluded shared belief that was apparently the product of Sanders' disturbed mind. A day after nearly being committed to a psychiatric hospital, Sanders and his followers barricaded themselves in a small house after taking a local policeman as hostage. There was an armed standoff with local authorities, and the hostage was brutally murdered. A police charge on the house ended with the deaths of all the cult's members.[2]

The events set in motion by Jones, Manson, and Sanders show very clearly that a leader's mental disturbance can play an important role in the emergence of violent behavior in a charismatic group. Because of the relative ease with which control can be exercised in such groups, the leader's fantasies can be translated into ritual actions that, although murderous and bizarre, make sense within the cult's delusional system.

The larger charismatic groups of the 1970s, on the other hand, were relatively free from violence. When they became rooted in the United States, they were usually run by a reasonably well-organized bureaucratic structure that served to mute the impact of their leaders' idiosyncrasies, and they were also exposed to exchanges with the general public, however distorted by mutual resentment. In addition, they had considerable visibility so that local and state authorities were fairly aggressive in scrutinizing potential areas of illegal activity and intervening when signs of violent behavior appeared.

Violence and Domestic Political Groups

Violence may also rise up in frankly political charismatic groups, but this is uncommon in the United States since political groups may come under the jurisdiction of federal laws against armed political action and violation of civil rights. Nonetheless, some outbreaks have occurred in recent years and these have attracted public attention. That they had so little impact on the tenor of national politics reflects the degree to which a stable and conservative body politic can suppress such activity. One episode took place in 1981, with an assault on a Brinks armored truck by members of the left-wing Weathermen. Four of the remaining adherents of this radical, zealous group killed two guards in an attempt to obtain money to support their continuing political activities.[3] The Weathermen had been responsible for several dozen bombings and at least five deaths in the early 1970s but had disappeared from public notice for six years. Some had still sustained a commitment to anarchy and radical socialism while in hiding. This illustrates an important characteristic of terrorist groups—their ability to retain interpersonal cohesiveness and allegiance to a political ideal during a protracted period of quiescence and then to reemerge with no less zeal. It parallels the commitment maintained by peaceable charismatic religious groups to their own precepts in the face of privation, and demonstrates the remarkable strength of this form of social organization.

Alienation is felt at both ends of the political spectrum, and terrorist political groups in the United States have arisen on the far right as well. One neo-Nazi charismatic goup, the Order, operated in the western United States in the early 1980s, practicing quasireligious rituals among its close-knit, secret membership. Like the Weathermen, its adherents carried out assaults on armored cars to obtain funds, and were also responsible for cold-blooded murder in gunning down Allen Berg, a Jewish talk show host who had provoked the sect's strong anti-Semitism. It was part of their dogma that Jews are the offspring of Satan and should therefore be killed.[4] Because of the political nature of their beliefs, and the violent acts they committed, members of the Order were pursued by federal authorities until key members were jailed.

Both the Order and the Weathermen were deeply imbued with a tradition of violence drawn from historical models: Nazism in the case of the Order, a loose amalgam of anarchism and revolutionary socialism for the Weathermen. This was central to their ideology, not simply an instrument for implementing policy. Even violent tradition can help sustain a charismatic group over time.

Violence and International Terrorism

Zealous groups that assume control over political organizations are often able to carry out large-scale systematic plans, even using the power of the state for their ends. If they capture the apparatus of the state, they gain legitimacy by institutionalizing their philosophy of government.

There is no more compelling recent example of ideologic zeal wedded to state power than the regime of the Ayatollah Khomeini. Reading about Iran in the newspapers, we have witnessed the sacrifices made by so many believers and the sharp splitting of good from evil—those within the fold and those outside. To avenge the attack on his country by Saddam Hussein of Iraq in 1980, Khomeini persisted in a holy war that killed hundreds of thousands of his young countrymen, ignoring all attempts at a negotiated peace. Under his regime the values of a partially Westernized society reverted to fundamentalist Islam, without which the war could not be waged in the same way.

Khomeini's domination of the country was nowhere more evident than in the fueling of his military machine by youths of twelve to seventeen years, impressed into what was virtual ritual suicide. Many went unarmed into battle wearing blood-red headbands or carrying books imprinted with sacred red marks, the color symbolizing their ticket to heaven. These victims of the nation's charismatic mission were recruited for martyrdom by local clergy and sent to the front in Iraq against heavy armor. As they ran across open fields of battle large numbers lost their limbs and lives in detonating land mines and thus clearing the terrain for regular troops. Often they were bound together by ropes in groups of 20 to prevent the faint of heart from deserting. In the end, though, it was their fanatical commitment that drove these youths into battle, supported by their families, who accepted their martyrdom with profound religious commitment.[5] Not only had the state assumed the role of the charismatic group, but it also drew on a tradition of martyrdom in fundamentalist Shiite Islamic faith.

Both the human sacrifices in Iran and the waves of terrorism that swept across the Middle East during that same period represent an awakening of Islamic commitment expressed with charismatic zeal and often with violence: airport raids, air and sea piracy, assaults on diplomatic targets, hostage taking, and protracted guerrilla warfare. Such events are likely to continue until the various movements are absorbed into the mainstream, subdued by more conservative Islamic forces, or until they triumph over their adversaries.

Terrorist violence has also arisen in several forms in Western cultures. In the 1970s, the German Baader-Meinhof Gang, the Italian Red Brigades, the French Action Directe, and the Weathermen all embodied a similar zealous commitment to a revolutionary world view, rooted in a blend of international socialism and anarchism. These groups not only cooperated with each other but also worked with Islamic fundamentalists and the Irish Republican Army, despite incongruities in their respective ideologic positions, in an international "terror network."[6]

What circumstances contribute to the rise of violence in charismatic groups? Among the danger signs for potential violence are these:

1. A *deluded leader who is prone toward paranoia* is likely to incite members to violence, and his ideas are more likely to be translated into action if no intermediate level of bureaucracy exists to mute his impact on the membership.
2. When zealous groups are *removed from open communication* with the body politic, bizarre plans that ignore usual social constraints on violence may come forth untempered.
3. If zealous groups acquire *police power* by taking over the appartus of the state, they gain legitimacy in using force to pursue their ends. Aggressive activity is no longer the product of a deviant minority, but rather the formal prerogative of the state.
4. A group that is beleaguered and *fighting for the symbol of its transcendent mission,* be it a fortified residence, a religious icon, or a political standard, may turn to violence to protect its symbolic mission. This is accentuated when the identity and survival of the group are threatened by real assailants, such as the police or other representatives of the state.
5. Some groups are associated with *a historical tradition of violence,* and thus are inclined to carry that tradition forward, particularly when under stress.
6. When a charismatic group becomes *allied with another movement that preaches violence* it is likely to be drawn into collaborative hostile acts.

This epilogue has addressed some of the potential dangers of cult-like groups. We should note, however, that most influential ideologies, religious or political, have emerged from the crucibles of such movements. Revolution, often an unavoidable vehicle for social change, rarely comes without charismatic leadership, intense cohesiveness, and shared, zealous beliefs. Once a charismatic group is established, though, it is hard to predict the vicissitudes of these forces. They may come into conflict with the most noble principles of the society, or they may enhance the way the body politic serves its members. Because of this, only the passage of time can determine whether a given charismatic group will be judged good, evil, or trivial.

APPENDIX A

THE CHARISMATIC GROUP:
A SUMMARY

If there is a science to the study of the charismatic group, then the student may find it useful to refer to some operating principles. To this end, the following summary has been prepared.

The charismatic group is a close-knit community defined by the following primary characteristics: It has a strongly held belief system and a high level of social cohesiveness; its members are deeply influenced by the group's behavioral norms and impute a transcendent (or divine) role to their leader. These groups may differ among themselves in the particulars of their ideology and ritual behavior, but they do have several traits in common, some listed below. Certain groups may conform only in part to this model and to that extent they are an expression of this phenomenon in modified form.

Entry into the Group

Charismatic groups are likely to emerge at a time when the values of a society are felt to be inadequate for addressing major social issues. Individuals are more prone to join if they are unhappy because of situational problems or chronic distress and if they have limited affiliative ties to family and friends.

Groups generally engage new members by creating an atmosphere of unconditional acceptance and support and offering a world view that promises a solution for all existential problems. Engagement (or conversion) entails experiences of intensely felt emotion or perceptual change. It also provides a relief of neurotic distress and a feeling of well-being. For the convert, these experiences serve to validate the group's mission.

The Experience of Membership

The group's leader is reputed to have the potential of bringing a resolution to the problems of humanity. In interacting with followers, the leader is also drawn into believing the grandiose role accorded him, and then justifies his behavior by referring to the transcendent mission suggested by the group's philosophy. This can cause him to make demands on his followers that outsiders would see as petulant and abusive.

The group attributes special meaning, colored by its philosophy, to everyday lan-

197

guage and events; this meaning is usually related to dogma or written code attributed to the group's leader or progenitor.

Recruits experience a *relief effect* with membership. That is, the closer they feel to their fellow members and the group's values, the greater the relief in their emotional distress; the more they become emotionally distanced from the group, the greater their experience of distress. This relief effect serves as the basis for reinforcing compliance with the group's norms, as it implicitly rewards conformity with enhanced well-being and punishes alienation with feelings of distress. It also keeps members from leaving the group because they are conditioned to avoid the distress that results from relinquishing the benefits of the relief effect.

Group behavioral norms generally structure all areas of members' lives, their work, sexuality, socialization, and intellectual pursuits. Activities in these areas are preferentially carried out with other members, so that outsiders are generally shunned as friends and colleagues.

Membership is characterized by levels of "sanctity," so that a member is continually striving to achieve a higher level of acceptance by conforming all the more with the group's expectations. Such conformity generally results in members' experiencing considerable privation.

The Charismatic Group as a Social System

The group operates as a close-knit social system to assure its stability. It does this by manipulating the activities and views of its members. Members' activities are monitored closely, either by formally designated observers or other general members. Compliance with the group's norms is assured by the members' need to avoid estrangement and resulting dysphoria if they appear to question these values. Scapegoating of recalcitrant members helps to maintain a sense of goodness and trust among members.

Information is managed to minimize dissonance between the views of the group and the contrasting attitudes of the general society. The group may therefore engender attitudes and views that fly in the face of reality to prevent destabilization in members' commitment. Implicit "evidence" of the credibility of the group's ethos is also provided by new members, and aggressive recruitment therefore helps stabilize the entire system.

Boundary control is exercised by the group to protect it from threatening incursions from without. The group will therefore engender a suspicious attitude toward the general society to protect its members from assimilation. A clear difference is drawn between members and nonmembers, in terms of their innate value as people. Nonmembers are accorded less moral weight, and may be deceived or snubbed to assure the stability of the group as a social system.

Charismatic groups come into conflict with the surrounding society in a number of ways. They disregard the concern of the families of new converts. They behave in a defensive and paranoid way toward outsiders suspected of being hostile to the group. They aggressively maintain ideologic positions at variance with those of the general culture.

After their initial most zealous phase, charismatic groups may follow any of these courses: They may become bureaucratized with the charisma of the original leader ascribed to the group's leadership hierarchy. They may assimilate into the broader society if the group's self-protectiveness and isolation are not sustained by the leadership. They may come into direct conflict with the surrounding society because of differences in ideology and defensiveness on both sides, potentially leading to violence. To escape a negative outcome, these groups may also migrate to an isolated setting.

APPENDIX B

CHRONOLOGY OF THE STUDIES

Findings from several of my studies are discussed at different points. To clarify the sequence of this work, the actual research projects are listed here in chronological order.

Year Conducted	Research Project, Site, and Subjects	Principal References
1970–72	Marijuana: physiology, psychology, and social behavior. National Institute of Mental Health (12 volunteers; 36 volunteers)	Galanter et al., 1972 Galanter et al., 1973 Galanter et al., 1974
1974	Divine Light Mission, active members. New York, Orlando, Florida (119 members)	Galanter, 1978 Galanter and Buckley, 1978
1977	Unification Church, active members. New York City (237 members)	Galanter et al., 1979 Galanter, 1981
1978	Unification Church, Induction Workshops. Boston, California, Washington, D.C., New York State (104 recruits)	Galanter, 1980
1980–1981	Unification Church, study of marital engagement. New York City, Boston (321 engaged members)	Galanter, 1983(a)
1981	Unification Church, drop-outs. U.S., National (66 ex-members)	Galanter, 1983(b)
1982	Federation of Parents for Drug-Free Youth. Atlanta, Georgia (135 parent members)	Galanter et al., 1984
1982–1986	Institutionally based self-help treatment for alcoholism. Bronx Municipal Hospital Center (282 experimental patients and controls)	Galanter et al., 1987
1983–1985	Unification Church, study of married couples. U.S., National (321-member follow-up)	Galanter, 1986

| 1983–1986 | Recovery, Inc., self-help for psychiatric problems. U.S., National (one member and leader in each of 211 groups) | Galanter, 1988 |
| 1988 | AA-based program for addicted physicians (100 physicians). | Galanter et al., 1989 |

NOTES

1. The Charismatic Group

1. S. Freud (1921), p. 16.
2. W. James (1902).
3. D. Hume (1779).
4. C. Darwin (1871).
5. E. O. Wilson (1975).
6. S. Wright (1945).
7. M. Galanter (1978, 1983a).
8. A. Jolly (1972).
9. S. J. Suomi (1972); S. J. Suomi et al. (1978); J. M. Smith (1964), S. Wright (1945).
10. L. von Bertalanffy (1950).
11. *U. S. News and World Report,* December 4, 1978, pp. 28–29.

2. Group Cohesiveness

1. Reference should be made here to G. H. Mead (1962), who showed that mind and self are generated in a social process. He posited a "generalized other," namely the organized community or social group that gives the individual a unity of self.
2. D. Cartwright and A. Zander (1962), p. 74.
3. M. Bowen (1978); L. Wynne et al. (1958).
4. D. Reiss (1971).
5. A. Deutsch (1980).
6. W. Bion (1959), p. 30.
7. A. K. Rice (1965). In the United States, these programs are run by the A. K. Rice Institute, with headquarters in Washington, D. C.
8. L. Coser (1974); A. L. Greil and D. R. Rudy (1984).
9. S. Freud (1921), p. 16.
10. The term new religious movements reflects a certain respect for these groups. It has been popularized by more sympathetic authors. The term cult, on the other hand, has often been used pejoratively by authors more concerned with the potential danger of these groups.

11. The names of individual group members and the details of their backgrounds are altered throughout to protect their identities.
12. J. G. Melton and R. L. Moore (1982).
13. J. V. Downton (1979).
14. J. V. Downton (1979); T. Pilarzyk (1978), p. 30.
15. M. Galanter and P. Buckley (1978).
16. Respondents' average age was 25. By eliminating "none," and "other" responses, the relative distribution of major religious denominations among the remaining sample prior to joining was obtained: 44% Protestant, 32% Catholic, and 21% Jewish. Comparable figures for the nation overall (*Yearbook of American Churches*, 1972, U. S. Church membership) were 57%, 38%, and 2% respectively.
17. C. Cameron (1973), p. 22.
18. T. Pilarzyk (1978), p. 38.
19. J. C. Ross (1982); D. G. Bromley and A. D. Shupe (1979).
20. M. Galanter et al. (1972).
21. Subjective symptoms not related to the group experience, however, differentiated the three experimental conditions. Thus, for symptoms such as "mouth feeling dry," "feeling dreamy," and "head feeling heavier," both marijuana and placebo are significantly different from the no drug condition, although the effect of active marijuana was stronger (Galanter et al. 1974).
22. B. J. Albaugh and P. O. Anderson (1974).
23. R. L. Bergman (1971).
24. F. Kass et al. (1980).
25. The internal reliability of the scales developed for this study and those in ensuing studies was assessed by computing the coefficient alpha, reflecting the average correlation of the test items. By this technique, the scales all had satisfactory coefficients of internal reliability. For example, for the Psychological Distress Scale, .78; group cohesiveness in relation to ten members, .75, in relation to all members, .75 in relation to nonmembers, .78; religious creed—used in the Unification Church study, .81. (Galanter, 1981). Specific points on all these scales were labeled as follows: 1—not at all; 2—a little bit; 3—moderately; 4—a lot; 5—very much.
26. Further details on symptom decline are found in Galanter (1978). Members actually had a relatively high incidence of drug use prior to joining. For example, the overwhelming majority had smoked marijuana (92%); most had used hallucinogens (68%), and a certain number used (14%) heroin too. With the exception of alcohol, the level of use for all drugs queried was two to four times that reported by a representative national sample of college students for the same period. The same number of Divine Light members (86%), though, had used alcohol, as had respondents in the national sample (National Commission on Marijuana and Drug Abuse, 1973).
27. Mean scores for the Social Cohesiveness Scale toward each of the three target groups reflected this difference: for ten members, 34.4 ± 3.4; for ten nonmembers 26.4 ± 4.7; for all members, 32.4 ± 3.6 ($F = 214.7$, 2/116 df, $p < .01$).
28. Typical declines in symptom scores after joining were 41% for anxiety and 42% for depression. A stepwise multiple regression analysis was performed using selected items on social cohesiveness toward sect members. These predicted 37% of the variance in scores on the Psychological Distress Scale (Galanter, 1982).

29. In one item, subjects indicated whether or not they had in the past "experienced serious emotional problems" before joining the group. Thirty-nine percent answered affirmatively.

3. Shared Beliefs

1. R. M. Kanter (1972).
2. W. M. Kephart (1976) reviews the history of this and related nineteenth-century communities.
3. R. M. Kephart (1976), p. 58.
4. P. B. Noyes (1927), pp. 126–127.
5. Oneida *Circular,* July 17, 1863.
6. R. J. Lifton (1961). R. Ofshe (1974) described Synanon games, and E. H. Schein (1956) examined inefficiencies in the Chinese brainwashing techniques.
7. A. Leighton and D. Leighton (1941).
8. B. Kaplan and D. Johnson (1964). I. Lubchansky et al. (1970) provide a similar framework for urban Hispanic faith healing in the United States.
9. R. S. Lynd and H. B. Lynd (1929); T. Caplow et al. (1981).
10. M. E. Pattison et al. (1973).
11. S. Schacter and J. E. Singer (1962).
12. M. E. Pattison and M. L. Pattison (1980).
13. J. Frank (1973).
14. L. Mosher and A. Menn (1978).
15. L. Mosher and A. Menn (1978), pp. 716–719.
16. R. J. Wendt et al. (1983).
17. R. Liberman (1973); A. Brier and J. S. Strauss (1983); W. T. Carpenter (1977).
18. L. Mosher and A. Menn (1983).
19. J. Lofland and R. Stark (1965) used the term religious seekers in a similar way in their early description of the new religious movements.
20. This issue is illustrated in studies on cognitive dissonance such as those by L. Festinger and J. M. Carlsmith (1959) and M. R. Lepper et al. (1973).
21. E. Barker (1974) used membership lists to generate a random sample in her study of the Moonies.
22. Typical items were, "Have you been feeling emotionally stable and sure of yourself?" and "How happy, satisfied, or pleased have you been with your personal life?" answered on a six-point scale (Dupuy, 1973). Respondents' GWB scores ($X = 74.4 \pm 17.2$) were significantly below those of the comparison group (83.4 ± 16.2, $p < .001$). They were also highly inversely correlated ($r = -.64$, $p < .001$) with the Psychological Distress Scale scores.
23. M. Galanter et al. (1979). Dr. John Ware of the Stanford Research Institute had not only undertaken the administration of the General Well-Being Schedule to 1,196 representative adults from Dayton, Ohio, but had also cross-tabulated his population's scores by age and sex, making it possible to draw out a sample with very much the same demographic distribution of our own respondents.
24. Comparison responses obtained for the periods right before and after first contacts with the church (Galanter, 1981) reflected a marked increase in the intensity of religious commitment on joining.

25. Cohesiveness items accounted for 30% of the variance in GWB scores in a stepwise multiple of regression analysis ($R = .55$, $F = 2.49$, 6/230 df), but when religion items were added to the regression equation, another 6% of the variance was predicted ($R = .62$, $F = 2.52$, 8/228 df) (Galanter, 1981).
26. F. Heider (1958).
27. W. Proudfoot and P. Shaver (1975).
28. D. J. Bem (1972), p. 2.
29. H. H. Kelley (1967), p. 200.
30. M. Galanter et al. (1979); M. Galanter (1980).
31. N. J. Cameron (1943).
32. S. E. Asch (1952).
33. R. Ofshe (1976).
34. R. Lifton (1961).

4. Altered Consciousness

1. W. James (1902).
2. A. M. Ludwig (1966).
3. C. T. Tart (1975).
4. R. K. Wallace (1970).
5. M. Galanter et al. (1973); Roth et al. (1973).
6. J. V. Hardt and J. Kamiya (1978).
7. Meditation was "usually" experienced during daily activities by 72% of members with prior drug problems vs. only 47% without such problems ($X^2 = 2.43$, $p < .05$).
8. Most of these findings on transcendent experiences were reported in M. Galanter and P. Buckley (1978). These items were also used for queries regarding experiences during conversion (Buckley and Galanter, 1979).
9. In a stepwise multiple regression analysis, the significant predictors of symptom decline included the members' frequency of meditation and the occurrence of transcendental experiences during meditation. Other significant predictors in this analysis were group cohesiveness and level of participation in Divine Light activities. These variables accounted for 48% of the variance in symptom decline since conversion.
10. *The New York Times* Magazine, February 6, 1975, p. 12; it is also the source of the figures on TM.
11. H. Benson and R. K. Wallace (1972) and H. Benson (1974).
12. *The New York Times,* January 1, 1984, p. A14.
13. The term also applies to certain drugs that do not lead to addiction or abuse. Chlorpromazine, a neuroleptic, is a tranquilizer used in the treatment of schizophrenia. One may well study the social impact on a mental ward when patients are medicated with this drug.
14. R. E. Schultes (1972); M. D. DeRios and D. E. Smith (1977); A. Paredes (1975).
15. E. M. Brecher (1972).
16. W. N. Pahnke (1966).
17. A. Deutsch (1975).
18. Parent Group members' cohesion scores toward the overall membership were

tabulated. They were no different from those of Unification members' scores toward their overall membership on mean item scores ($3.72 \pm .96$ vs. 3.66 ± 1.04). Parent group scores for nonmembers whom they knew best, however, were much higher than those of the Moonies (3.66 ± 1.14 vs. 2.62 ± 0.91; $t=9.65$, $p<.001$) (Galanter et al., 1984).

19. M. Orne (1969).
20. M. Galanter et al. (1978).
21. F. I. Melges et al. (1974).
22. J. G. Melton (1978).
23. R. C. Ness and R. M. Wintrob (1980).
24. W. J. Samarin (1959); E. M. Pattison (1974).
25. J. G. Melton (1978), p. 248.
26. F. D. Goodman (1972).
27. Lisa Alther, *The New York Times* Magazine, June 6, 1976, p. 18 ff.
28. R. Lane (1976) described the development of the Catholic Charismatic Movement.
29. *The New York Times,* September 8, 1974, p. A1 ff, and May 10, 1981, p. A26, among other related news items.
30. A. Greeley (1975).
31. E. Bourguignon (1974).
32. W. LaBarre (1970).
33. M. A. Kirsch and L. L. Glass (1977).
34. Irvin Yalom, a group therapy researcher, also experienced difficulties in attempts to establish a working arrangement with est (*American Journal of Psychiatry,* 134:213, 1977).
35. The membership figure and the quotation from the est trainer are from *Time* Magazine, June 7, 1976, pp. 53–54.
36. E. Babbie and D. Stone (1976).
37. J. Simon (1978).

5. Biology and Behavior

1. C. Darwin (1889).
2. M. T. Ghiselin (1969), p. 188.
3. C. Darwin (1889), p. 402.
4. K. Z. Lorenz (1974).
5. N. Tinbergen (1951); E. Weigert (1956); J. Bowlby (1957).
6. E. O. Wilson (1975).
7. M. Ruse (1981); J. D. Baldwin and J. I. Baldwin (1981).
8. W. D. Hamilton (1975); M. J. Smith (1964).
9. R. L. Trivers (1971); B. C. R. Bertram (1982).
10. C. J. Lumsden and E. O. Wilson (1981).
11. Mean scores for the workshop registrants were 61.9 (those who joined), 67.2 (late dropouts), and 74.7 (early dropouts). Persons who were members for two years had a mean score of 74.4. The comparison group drawn from the general population had a mean score of 83.4. These data and others on the inductees

will be reviewed in detail in a subsequent chapter on the experience of Unification Church members.

12. A stepwise multiple regression analysis was done using items reflecting social cohesiveness as predictors, and the decline in members' scores for psychological distress after joining as the dependent variable. Cohesiveness items predicted 37% of the variance in the decline in distress.

13. In a multiple regression analysis where scores on the General Well-Being Schedule were used as the dependent variable, social cohesiveness items accounted for 30% of the variance. When items on religious belief were added to the regression equation, an additional 6% of the variance was accounted for. These data and others cited here are reviewed in M. Galanter (1981). See also National Center for Health Statistics (1977).

14. M. Galanter (1983).

15. T. H. Holmes and R. H. Rahe (1967).

16. These studies are described later. In brief, life events accounted for 15% of the variance in general well-being scores during the engagement. When affiliateness items were added to the regression equation, an additional 20% of variance was accounted for. After marriage, altogether 32% of the variance was accounted for, using a somewhat modified procedure (Galanter, 1983, 1985).

17. Point biserial correlations were obtained between the item in which respondents reported whether or not they had a history of "serious emotional problems" and their scores on each of the following two scores: (a) psychological distress and (b) social cohesiveness. There was no significant correlation in either case, among either the Moonies or the Divine Light members (Galanter, 1981).

18. The product-moment correlation (r) between this item and the decline on the psychological distress scale was .45 $(p < .01)$ (Galanter, 1978).

19. M. Galanter (1984).

20. B. G. Campbell (1974), pp. 376–381.

21. W. D. Hamilton (1975).

22. A. Jolly (1972), p. 128.

23. T. Dobzhansky and O. Pavlovsky (1971).

24. D. Pilbeam (1972).

25. A. Jolly (1972), p. 126.

26. H. F. Harlow and M. K. Harlow (1969).

27. S. J. Suomi, et al. (1976); S. J. Suomi et al. (1978).

28. R. Gardner (1982).

29. J. A. Hobson and R. W. McCarley (1977).

30. A. R. Radcliffe-Brown (1939).

6. The Cult as a Social System

1. Von Bertalanffy (1968), F. Baker (1970), and J. G. Miller (1975) provide good introductions to systems theory and its relationship to social psychology.

2. American Psychiatric Association, DSM III (1980).

3. APA DSM III (1980), p. 253.

4. J. Simon (1978).

5. L. L. Glass et al. (1977); M. A. Kirsch and L. L. Glass (1977).

6. T. Strentz (1980) provides the background on clinical interviews of hijacking.
7. D. Lang (1974).
8. A. Freud (1966).
9. A. Deutsch (1980).
10. M. Galanter (1983a).
11. M. Galanter (1983b).
12. A case reported by H. Basedow, cited by W. B. Cannon (1965).
13. R. A. DeSilva (1982).
14. J. G. Miller (1965).
15. *Newsweek,* June 14, 1976, p. 44.
16. G. Moorhouse (1981); K. Rothmyer (1984).
17. J. G. Clark (1979); M. Singer (1978).
18. J. T. Ungerleider and D. K. Wellisch (1979).
19. M. Galanter (1983b).

7. *Trouble at the System's Boundary: Jonestown and MOVE*

1. J. M. Weightsman (1983), p. 47. J. P. Nugent (1979), pp. 77–78.
2. *Keesing's Contemporary Archives,* May 25, 1979, p. 29627.
3. *Time* Magazine, December 4, 1978, p. 21.
4. C. Winfrey (1979).
5. J. M. Weightsman (1983), p. 98.
6. Both letters are quoted in *The New York Times,* November 29, 1978, p. A1.
7. J. R. Hall (1981), p. 188.
8. J. M. Weightsman, p. 29.
9. *Time* Magazine, December 4, 1978, p. 28.
10. Gerald Parks, quoted by J. M. Weightsman (1983), p. 54.
11. Deborah L. Blakey, affidavit, quoted by J. M. Weightsman (1983), p. 57.
12. J. M. Weightsman (1983), p. 49.
13. P. Kerns and D. Wead (1979), p. 191.
14. *Time* Magazine, December 4, 1978, p. 19.
15. *Keesing's Contemporary Archives,* May 25, 1979, p. 29627.
16. *Newsweek,* May 27, 1985, p. 24.
17. *Time* Magazine, May 27, 1985, p. 21.
18. *The New York Times,* May 20, 1985, p. A5.
19. *Time* Magazine, May 27, 1985, citation of *Philadelphia Inquirer.*
20. *Newsweek,* May 27, 1985, p. 24.
21. *Time* Magazine, May 27, 1985, p. 22.

8. *Religius Sect: The Unification Church*

1. This and the ensuing statement were quoted in *The New York Times* January 22, 1979, p. A1 ff.
2. *The New York Times,* September 16, 1974, p. 1.
3. *The New York Times,* September 16, 1974, p. 26.
4. *Boston Globe,* May 23, 1979, pp. 37–38.

5. *The New York Times,* July 22, 1979, p. A1.

6. Berkeley Rice, The Pull of Sun Moon, *The New York Times* Magazine, May 30, 1976.

7. *The New York Times,* September 19, 1977, p. 22.

8. B. Falk, Suburbia Today, Gannett Newspapers, December 27, 1981, p. 6 ff.

9. *The New York Times,* April 2, 1984, p. C15.

10. C. Welles, *New York* Magazine, September 27, 1976.

11. B. Falk, Suburbia Today, Gannett Newspapers, December 17, 1981, p. 6 ff.

12. *The New York Times,* October 16, 1981, p. A1.

13. *The New York Times,* July 5, 1985, p. B3.

14. *The New York Times,* July 27, 1985, p. A10.

15. M. Galanter (1982).

16. Models for recruitment have also been proposed by J. Lofland and R. Stark (1965); D. A. Snow and C. L. Philips (1980); B. Kilbourne and J. T. Richardson (1984).

17. F. Conway and J. Siegelman (1978) in their popular book, *Snapping,* reflect the negative view of the induction techniques. D. Bromley and A. Shupe (1979) studied the evolution of such highly negative views in the media.

18. J. M. Carlsmith et al. (1966).

19. See M. Galanter (1980) for a full report on the methodology of this induction study.

20. E. Barker (1984), p. 146.

21. Longstanding members scored lower than a community sample on GWB (74.4 ± 17.2 vs. 83.4 ± 16.2, $t = 6.24$, $p < .001$). Those who left the workshops after the first weekend had scores that were not significantly different from the ones of long-term members. Those who stayed after the first weekend, however, did have lower scores (67.2 ± 19.2 vs. 74.7 ± 17.2, $t = 1.95$, $p < .05$), and those who actually joined had scores even lower (61.9 ± 20.1, $t = 1.89$, $p < .05$). The workshop guests who continued beyond the second day scored as high on the cohesion scales as longstanding members (mean score, 23.7 ± 3.9), even as early as day 2. The early dropouts, on the other hand, did not score as high ($t = 5.76$, $p < .001$). Early dropouts scored lower on the creed scale than those who continued (mean score, 22.3 ± 7.2 and 26.0 ± 6.0, respectively, $t = 2.39$, $p < .01$).

22. There were no significant differences at any of the test points between the two groups with regard to affiliation toward fellow group members, but significant differences existed at all points with regard to affiliative feelings toward outsiders; the early and late dropouts scored significantly higher on the outside affiliations scale than the joiners. For example, outside affiliations scores on day 2 were 15.8 ± 6.6 and 7.4 ± 6.2, respectively; $t = 2.80$, $p < .01$.

23. For example, if subjects were ranked according to the degree of diminished distress, the quartile who improved most showed a 128% increase in their reported religiosity scores over the course of conversion, while those who improved least showed a 76% increase ($t = 3.67$, $p < .01$). Similar results were obtained on Divine Light members, reported in a previous chapter.

24. A. S. Parsons (1984).

25. M. Galanter (1983a).

26. No doubt some of them dropped out within the year following the engagement.

On these I have no data. Particulars on each of the engaged subgroups and their scores may be found in M. Galanter (1983a).

27. Their mean score on GWB items was considerably lower (53.9 ± 17.8 vs. 70.6 ± 14.1; $t = 3.48$, $p < .001$), within the range of clinically significant distress (National Center for Health Statistics, 1977).

28. B. I. Murstein (1972); W. J. Goode (1970).

29. T. H. Holmes and R. H. Rahe (1967).

30. These latter events were evaluated by each subject in relation to the amount of readjustment they required, the format originally defined for the Holmes and Rahe scale. The adaptation of the scale follows the model proposed by B. S. Dohrenwend (1978).

31. The following variables were used as predictors in the first analysis: the 15 items from Holmes and Rahe most frequently experienced by respondents and the five UC-related life changes most frequently experienced. In the second analysis 10 items reflecting affiliativeness toward the UC were added to the list of predictors. In each stage, predictors were entered into the regression equation only as long as each accounted for a portion of the variance significant at the 5% level. The percentages of variance predicted in these two analyses are reported in the text.

32. S. Milgram (1975).

33. L. Festinger et al. (1956).

34. *Life* Magazine, August 1982, pp. 91–96.

35. Ibid.

36. *The New York Times*, July 2, 1982, p. B4.

37. Other life events included the issue of pregnancy, the marriage itself, assuming responsibility for rent and household bills, and adjusting to an active sexual life with one's spouse. All were rated on a five-point scale that ranged from very agreeable to very disagreeable. The methodology and results of this entire study are elaborated in M. Galanter (1986).

38. D. P. Mueller et al. (1977); I. Grant et al. (1981).

39. In the one analysis, items on the cohesiveness and religiosity scales were entered; they accounted for 21% of the variance in GWB scores. In a second analysis, maritally related life events scored for their disagreeable nature were entered as predictors; these variables themselves accounted for 14% of the variance in GWB scores. Finally, both sets of predictors (20 in all) were used for a third analysis, and in that analysis accounted for 32% of the variance in well-being.

40. *The New York Times*, January 22, 1979, p. A14.

41. Ibid.

42. T. Robbins (1979–1980). M. Galanter (1982).

43. These comparisons were made in my follow-up, M. Galanter (1986), on the engaged sample, M. Galanter (1983a).

44. In 1985, two years after the follow-up survey on married members was conducted, I was able to obtain a second follow-up on the cohort that had been engaged in 1979, with the assistance of informants in the church and with church cooperation. The results again confirmed the tenacity of commitment in this group who were now members for an average of fifteen years: 71% were

still married to the spouse to whom they were originally matched. Of the total sample, 81% were documented as active. Only 10% were known to have dropped out. Of an additional 9% who could not be located, some were probably active but stationed in remote settings.

45. Specifically, active members (Galanter et al., 1979) scored lower than these dropouts (74.4±17.2 vs. 81.9±16.7; t=3.16, p<.01) (Galanter, 1983b), whose scores were, in turn, not significantly different from those of a matched community group (82.3±15.7). It should be noted, however, that there may be a variety of reasons for this: Members with a more benign disposition may have tended to drop out; also, members may be inclined to drop out only *after* they have improved; alternatively, members may have improved after they left. All three reasons may have played a part in this observation.

46. To corroborate these designations, participants were asked to rate the degree of force their family or its representatives had used in attempting to remove them from the sect. For clarifying the use of coercion by the Unification Church itself, respondents were also asked to use the same scale to indicate the degree to which force had been used on them by other members to retain them in the group. Those who were designated as deprogrammed reported much more coercion in a variety of ways. Nine of the ten indicated their freedom was overtly limited by their family both before the time of departure and afterward. They also reported more limitations on them by members before they left.

47. Those who were deprogrammed scored lower on cohesiveness toward the members they knew best (2.61±.40 vs. 3.29±.71; t=2.76, p<.01), and higher on affiliative feelings toward the nonmembers they knew best (4.45±.25 vs. 4.01±.56; t=3.80, p<.001). They also had a lower mean score on the creed scale (1.33±.50 vs. 2.55±1.35; t=2.79, p<.01).

48. Similar observations were made by E. Barker (1984) over the course of her contacts with the Unification Church.

9. Charismatic Healing Groups: The AA Example

1. M. Weber (1947); H. Gerth and C. W. Mills (1946).
2. Bill W.'s tale is available in a number of sources, among them E. Kurtz (1979) and R. Thomsen (1975).
3. *Alcoholics Anonymous Comes of Age* (1957).
4. Bill W. Letter to Carl Jung. *The AA Grapevine*. New York, 1963.
5. Alcohol, Drug Abuse, and Mental Health Administration. *ADAMHA News,* May 1985; M. Bean (1975).
6. H. Trice and J. M. Beyer (1983).
7. R. Lifton (1961), pp. 429–430; N. K. Denzin (1987).
8. L. A. Alibrandi (1978).
9. E. A. Bohince and A. C. Orenstein (1950).
10. Alcoholics Anonymous (1976).
11. R. Lifton (1961), p. 425.
12. Cited by R. Thompson (1975), p. 365, and the New York *Village Voice,* July 23, 1985, p. 64.
13. R. Kanter (1972), p. 113.

14. C. Emrick, et al. (1977).
15. *ADAMHA News,* May 1985.
16. M. Galanter (1980).
17. E. M. Pattison (1976); *The New York Times,* November 22, 1983, p. C1, ff. 1983, p. C1, ff.
18. D. R. Rudy (1986).
19. D. Robinson (1979).
20. G. Vaillant (1982).
21. M. Bean (1975), p. 49.
22. *The AA Way of Life* (1967).
23. H. Suwaki (1979).
24. *ADAMHA News,* May 1985.
25. M. D. Maxwell (1984).
26. M. Galanter et al. (1984).
27. M. Galanter (in press).
28. M. Galanter (1984); M. Galanter et al. (1987).
29. F. Adler (1974).
30. C. Emrick et al. (1977).
31. A. Maslow (1967).
32. R. Ofshe (1976).
33. *The New York Times,* March 9, 1982, p. A17.
34. Ibid.
35. Ibid.
36. Ibid.
37. *The New York Times,* December 4, 1978, p. A16.

10. Epilogue

1. V. Bugliosi and C. Gentry (1974).
2. *The New York Times,* January 14, 1983, p. A1 ff; January 15, 1983, p. 4.
3. *The New York Times,* October 21, 1981, p. A, October 22, 1981, p. 1.
4. *The New York Times,* December 17, 1985, p. A18.
5. *The New York Times* Magazine, February 12, 1984, p. 21 ff, *Time* Magazine, April 2, 1984, p. 30.
6. C. Sterling (1981).

BIBLIOGRAPHY

Adler, F., *A Systems Approach to Drug Treatment*. Philadelphia: Dorrance and Co., 1974.

Albaugh, B. J., and Anderson, P. O. Peyote in the treatment of alcoholism among American Indians. *American Journal of Psychiatry* 131: 1247–50, 1974.

Alcoholics Anonymous. New York: Alcoholics Anonymous World Services, Inc., 1939.

Alcoholics Anonymous Comes of Age. New York: Alcoholics Anonymous Publishing, 1957.

Alcoholics Anonymous (3rd ed.). New York: Alcoholics Anonymous World Services, 1976.

Alibrandi, I. A. The folk psychotherapy of Alcoholics Anonymous. In S. Zimberg, J. Wallace, and S. B. Blume (eds.). *Practical Approaches to Alcoholism Psychotherapy*. New York: Plenum Publishing, 1978, 163–80.

American Psychiatric Association, *Diagnostic and Statistical Manual of Mental Disorders* (3rd ed.). Washington, D.C.: American Psychiatric Association, 1980.

Asch, S. E. *Social Psychology*. Englewood Cliffs, N.J.: Prentice-Hall, 1952.

Babbie, E., and Stone, D. What have you gotten after you "get it"? An evaluation of awareness training participants. Presented at the 129th annual meeting of the American Psychiatric Association. Miami Beach, Fla., May 1979.

Baker, F. General systems theory, research, and medical care. In *Systems and Medical Care*. Edited by Sheldon A. Baker, F. McLaughlin, and Curtis P. McLaughlin. Cambridge: MIT Press, 1970.

Baldwin, J. D., and Baldwin J. I. *Beyond Sociobiology*. New York: Elsevier, 1981.

Barker, E. *The Making of a Moonie: Choice or Brainwashing*. Oxford, England: Basil Blackwell, 1984.

Bean, M. Alcoholics Anonymous. *Psychiatric Annals* 5:46–61, 1975.

Bem, D. J. Self-perception theory. In *Advances in Experimental Social Psychology*, Vol VI, L. Berkowitz (ed.). New York: Academic Press, 1972, 1–62.

Benson, H. Decreased alcohol intake associated with the practice of meditation: a retrospective investigation. *Annals of the New York Academy of Sciences*, 233:174–77, 1974.

Benson, H., and Wallace, R. K. Decreased drug abuse with transcendental meditation: a study of 1862 subjects. *Drug Abuse Proceedings of the International Conference*, Zarafonetis, C. J. D. (ed.). Philadelphia: Lea and Febiger, 1972, 369–76.

Bergman, R. L. Navajo peyote use: its apparent safety. *American Journal of Psychiatry* 128: 695–99, 1971.

Bertram, B. C. R. Problems with altruism. In Kings College Sociobiology Group, Cambridge (eds.), *Current Problems in Sociobiology*. Cambridge: Cambridge University Press, 1982, 260–65.

Bion, W. R. *Experiences in Groups*. New York: Basic Books, 1959.

Bohince, E. A., and Orenstein, A. C. Master's thesis (1950). Cited in C. Emrick, et al., 1977.

Bourguignon, E. Cross-cultural perspectives on the religious uses of altered states of consciousness. In *Religious Movements in Contemporary America*, I. I. Zaretsky and M. P. Leone (eds.). Princeton: Princeton University Press, 1974, 228–43.

Bowen, M. *Family Therapy in Clinical Practice*. New York: Jason Aronson, 1978.

Bowlby, J. Symposium on the contribution of current theories to an understanding of child development: An ethological approach to research in child development. *British Journal of Medical Psychology* 30: 230–40, 1957.

Brecher, E. M. *Licit and Illicit Drugs*. Boston and Toronto: Little, Brown and Company, 1972.

Brier, A. and Strauss, J. S. Self-control in psychotic disorders. *Archives of General Psychiatry* 40: 1141–45, 1983.

Bromley, D. G., and Shupe, A. D. *Moonies in America: Cult, Church, and Crusade.* Beverly Hills, Calif.: Sage Publications, 1979.

Bromley, D. G., Shupe, A. D., Jr., and Ventimiglia, J. C. Atrocity Tales, The Unification Church and the social construction of evil. *Journal of Communication* 29: 42–53, 1979.

Buckley, P., and Galanter, M. Mystical experience, spiritual knowledge, and a contemporary ecstatic religion. *British Journal of Medicine and Psychology* 52: 281–89, 1979.

Bugliosi, V., and Gentry, C. *Helter Skelter*. New York: Norton, 1974.

Cameron, C. *Who is Guru Maharaj Ji?* New York: Bantam Books, 1973.

Cameron, N. A. The paranoid pseudo-community. *American Journal of Sociology* 49: 32, 1943.

Cannon, W. B. "Voodoo" Death. Reprinted in abridged form from *American Anthropologist* XLIV (1942), 169–81, by permission of the American Anthropological Association. In *Reader in Comparative Religion: An Anthropological Approach*, W. A. Lessa and E. Z. Vogt (eds.). New York: Harper & Row, 1965.

Campbell, B. G. Human Evolution: Introduction to Man's Adaptations. Chicago: Aldine Publishing, 1974.

Caplow, T., Bahr, H. M., Chadwick, B. A. Piety in Middletown. *Society* 18: 34–37, 1981.

Carlsmith, J. M., Collins, B. E., and Helmreich, R. L. Studies in forced compliance: I. The effect of pressure for compliance on attitude change produced by face-to-face role playing and anonymous essay writing. *Personality and Social Psychology* 4: 1–13, 1966.

Carpenter, W. T., Jr., McGlashan, T. H., and Strauss, J. S. The treatment of acute schizophrenia without drugs: an investigation of some current assumptions. *American Journal of Psychiatry* 134:14–20, 1977.

Cartwright, D., and Zander A. (eds.). *Group Dynamics: Research and Theory*. Evanston, Ill.: Row, Peterson, 1962.

Clark, J. G. Cults. *Journal of the American Medical Association* 242: 279–81, 1979.

Conway, F., and Siegelman, J. *Snapping*. New York: Dell Publishing, 1978.

Coser, L. *Greedy Institutions: Patterns of Undivided Commitment*. New York: Free Press, 1974.

Darwin, C. *The Descent of Man, and Selection in Relation to Sex* (1871). New York: D. Appleton, 1889.

DeRios, M. D., and Smith, D. E. Drug use and abuse in cross cultural perspective. *Human Organization* 36: 1, 14–21, 1977.

DeSilva, R. A. Central nervous system risk factors for sudden cardiac death. In H. M. Greenberg and E. M. Dwyer (eds.). Sudden cardiac death. *Annals of the New York Academy of Science* 382: 143–61, 1982.

Denzin, N. K. *The Recovering Alcoholic*. Newbury Park, Calif.: Sage Publications, 1987.

Deutsch, A. Tenacity of attachment to a cult leader: A psychiatric perspective. *American Journal of Psychiatry* 137: 1569–73, 1980.

Deutsch, A. Observations on a sidewalk Ashram. *Archives of General Psychiatry* 32: 166–75, 1975.

Dobzhansky, T., and Pavlovsky, O. Experimentally created incipient species of *Drosphila*. *Nature* 230: 289–92, 1971.

Dohrenwend, B. S. et al. Exemplification of a method for scaling life events. The PERI life events scale. *Journal of Health and Social Behavior* 19: 205–29, 1978.

Downton, J. V. *Sacred Journeys: The Conversion of Young Americans to the Divine Light Mission*. New York: Columbia University Press, 1979.

Dupuy, H. J. The psychological section of the current health and nutrition examination survey. In *Proceedings of the Public Health Conference on Records and Statistics* (1972). DHEW Publication (HRA) 74-1214. Rockville, Md.: National Center for Health Statistics, 1973.

Emrick, C. D., Lassen, C. L., and Edwards, M. T. Nonprofessional peers as therapeutic agents. In A. S. Gurman and A. M. Razin (eds.). *Effective psychotherapy*. Oxford: Pergamon Press, 1977, 120–161.

Ezriel, H. A psychoanalytic approach to group treatment. *British Journal of Medical Psychology* 23: 59–74, 1950.

Festinger, L., and Carlsmith, J. M. Cognitive consequences of forced compliance. *Journal of Abnormal Social Psychology* 58: 203–10, 1959.

Festinger, L., Riecken, H., and Schachter S. *When Prophecy Fails*. Minneapolis: University of Minnesota Press, 1956.

Frank, J. *Persuasion and Healing*. New York: Schocken, 1973.

Freud, A. *The Ego and the Mechanisms of Defense*. New York: International Universities Press, 1966.

Freud, S. Group psychology and the analysis of the ego (1921). In *The Standard Edition of the Complete Psychological Works of Sigmund Freud*, Vol XVIII, J. Strachey (ed.). London: Hogarth Press, 1955.

Freud, S. Group psychology and the analysis of the ego. London: The Hogarth Press, 1948.

Galanter, M. The "relief effect": A sociobiological model for neurotic distress and large-group therapy. *American Journal of Psychiatry* 135: 588–91, 1978.

Galanter, M. Psychological induction into the large-group: findings from a contemporary religious sect. *American Journal of Psychiatry* 137: 1574–79, 1980.

Galanter, M. Sociobiology and informal social controls of drinking. *Journal of the Studies on Alcohol* 42: 64–79, 1981.

Galanter, M. Charismatic religious sects and psychiatry: an overview. *American Journal of Psychiatry* 139: 1539–48, 1982.

Galanter, M. Engaged members of the Unification Church. *Archives of General Psychiatry* 40: 1197–1202, 1983(a).

Galanter, M. Unification Church ("Moonie") dropouts: Psychological readjustment after leaving a charismatic religious group. American Journal of Psychiatry 140: 984–88, 1983(b).

Galanter, M. Self-help large-group therapy for alcoholism: a controlled study. *Alcoholism: Clinical and Experimental Research* 8: 16–23, 1984.

Galanter, M. Moonies get married: A psychiatric follow-up study of a charismatic religious sect. *American Journal of Psychiatry* 143: 1245–49, 1986.

Galanter, M. Recovery: Self-help groups for the mentally ill. American Journal of Psychiatry, 145: 1248–53, 1988.

Galanter, M, and Buckley, P. Evangelical religion and meditation: psychotherapeutic effects. *Journal of Nervous and Mental Disease* 166: 685–91, 1978.

Galanter, M, Castaneda, R, and Salamon I. Institutional self-help for alcoholism clinical outcome. *Alcoholism: Clinical and Experimental Research* 11: 424–29, 1987.

Galanter, M, Gleaton, T. J., Marcus, C. E., and McMillin, J. Parent self-help groups for young drug and alcohol abusers. *American Journal of Psychiatry* 141: 889–91, 1984.

Galanter, M., Rabkin, R., Rabkin, J., and Deutsch, A. The "Moonies": a psychological study. *American Journal of Psychiatry* 136: 165–70, 1979.

Galanter, M., Stillman, R., Wyatt, R. J., Vaughan, T. B., Weingartner, H., Nurnberg, F. L. Marihuana and social behavior. *Archives of General Psychiatry* 30: 518–21, 1974.

Galanter, M., Talbott, G. D., Gallegos, K., Rubenstone, L. AA and professional care for addicted physicians. Presented at the annual meeting of the American Medical Society for Alcoholism and other Drug Dependencies. Atlanta Ga., April 1989.

Galanter, M., Weingartner, H., Vaughan, T. B., Roth, W. T., and Wyatt, R. J. Delta-9 tetrahydrocannabinol and natural marihuana: a controlled comparison. *Archives of General Psychiatry* 28: 278–81, 1973.

Galanter, M., Wyatt, R. J., Lemberger, L., Weingartner, H., Vaughan, T. B., and Roth, W. T. Effects on humans of delta^9-tetrahydrocannabinol administered by smoking. *Science* 175: 934–36, 1972.

Gardner, R. Mechanisms in manic-depressive disorder: An evolutionary model. *Archives of General Psychiatry* 39: 1436–41, 1982.

Gerth, H., and Mills, C. W. *From Max Weber*. New York: Oxford University Press, 1946.

Ghiselin, M. T. *The Triumph of the Darwinian Method*. Berkeley and Los Angeles: University of California Press, 1969.

Glass, L. L., Kirsch, M. A., and Parris, F. N. Psychiatric disturbances associated with Erhard Seminars Training I: Report of cases. *American Journal of Psychiatry* 134: 245–47, 1977.

Goode, W. J.: *World Revolution and Family Patterns*. New York: Macmillan Publishing Co., 1970.

Goodman, F. D. *Speaking in Tongues*. Chicago: University of Chicago Press, 1972.

Grant, I., Sweetwood, H. L., Yager, J., and Gerst, M. Quality of life events in relation to psychiatric symptoms. *Archives of General Psychiatry*, 38: 335–39, 1981.

Greeley, A. M. *The Sociology of the Paranormal: A Reconnaissance*. Beverly Hills, Calif.: Sage Publications, 1975.

Greil, A. R., and Rudy, D. R. Social cocoons: Encapsulation and identity transformation organizations. *Social Inquiry* 54: 260–78, 1984.

Hall, J. R. The Apocalypse at Jonestown. In *In Gods We Trust: New Patterns of Religious Pluralism in America* T. Robbins and D. Anthony (eds.). New Brunswick, N.J.: Transaction Books, 1981.

Hamilton, W. D. Innate social aptitudes of man: An approach from evolutionary genetics. In *Biosocial Anthropology*. R. Fox (ed.). New York: Wiley, 1975, 133–55.

Hardt, J. V., and Kamiya, J. G. Anxiety change through electroencephalographic alpha feedback seen only in high anxiety subjects. *Science* 201: 79–81, 1978.

Harlow, H. F., and Harlow, M. K. Effects of various mother-infant relations on Rhesus monkey behaviors. In *Determinants of Infant Behavior* IV, B. M. Foss, (ed.). London: Metheuen, 1969, 15–36.

Heider, F. *The Psychology of Interpersonal Relations*. New York: Wiley, 1958.

Hobson, J. A., McCarley, R. W. The brain as a dream state generator: An activation-synthesis hypothesis of the dream process. *American Journal of Psychiatry* 134: 12, 1335–48, 1977.

Holmes, T. H., and Rahe, R. H. The social readjustment rating scale. *Journal of Psychosomatic Research* 11: 213–18, 1967.

Hume, D. *An Enquiry Concerning the Human Understanding* (1779). Oxford: Clarendon Press, 1894.

James, W. *The Varieties of Religious Experience* (1902). New York: Modern Library, 1929.

Jellinek, E. M. *The Disease Concept of Alcoholism*. New Haven: College and University Press, 1960.

Jolly, A. *The Evolution of Primate Behavior*. New York: Macmillan, 1972.

Kanter, R. M. *Commitment and Community: Communes and Utopias in Sociological Perspective*. Cambridge: Harvard University Press, 1972.

Kaplan, B., and Johnson, D. The Social Meaning of Navajo Psychopathology and Psychotherapy. In *Magic Faith in Healing*, A. Kiev (ed.). New York: Free Press, 1964, 203–29.

Kass, F., Skodol, A., and Charles, E. Therapists' recognition of psychopathology: a model for quality review of psychotherapy. *American Journal of Psychiatry* 137: 87–90, 1980.

Kelley, H. H. Attribution theory in social psychology. In *Nebraska Symposium on Motivation*, Vol XV, D. Levine (ed.). Lincoln: University of Nebraska Press, 1967, 192–238.

Kephart, W. M. *Extraordinary Groups: The Sociology of Unconventional Life-Styles.* New York: St. Martin's Press, 1976.

Kerns, P., and Wead, D. *Peoples Temple: Peoples Tomb.* Plainfield, N.J.: Logos, 1979.

Kilbourne, B., and Richardson, J. T. Psychotherapy and new religions in a pluralistic society. *American Psychologist* 39: 237–51, 1984.

Kirsch, M. A., and Glass, L. L. Psychiatric disturbances associated with Erhard Seminars Training: II. Additional cases and theoretical considerations. *American Journal of Psychiatry* 134: 1254–58, 1977.

Kolata, G. B. Human evolution: Life-styles and lineages of early hominids. *Science* 187: 940–42, 1975.

Kurtz, E. *Not God: A History of Alcoholics Anonymous.* Garden City, Minn.: Hareldon Educational Services, 1979.

LaBarre, W. *The Ghost Dance.* New York: Doubleday, 1970.

Lane, R., Jr. Catholic charismatic renewal. In *The New Religious Consciousness*, C. Y. Glock and N. Bellah (eds.). Los Angeles: University of California Press, 1976.

Lang, D. A reporter at large. *New Yorker*, November 1974, 56–126.

Leighton, A., Leighton, D. Elements of psychotherapy in Navajo religion. *Psychiatry* 4: 515–23, 1941.

Lepper, M. R., Greene, D., and Nesbitt, R. E. Undermining children's intrinsic interest with extrinsic reward: a test of the "over-justification" hypothesis. *Journal of Personality and Social Psychology* 28: 129–37, 1973.

Lewin, K. *A Dynamic Theory of Personality.* New York: McGraw-Hill, 1935.

Liberman, R. P., Teigen, J., and Patterson, R. Reducing delusional speech in chronic paranoid schizophrenics. *Journal of Applied Behavioral Analysis* 6: 57–64, 1973.

Lifton, R. J. *Thought Reform and the Psychology of Totalism.* New York: Norton, 1961.

Lockard, J. S., McDonald, L. L., Clifford, D. A., and Martinez, R. Panhandling: Sharing of Resources. *Science* 191: 406–8, 1976.

Lofland, J., and Stark, R. Becoming a world-saver: a theory of conversion to a deviant perspective. *American Sociology Review* 30: 862–75, 1965.

Lorenz, K. Analogy as a source of knowledge. *Science* 185: 229–34, 1974.

Lorenz, K. *On Aggression.* New York: Harcourt Brace, 1966.

Lubchansky, I., Egri, G., and Stokes, J. Puerto Rican spiritualists view mental illness: the faith healer as a paraprofessional. *American Journal of Psychiatry* 127: 312–21, 1970.

Ludwig, A. M. Altered states of consciousness. *Archives of General Psychiatry* 15: 225–34, 1966.

Lumsden, C. J., and Wilson, E. O. *Genes, Mind, and Culture.* Cambridge: Harvard University Press, 1981.

Lynd, R. S., and Lynd, H. B. *Middletown: A Study in American Culture.* New York: Harcourt and Brace, 1929.

Manatt, M. *Parents, Peers and Pot.* US DHEW Publication (ADM) 79-812, 1979.

Maslow, A. H. Synanon and eupsychia. *Journal of Humanistic Psychology* 7: 28–35, 1967.

Maslow, A. H. *Religions, Values, and Peak-Experiences.* New York: Viking Press, 1964.

Maxwell, M. A. *The Alcoholics Anonymous Experience.* New York: McGraw-Hill, 1984.

Maynard Smith, J. Group selection and kin selection. *Nature* 201: 1145–47, 1964.

Mead, G. H. *Mind, Self, and Society from the Standpoint of a Social Behaviorist.* C. W. Morris (ed.). Chicago: University of Chicago Press, 1962.

Melges, F. T., Tinklenberg, J., Deardorff, C. M., Davies, N. H., Anderson, R. E., and Owen, C. A. Temporal disorganization and delusional-like ideation. *Archives of General Psychiatry* 30: 855–61, 1974.

Melton, J. G. *The Encyclopedia of American Religions,* Vol. II. Wilmington, N.C.: McGarth Publishing Company, 1978.

Melton, J. G., and Moore, R. L. *The Cult Experience: Responding to the New Religious Pluralism.* New York: Pilgrim Press, 1982.

Menninger, K. *The Vital Balance.* New York: Viking Press, 1963.

Milgram, S. *Obedience to Authority.* New York: Harper Colophon Books, 1975.

Miller, J. G., Freedman, A. M., Kaplan, H. I., and Saddock, B. K. (eds.). In *Comprehensive Textbook of Psychiatry* II. Baltimore, Md.: Williams and Wilkins, 1975, 74–88.

Miller, J. G. Living systems: Basic concepts. *Behavioral Science* 10: 193–237, 1965.

Miner, H. Body ritual among the Nacirema. *American Anthropologist* 58: 503–7, 1956.

Moorhouse, G. The Moonies invade Gloucester. *Harper's* Magazine, January 1981, pp. 46–52.

Mosher, L. R., Menn, A., and Matthews, S. M. Soteria: Evaluation of a home-based treatment for schizophrenia. *American Journal of Orthopsychiatry* 45: 455–67, 1975.

Mosher, L. R. and Menn, A. Z. Community residential treatment for schizophrenia: a two-year follow-up. *Hospital and Community Psychiatry* 29: 715–23, 1978.

Mosher, L. R., and Menn, A. Z. Scientific Evidence and System Change: The Soteria Experience. In *Psychosocial Interventions in Schizophrenia,* H. Stierlin et al. (eds.). Heidelberg: Springer-Verlag, 1983, 93–108.

Mueller, D. P., Edwards, D. W., and Yarvis, R. M. Stressful life events and psychiatric symptomatology: change or undesirability? *Journal of Health and Social Behavior* 18: 307–17, 1977.

Murstein, B. I. Physical attractiveness and marital choice. *Journal of Personality and Social Psychology* 22: 8–12, 1972.

National Center for Health Statistics. *A Concurrent Validational Study of the NCHS General Well-Being Schedule.* Vital and Health Statistics Series 2, No. 73. Hyattsville, Md.: DHEW Publication No. (HRA) 78-1347, 1977.

Ness, R. C., and Wintrob, R. M. The emotional impact of fundamentalist religious participation: an empirical study of intragroup variation. *The American Journal of Orthopsychiatry* 50: 302–15, 1980.

Noyes, P. B. *My Father's House: An Oneida Boyhood* (1927). Gloucester, Mass.: Peter Smith, 1966.

Nugent, J. P. *White Night: The Untold Story of What Happened Before—and Beyond—Jonestown*. New York: Rawson and Wade, 1979.

Ofshe, R., Eisenberg, N., Coughlin, R., Dolinajec, G., Gerson, K., and Johnson, A. Social structure and social control in Synanon. *Voluntary Action Research* 3: 67–76, 1974.

Ofshe, R. Synanon: The People Business. In *The New Religious Consciousness*, C. Y. Glock and R. N. Bellah (eds.). Berkeley: University of California Press, 1976, 116–37.

Orne, M. Demand characteristics and the concept of quasi-controls. In Artifact in Behavioral Research, R. Rosenthal and L. Rosnow (eds.). New York: Academic Press, 1969, 143–79.

Pahnke, W. N. Drugs and mysticism. *International Journal of Parapsychology*. Vol. VIII, 2: 295–314, 1966.

Paredes, A. Social control of drinking among the Aztec indians of Mesoamerica. *Journal of the Studies on Alcohol* 36: 9, 1139–53, 1975.

Parsons, A. S. The Moonies: the triumph of family. *Smith Alumnae Quarterly*, Summer 1984, pp. 8–13.

Pattison, E. M. Nonabstinent drinking goals in the treatment of alcoholism. *Archives of General Psychiatry*. 33: 923–30, 1976.

Pattison, E. M. Ideological support for the marginal middle class: faith healing and glossolalia. In *Religious Movements in Contemporary America*, I. I. Zaretsky and M. P. Leone (eds.). Princeton: Princeton University Press, 1974, 418–55.

Pattison, E. M., Labins, N. A., and Doerr, H. A. Faith healing: a study of personality and function. *Journal of Nervous and Mental Disease* 157: 367–409, 1973.

Pattison, E. M., Pattison, M. L. "Ex-gays": religiously-mediated change in homosexuals. *American Journal of Psychiatry* 137: 1553–62, 1980.

Penfield, W. *The Mystery of the Mind*. Princeton: Princeton University Press, 1975.

Pilarzyk, T. The origin, development, and decline of a youth culture religion: An application of sectarianization theory. *Review of Religious Research* 20 (Fall 1978).

Pilbeam, D. *The Ascent of Man: An Introduction to Human Evolution*. New York: Macmillan, 1972.

Proudfoot, W., and Shaver, P. Attribution theory and the psychology of religion. *Journal for the Scientific Study of Religion* 14: 317–30, 1975.

Radcliffe-Brown, A. R. *Taboo*. Cambridge: Cambridge University Press, 1939.

Reiss, D. Varieties of consensual experience. *Family Process* 10: 1–35, 1971.

Rice, A. K. *Learning for Leadership*. London: Tavistock Publications Ltd., 1965.

Robbins, T. Religious movements, the state, and the law: reconceptualizing "the cult problem." *New York University Review of Law and Social Change* 19: 33–49, 1979–1980.

Robinson, D. *Talking Out of Alcoholism. The Self-Help Process of Alcoholics Anonymous*. Baltimore, Md.: University Park Press, 1979.

Ross, J. C. Errors on "Moonies." *American Journal of Psychiatry* 140: 643–44, 1983.

Roth, W. T., Galanter, M., Weingartner, H., Vaughan, T. B., and Wyatt, R. J. Marijuana and synthetic delat-9-trans-tetrahydrocannabinol: Some effects on the auditory evoked response and background EEG in humans. *Biological Psychiatry* 6: 221–23, 1973.

Rothmyer, K. Mapping out Moon's media empire. *Columbia Journalism Review*, November–December, 1984, pp. 23–31.

Rudy, D. R. *Becoming Alcoholic: Alcoholics Anonymous and the Reality of Alcoholism.* Carbondale: Southern Illinois University Press, 1986.

Ruse, M. Sociobiology: Sound science or muddled metaphysics. In *Is Science Sexist? and Other Problems in the Biomedical Sciences.* Boston: D. Reidel, 1981.

Samarin, W. J. Glossolalia as learned behaviour. *Canadian Journal of Theology* 15: 60–64, 1959.

Schacter, S., and Singer, J. E. Cognitive, social, and physiological determinants of emotional state. *Psychology Review,* 69: 379–99, 1962.

Schein, E. The Chinese indoctrination program for prisoners of war. *Psychiatry* 19: 149–172, 1956.

Schultes, R. E. An overview of hallucinogens in the western hemisphere. In *Flesh of the Gods,* P. Furst (ed.). New York: Praeger, 1972.

Simon, J. Observations on 67 patients who took Erhard Seminars Training. *American Journal of Psychiatry* 135: 686–91, 1978.

Singer, M. Therapy with ex-cult members. *National Association of Private Psychiatric Hospitals Journal* 9(4): 14–18, 1978.

Smith, M. J. Group selection and kin selection. *Nature* 201: 1145–47, 1964.

Snow, D. A., and Phillips, C. L. The Lofland-Stark conversion model. *Social Problems* 27: 430–47, 1980.

Stark, R., and Bainbridge, W. S. Networks of faith: Interpersonal bonds and recruitment to cults and sects. *American Journal of Sociology* 85: 1376–95, 1980.

Sterling, C. *The Terror Network.* New York: Holt Rinehart, 1981.

Strentz, T. The Stockholm Syndrome. *Annals of the New York Academy of Sciences* 347: 137–50, 1980.

Suomi, S. J., Harlow, H. F., and McKinney, W. T., Jr. Monkey psychiatrists. *American Journal of Psychiatry* 128: 927–32, 1972.

Suomi, S. J., Seaman, S. F., Lewis, J. K., DeLizio, R. D., and McKinney, W. T. Effects of imipramine treatment of separation-induced social disorders in Rhesus monkeys. *Archives of General Psychiatry* 35: 321–25, 1978.

Suomi, S. J., DeLizio, R., and Harlow, H. F. Social rehabilitation of separation-induced depressive disorders in monkeys. *American Journal of Psychiatry* 133: 1279–85, 1976.

Suwaki, H. 'Naikan' and Danshukai for the treatment of Japanese alcoholic patients. *British Journal of Addictions* 74: 15–19, 1979.

Tart, C. T. *States of Consciousness.* New York: E. P. Dutton, 1975.

The AA Way of Life. New York: Alcoholics Anonymous World Services, 1967.

Thomsen, R. *Bill W.* New York: Harper and Row, 1975.

Tinbergen, N. *The Study of Instinct.* London: Oxford University Press, 1951.

Trice, H., and Beyer, J. M. The routinization of charisma in two social movement organizations. Paper presented at the Academy of Management Meetings, Dallas, 1983.

Trivers, R. L. The evaluation of reciprocal altruism. *Quarterly Review of Biology* 46: 35–37, 1971.

Ungerleider, J. M., and Wellisch, D. K. Coercive persuasion (brainwashing), religious cults, and deprogramming. *American Journal of Psychiatry,* 136: 279–82, 1979.

Vaillant, G. E., and Milofsky, E. S. Natural history of male alcoholism. *Archives of General Psychiatry* 39: 127–33, 1982.

von Bertalanffy, L. *General Systems Theory.* New York: George Braziller, 1968.

Wallace, R. K. Physiological effects of transcendental meditation. *Science* 167: 1751–54, 1970.

Weber, M. *The Theory of Social and Economic Organization.* New York: Macmillan, 1947.

Weigert, E. Human ego functions in the light of animal behavior. *Psychiatry* 19: 325–32, 1956.

Weightsman, J. M. *Making Sense of the Jonestown Suicides.* Lewiston, N.Y.: Edwin Mellon Press, 1983.

Weiner, N. *Cybernetics.* New York: Wiley, 1948.

Wendt, R. J., Mosher, L. R., Matthews, S. M., and Menn, A. Z. Comparison of two treatment environments for schizophrenia. In *Principles and Practices of Milieu Therapy,* J. G. Gunderson, O. A. Will, Jr., and L. R. Mosher (eds.). New York: Jason Aronson, 1983.

Wilson, E. O. *Sociobiology: The New Synthesis.* Cambridge: Harvard (The Belknap Press), 1975.

Winfrey, C. Why 900 died in Guyana. *New York Times* Magazine, February 26, 1979, p. 45.

Wolin, S. T., Steinglass, P. Interactional behavior in an alcoholic community. *Medical Annals of the District of Columbia* 43: 183–87, 1974.

Wright, S. Tempo and mode in evolution—a critical review. *Ecology* 26: 415–19, 1945.

Wynne, L. C., Ryckoff, I. M., Day, J., and Hirsch, S. Pseudomutuality in the family relations of schizophrenics. *Psychiatry* 21: 205–22, 1958.

INDEX